BECOMING A CLINICAL PSYCHOLOGIST

BECOMING A CLINICAL PSYCHOLOGIST

ROBERT HENLEY WOODY
AND
MALCOLM ROBERTSON

International Universities Press, Inc.
Madison, Connecticut

Library of Congress Cataloging-in-Publication Data

Woody, Robert Henley.
Becoming a clinical psychologist / Robert Henley Woody and Malcolm Robertson.
p. cm.
Bibliography: p.
Includes indexes.
ISBN 0-8236-0491-8:
1. Clinical psychology—Practice. 2. Clinical psychology--Vocational guidance. I. Robertson, Malcolm. II. Title.
RC467.95.W66 1988
157′.9′023—dc19 88-12890
CIP

Manufactured in the United States of America

We recognize that our careers and this book have been facilitated by the support and love of our families. We dedicate this book to our spouses, Jane Divita Woody and Joan M. Robertson, and to our children, Jennifer, Robert, and Matthew Woody, and Tim, Suzanne, Greg, Chris, and Michelle Robertson.

Contents

Introduction

In writing BECOMING A CLINICAL PSYCHOLOGIST, we have recognized over and over that the quest is both personal and professional. It is likely that most students and perhaps even practitioners with newly acquired doctorates, believe that "taking the right courses will assure success as a clinical psychologist." To the contrary and as is quickly recognized upon gaining experience as a practitioner, the courses completed for undergraduate and graduate degrees are only an introduction to the "becoming" process. In the professional realm, changes in societal preferences, redefinitions of psychological practices, research advances, and emerging priorities lead to a requirement of continued education and training throughout one's career. In the personal realm, the stages of life lead to an interface of one's need fulfillment and motivation with career-related decisions. Comments have been included to provide the reader with a stimulus for personal development, i.e., a unification of the personal and professional self concepts.

The contents have a twofold purpose. First, it is believed that even a seasoned clinical psychologist can benefit from a review of the "becoming" process and recognition of the advances and changes that have occurred in clinical psychology since he/she received professional training. Second, students of psychology, especially those who are considering a career commitment to clinical psychology, need a perspective of the field that has both breadth and depth—with a meaningful merger of academic and practice issues. Therefore, this book should be suitable for the established professional's growth and the student's search for knowledge and insight.

Part I is devoted to preparation of the practitioner and entry into the field. Chapter One traces the evolution of clinical psychology. Chapter Two describes training, including specialization. Chapter Three offers practical information about employment opportunities. Chapter Four reveals the public policy, governmental, and professional–organizational forces that shape the practice of clinical psychology.

Part II covers theories and methods for practice. Chapter Five presents an introduction to theories and strategies of psychotherapy, and Chapter Six continues into effectiveness of and special modalities for psychotherapy. Chapter Seven explores the critical issues of assessment, as applied to normal and abnormal conditions. Chapter Eight describes psychodiagnostic principles and the process of diagnosis. Chapter Nine continues the psychodiagnostic thrust, delineating the primary types of assessment methods. In an Afterword, we prognosticate about the future of clinical psychology.

In writing this book, we have gained an understanding of what has moved us forward through our careers. In substance, clinical psychology can afford intriguing theories and principles, and an opportunity to explore their significance with a wide variety of people and for diverse behavior problems. On a personal level, clinical psychology offers an opportunity to apply new ideas for personal enrichment, and to enhance lifestyle (including mental and physical health) through what one encounters while "on the job." For employment, clinical psychology appears to be well-entrenched in the economic system, and while there are changes in job definitions and opportunities, clinical psychology continues to elevate its status. For society, it seems clear that clinical psychology is recognized and endorsed for its contributions. The outcome for the authors is likely to be the same for the readers—an appreciation of BECOMING A CLINICAL PSYCHOLOGIST.

Robert Henley Woody
Omaha, Nebraska

Malcolm Robertson
Kalamazoo, Michigan

PART I

PREPARATION OF THE PRACTITIONER AND ENTRY INTO THE PROFESSION

Chapter 1

The Birth and Growth of Clinical Psychology

1890–1910: THE BEGINNING

The profession of clinical psychology was launched in the last decade of the 19th century by a few maverick psychologists who broke ranks with their scientific colleagues and left the hallowed laboratories of academia for an uncertain future in the marketplace. Before this time, scientific psychology was primarily the study of the elements of consciousness, and most psychologists were opposed to clinical applications (Reisman, 1981). Shortly before 1900 the vision of a profession of psychology was articulated by Lightner Witmer who boldly proposed that psychologists use their knowledge and tools to improve the quality of life (Reisman, 1976). He spoke of a new profession, which he called clinical psychology, although the name had been used earlier in France in a general sense (Garfield, 1982). According to Witmer, the laboratory would be a clinic, and in 1896 he founded the first psychological clinic at the University of Pennsylvania. The tools would be psychological tests; the subjects would be handicapped children; and the method would be a single-subject format based on the systematic administration and evaluation of tests. The practical value would be a remedial plan designed for each child; and the scientific value would be in the new knowledge derived from the cumulative findings of many single case studies. By 1904, James McKeen Cattell stated that psychology would be not only a science but also a profession (Cattell, 1937). In 1907, Witmer summed up his position as follows:

"where genetic psychologists were looking for laws and universals, the clinicians were looking at persons and trying to solve problems" (cited in Charles, 1970, p. 31).

If Witmer's proposal struck a quixotic note at the time, his parochial statement that other professionals lacked the unique training of psychologists strained the credulity of even those sympathetic to his mission. Though the statement was one of high purpose, it was based on faith rather than fact—at that time no psychologist possessed the unique training endorsed by Witmer. The question of training aside, there was no one else doing what Witmer called on psychologists to do.

The response within psychology ranged from dismay to opposition. Except for a few colleagues of like mind, the response of the establishment was predictable: the proposal of psychology as a profession was a repudiation of psychology as a pure science; if taken seriously, it would be an irreversible setback. The implications of Witmer's proposal were not lost upon the other professional groups. Educators, social workers, and physicians viewed the move as a threat to their professional sovereignty. With some justification they argued that psychologists lacked a professional identity in the public's eye.

Yet predictions of the profession's early demise never materialized. The belief prevailed that psychology could be, ought to be, and would be a profession.

By 1910, five universities had clinics; three had some semblance of a professional training curriculum; and a forerunner of today's clinical psychology internship had been established by Henry Goddard at the Vineland Training Center in Vineland, New Jersey (Reisman, 1976). From that point on, clinical psychology never looked back.

1910–1930: THE EARLY YEARS

If the preceding 20 years might be characterized by a new breed of psychologist in search of a client population, the ensuing two decades could be characterized by a client population in search of the professional psychologist.

Two events contributed to the profession's gathering momentum. First was the strong demand for psychological testing and evaluation in schools and in the military service during World War I. Psychological tests were an efficient method of classifying the large number of military recruits. Educators also saw the value of psychological tests as a practical tool to assess intellectual growth and academic achievement in children. With the development of measures for intelligence, aptitudes, interests, and personality, psychological testing became commercially as well as professionally successful (Goldenberg, 1983, chapter 2). Second was the limited number of university programs to train psychological practitioners. In short, a fast growing need pressing against insufficient resources led inevitably to an upsurge in university-based clinics and training programs. By 1914, 19 universities had psychological clinics to train clinical psychologists and another 68 would be added over the next 20 years (cited in Kirsch and Winter, 1983).

Increasing numbers of psychologists sought a career in or career change to the clinical practice of psychology, though at this time most of their training was learning by doing. Continued penetration of the human service area by psychologists (though limited to an educational–remedial focus), was coupled with the fact that they were being accorded legal status in some states and allowed to sit on commissions for commitment to institutions for the retarded. Clinical psychologists were becoming a professional force.

As expected, opposition mounted both within and outside psychology. Physicians contended that a lack of psychoanalytic training weakened psychologists' claims to clinical competence. Educators were alarmed at the potential (and occasionally actual) abuse of tests. Social workers found fault with the excessive reliance on diagnosis. Scientific colleagues decried the lack of experimental rigor in "clinical studies."

Wisely, clinical psychologists chose first to confront the opposition within their own ranks. Confident of a growing numerical strength, the profession executed a tour de force. In 1917, the profession formed an independent American Association of Clinical Psychologists (AACP). The hand of the American Psychology Association (APA) was forced, and in the spirit of "divided we perish, united we stand," proffered an invitation to set up a clinical psychology section of APA with full rights and privileges. The AACP disbanded as precipitously as it had incorporated, and its members returned to the APA in 1919.

Flushed with its first political victory and buoyed by a newly acquired power base within APA, the clinical psychology section served notice that it would pursue parity both within and outside psychology. Top priority would be given to seeking a legal definition of professional psychology and to establishing university-based Ph.D. programs to train clinical psychologists.[1]

Scarcely 30 years had passed since the day that Lightner Witmer presented his clinical psychology proposal at an APA meeting, and the words of Joseph Jastrow, one of psychology's most respected elder statesmen, "Yet of all the applications, that of clinical psychology appears to me the most momentous" (cited in Reisman, 1976, p. 188).

1930–1940: THE TIME OF TRANSITION

As the twenties drew to a close, clinical psychologists faced a sharply curtailed job market due primarily to an economic depression, and secondarily to a still fuzzy notion of who was *really* a clinical psychologist. Nevertheless, the profession began the decade of the thirties on an upbeat note.

With an official section to represent its interests, clinical psychologists became a vocal, if small minority within APA. Approximately 20 percent of the APA membership listed clinical psychology as a research, teaching, or service interest (Goldenberg, 1983, chapter 2). Another statistic that seemed to bode well for the future was that some 40 percent of APA members had full-time employment outside academia. Although only one-fourth of this group were clinical practitioners, four times as many (those who could not or would not belong to APA) were doing clinical work. Reisman (1981) estimates that there were approximately 800 clinical psychologists at the beginning of the thirties, a number that would grow to nearly 30,000 by the end of the mid-eighties. With the increasing emphasis on service delivery, the profession's academically derived identity had to be stretched to include the community centered practitioner.

[1] An example of an idea whose time had not come was L. Crane's motion to have an exclusively professional training program with a Psy.D., doctor of psychology degree (Crane, 1925–1926). The motion died for lack of a second, and 40 years would pass before a similar motion would receive a considered hearing within APA.

With the worst of the Depression over and the job market brightening, clinicians began to take a close look at their role definition. Many felt boxed in by the traditional focus on the handicapped child. More importantly, they objected to a professional role that confined their practice to diagnosis and treatment planning. In short, they wanted another piece of the action, and the missing piece was *treatment*. After all, it was there in Witmer's blueprint—clinical psychologists would use their knowledge and methods to improve the quality of life, mentally, emotionally, and socially for individuals of all ages.

Opposition surfaced immediately and hewed pretty much to party lines. Psychiatrists quickly invoked the specter of charlatanism and admonished that in addition to psychoanalytic training a medical degree was the sine qua non for assuming full responsibility for the welfare of client/patients. Academic psychologists deplored yet another deviation from the strict canons of science. The conservative voices of the profession cautioned against rocking the boat by reaching for too much too soon.

The opposition was answered by a commitment to define standards of practice and establish accreditation procedures for training programs. In 1935, a hastily assembled APA Committee on Standards of Training (in a surprising display of collegial unanimity) reaffirmed the commitment to standards of practice and accreditation procedures. Next, the Committee attempted to defuse the opposition to the treatment issue by defining two levels of practitioners: a professional psychologist (Ph.D. and one year of supervised experience), and an assistant psychologist (M.A. and one year of supervised experience). The Committee then capped off its work with the statement that was to be a harbinger of future controversy, namely, that clinical psychology is the *art* (a term that would require endless disclaimers), and *technology* (another term that would be disavowed again and again) which deals with adjustment problems of human beings (cited in Reisman, 1976, p. 250). It was all there, the polarization within the profession over subdoctoral training, the territorial dispute with psychiatry, the scientist–practitioner conundrum, and the rivalry between the technocratic practitioners and the humanistic practitioners.

Although supported by the Committee on Standards, the clinical section of APA chafed under the slow-moving parent organization. In 1937, the clinicians left APA to join the American Association of Applied Psychologists (AAAP) (English, 1938). Despite the developing factionalism, by the end of the thirties clinical psychologists could take some pride in their contribution to diagnostic testing, which now encompassed psychopathology as well as the earlier achievements in intellectual, educational, and vocational assessment.

1940–1950: THE EXPANSION YEARS

In the 1940s, a new dimension was added to the growth of clinical psychology. As Sterling (1982) aptly put it, "Affluence pushed its nose under our tent" (p. 789). As might be expected, affluence created new problems about as fast as it solved old ones. But in the beginning and for some time after, it was a heady experience.

In recognition of the significant contributions made by clinical psychologists during World War II, the Veterans Administration (VA) turned to psychology for assistance in providing service to veterans who were psychiatric casualties. The VA alone required 4,700 clinical psychologists (Goldenberg, 1983, chapter 2).

The profession was faced with the enviable problem of how to use the Federal Government's largess to alleviate the shortage of training programs and trained practitioners. In 1944, a joint committee of APA and AAAP (the latter ended their walk-out a year later and returned to the fold) agreed to use VA, U.S. Department of Public Health (USDPH), and National Institute of Mental Health (NIMH) funds to expand already existing graduate facilities.

During this period the visibility of the profession rose dramatically. Undergraduate and graduate enrollments soared, and psychology departments were rapidly expanded by students drawn to a field that offered an oversupply of jobs, attractive salaries, the excitement of doing psychotherapy, and, for those who made it all the way, the status of a practitioner with a doctoral degree.

Between 1946 and 1949, the number of Ph.D. clinical

psychology programs rose from 22 to 42, and by the end of the decade approximately 60 doctoral programs were training close to 1,500 clinical graduate students (Kirsch and Winter, 1983), but applications still far outnumbered available spaces.

In 1947, the APA Committee on Training in Clinical Psychology, which was responsible for specifying curriculum content, setting standards of training, and placing its imprimatur on Ph.D. programs that met the standards, became alarmed at the prospect of the "clinical tail wagging the scientific dog." With the hope of striking an optimal balance between scientific and professional education, the APA formed a committee, chaired by David Shakow, to set forth guidelines for graduate training in clinical psychology (Shakow, Hilgard, Kelly, Luckey, Sanford, and Shaffer, 1947). Two years later, the historic Boulder Conference, a summit meeting of leading clinical psychology educators, was held to plan implementation of the Shakow Report. The intent was to close the schism between science and the profession. The conference mandated that a clinical psychologist be trained as a scientist and a practitioner in graduate as opposed to professional schools (Raimy, 1950). Then, with a passing reference to the need for innovative programming, the conference reaffirmed the existing Ph.D. model, in which the first and fourth years were set aside for scientific instruction and the second and third years for the professional program. Frank (1984) states that the emphasis on research training was designed to give clinical psychologists an independence from psychiatrists in clinical settings.

With the AAAP and two other separatist organizations reuniting with APA in 1945 (Frank, 1984), the discipline appeared to have resolved its internal politics. Wolfe (1946) captured the spirit of accord with the statement that "the object of the APA should be to advance Psychology as a science, as a profession, and as a means of promoting human welfare" (p. 3). At this juncture, clinical and counseling practitioners accounted for almost half of the psychology positions outside academia; salaries of Ph.D. clinicians had nearly doubled; the clinical division of APA now accounted for about 20 percent of the total membership (not counting a sizable number of associate members); and slightly more than 50% of those affiliated with APA expressed an interest in professional applications (Reisman, 1976). Although the practice of psychotherapy loomed as a potentially divisive issue among psychologists, psychiatry's opposition helped to close ranks, and APA's policy was that psychotherapy had a legitimate place in the training and practice of clinical psychologists. Besides, by the beginning of World War II nearly one-third of all clinical psychologists included psychotherapy in their practice (Kirsch and Winter, 1983).

Although two states, Connecticut and Virginia, had passed certification laws for Ph.D. clinical psychologists, APA decided that the matter was too critical to be left entirely to the states. First, it could not be assumed that all states would follow suit, or that standards would necessarily be uniform. With that in mind, the American Board of Examiners in Professional Psychology (ABEPP) was founded to provide national certification for the specialties of clinical, counseling, and industrial psychology.

The profession's strong suit was still assessment and diagnosis—though a healthy skepticism had taken hold, especially in response to the unfavorable research reviews of projective techniques (non- or semistructured test stimuli to which clients respond). The profession moved to loosen psychiatry's proprietary control of psychotherapy. The pioneering work of Carl R. Rogers (1942) not only gave psychologists a psychotherapy theory of their own, but also ushered in a period of productive research on the effect of different treatment procedures.

1950–1960: THE PERIOD OF CONSOLIDATION

The demand for clinical psychology was still strong. Clinical psychology had become the largest APA division. The number of APA-approved doctoral programs continued to grow. Close to half the psychology Ph.D.s graduated in clinical psychology (Goldenberg, 1983, chapter 2).

During this period 13 more states wrote certification laws. The American Psychiatric Association first offered and then withdrew its support of psychologist certification, a reversal that may have been triggered by the portents riding on a State of Michigan Supreme Court ruling that a clinical psychologist could serve as expert witness in a determination of mental illness (Reisman, 1976). The ABPP (the E had since been dropped) had 1,403 duly certified diplomates at this point, two-thirds of whom were clinical psychologists. Early on, APA preferred certification (i.e., qualified to use the title of psychologist) to licensing (i.e., qualified to practice psychology) to avoid premature definition of a practitioner's role, and to sidestep conflict with other mental health professions. It also encouraged voluntary rather than mandatory certification so as not to give the appearance of discriminating against nonclinically trained psychologists.

The profession reaffirmed its commitment to develop the area of psychotherapy. In addition to Carl Rogers' (1942, 1951) seminal ideas, a systematic blending of learning principles and psychodynamic concepts was being fashioned by several psychologists, notably John Dollard and Neal Miller (1950). And, as was true of psychodiagnosis, the first rush of enthusiasm was now tempered by skepticism over uncritical claims of success rates for psychotherapy.

Mindful of its responsibility to uphold the integrity of the discipline and to safeguard the welfare of society, APA promulgated its first code of professional ethics in 1951. Then, to show that scientific and professional psychology were compatible, APA chose two eminent scientist-practitioners, first Carl Rogers and then Paul Meehl, to receive the Gold Medal Award for significant contributions to the science of psychology.

1960–1970: THE TIME OF CONFLICT AND GROWTH

If the fifties were the halcyon days, the sixties was a more complex decade. There were 35,000 psychologists (APA membership was 27,000, compared to 31 members at its inauguration in 1892), one-third of whom identified themselves as clinical psychologists (Reisman, 1976). The number of Ph.D.-approved programs had almost tripled since the forties, and all but three states had statutory certification. Generous grants were still available for training and research, and federal funds continued to be readily available.

Employers bid competitively with each other to fill newly created clinical psychology positions. Graduate students were hired in both Ph.D. and M.A. levels almost immediately following graduation. Even factoring in new graduate programs and the expansion of existing ones, manpower shortages were projected to rise sharply at national, state, and local levels. Noteworthy is Wright's (1983) observation that in the late 1960s there were seven positions for every clinical psychology graduate compared to a 1:1 ratio in the 1980s.

On the other hand, the issue of the conflicting priorities of a science and a profession were still unresolved. Garfield (1966) spoke of clinical psychology's "dual identity of a science and a profession as a source of uniqueness and enrichment, as well as a source of divisiveness and discontent" (p. 353).

In effect the discipline of psychology had two masters, one with power and the other with money, and each threatened the other's vested interests. The pure science faction resented the money being put into strictly professional pursuits, and charged that professional concerns preempted the training of clinical psychology students. Those on the professional (clinical) side of the aisle felt shortchanged in terms of influence and control within APA, as they discovered that a majority of numbers did not equate with majority clout.

A few prestigious departments summarily dropped their clinical programs. A separatist group, the Psychonomic Society, was organized for the pursuit of psychology as a pure science, and in 1960 held its first meeting at the University of Chicago. Some clinical programs were transferred to colleges of education and medicine. In professional circles talk was heard of leaving APA to form an independently funded organization that would put the full force of its resources behind the promotion of psychology as a profession (a maneuver that had been successful twice before). From both sides came suggestions that APA be split into separate organizations, each free to pursue its priorities. Albee (1970) proposed an American Scientific Psychological Association and an American Professional Psychological Association coexisting side by side.

To stem the tide of the separatist movement and to cool down the in-house feuding, the National Conference on the

Professional Preparation of Clinical Psychologists was held in Chicago in 1965. Its purpose was to redress the complaints of the practitioner group without subverting the Boulder model of the scientist–practitioner. The recommendations for more and different professional preparation were largely ignored, even though implicit in the Boulder legacy was permission to experiment with training models.

As with the two previous conferences held in the fifties, there was struggle between those who supported the current Boulder model but with additional professional training, and others who wanted major changes in the education of clinicians. As chairman of the 1965 APA Committee on Scientific and Professional Aims, Kenneth Clark made a plea for a practitioner-oriented training program that would grant a Psy.D. degree. Three years later, with support from several APA divisions, state psychological associations, and professional societies, the National Council on Graduate Education endorsed Clark's proposal (Caddy, 1981). It was an idea whose time had come, although Crane (1925–1926), Poffenberger (1938), and Louttit (1939) had proposed alternative degree programs for clinicians, and Gardner in the forties had proposed a School of Professional Psychology (Harrower, 1947).

By the end of the sixties two solutions were in place: The first, and the first officially endorsed Psy.D. program, was a two-track system at the University of Illinois (Peterson, 1968). One track was the traditional Ph.D. with primary emphasis on developing research and teaching skills, and the other was a Psy.D. with primary emphasis on teaching clinical skills, with applications to either program filtered through the same stringent admission criteria. The other solution was the California School of Professional Psychology's six-year career ladder divided into four degree rungs (A.A., B.A., M.A., and Ph.D.), with admission criteria that considered personal suitability as well as academic aptitude.

With its corporate image burnished by a new eight-story headquarters building in Washington, DC, APA stood ready to lend its skill bank and resources to solving the great social problems of the sixties: racism, poverty, overpopulation, and the assault on society's traditions by an alienated and disenchanted youth.

Within the mental health community, clinical psychology had effected a rapprochement with allied professions through membership in interdisciplinary organizations coupled with a wider participation in the delivery of mental health services. Indicative of an advancing professional maturity was the expansion of both predoctoral and postdoctoral opportunities for specialty concentrations, such as clinical, counseling, child clinical, clinical–community psychology, and subspeciality areas such as neuropsychological assessment, forensic psychology, crisis intervention, group therapy, and marital–family therapy.

For many, perhaps most in the profession, the high point of this decade was the community mental health movement, which Hobbs (1964) called the third revolution, the first being humane treatment of the insane and the second belonging to Freud. What the grants from VA, NIMH, and USDPH did for professional education in the forties and fifties, the infusion of federal monies into the country's mental health system did for career opportunities and advancement in the sixties. For the client population the salutary effect was a significant expansion of publicly supported mental health services at the community level. As a consequence, services were now available to a broader spectrum of psychological disorders, and the more seriously disturbed persons could be treated in their own community as an alternative to being isolated in an institution.

With the progress of the past 20 years, clinical psychology was in a good position to take advantage of the windfall created by nationwide funding for the construction and implementation of comprehensive mental health centers (CMHC). Salaries and career benefits improved to keep pace with the rising shortage of mental health professionals to staff the newly created CCMHs. Within the centers, the broad spectrum of mental health services created diversification in terms of job opportunities. Those with a strong clinical bent could hone their diagnostic and therapeutic skills; clinical–community psychologists were phased into prevention, consultation, and education; research skills were needed for program evaluation; others with managerial and organizational talents could find positions in administration and program development;

and the pedagogically inclined found opportunities for the supervision of psychology trainees and paraprofessionals.

Funds from the Community Mental Health Centers Act (1963) not only made mental health services more accessible, but also provided new services, such as partial hospitalization, crisis intervention, and consultation and education (Bellak and Hersen, 1980). The CMHCs also gave an impetus to experimenting with brief or time-limited forms of therapy, as well as the development of new treatment approaches, such as existential, gestalt, behavioral, rational–emotive, and transactional analysis.

However, during this period, time and again clinical research studies demonstrated that the value of diagnostic and therapeutic techniques left much to be desired (Garfield, 1966). Albee (1970) observes that: "professional ingenuity in inventing new forms of psychotherapy has at least kept pace with the efforts of evaluators to catch up and expose it!" (p. 1075). Furthermore, the enthusiasm and pride that accompanied formation of national certification through ABPP had waned, and applications to all the specialty areas had tailed off noticeably. A survey by Robyak and Goodyear (1984) disclosed that the largest percentage of ABPP diplomates in clinical psychology graduated in the fifties. The rapid formation of state certification provided a means to obtaining credentials that, in contrast to ABPP, had legal status, grass roots relevancy, less rigorous preparation, and was less expensive.

In addition, discouragement persisted over the failure to loosen the grip of the medical model (which viewed psychological disorder as an illness) on the thinking of mental health professionals, including many clinical psychologists (Albee, 1966–1967). Despite being the only human service profession to combine a science of human behavior with a professional discipline, psychology continued to come up short against a model whose credibility rested largely on metaphor and analogy.

Also, there was the unsettling discrepancy between what clinical psychologists were supposed to be and what in fact they did. Although trained as a scientist–practitioner, the large majority of clinicians wanted to be doctor–practitioners rather than doctor–scientists. [As Katkin (1982) notes, the scientist–practitioner model may be pronounced with a silent "scientist."] Such clinicians could talk knowledgeably about research, but they seldom did it and rarely published. Graduate clinical psychology programs simply failed to instill the sense of excitement necessary to doing research (Strupp, 1982). In practice, the modus operandi of the Ph.D. clinical psychologist differed only slightly from on the one hand that of the more highly paid psychiatrist, and on the other, the psychiatric social worker with much less training. Although the Ph.D. clinician was gaining parity with psychiatrists by having therapeutic and managerial responsibilities commensurate with professional training, de facto discrimination was still evident in both salary and administrative authority.

The definitional problem was also played out in the graduate schools, where clinical psychology students learned to finesse their way through the often conflicting requirements of the scientific and professional program components. Meanwhile, George Albee (1966–1967) was warning us that in 10 to 20 years most clinical psychologists would be leaving the CMHCs for university teaching or the private sector.

1970–1980: THE MATURING YEARS

The profession began the seventies with a quarter century of rapid growth behind it. Much that transpired in this decade had to do with improving the image of clinical psychology and enlarging the scope of clinical practice. A convincing case had to be made to the sister professions (psychiatry, psychiatric nursing, and social work), legislative bodies, and the public at large that the clinical psychologist was not a technician who only administered diagnostic tests, but was an independently functioning, professionally accountable practitioner. What followed was a deemphasis on diagnostic testing in favor of therapeutic interventions. Kelly (1961) pointed to a shift in this direction beginning in the late fifties, and Cleveland (1976) cites several cogent reasons for the decline of diagnostic testing.

In the seventies, a typical distribution of a Ph.D. clinician's time was 50 percent therapy, 20 percent assessment–diagnosis, 20 percent supervision–consultation, and 10 percent administration. Another part of upgrading the image was to point out that a clinical psychologist worked not only as a salaried public servant, but also as a private, fee-for-service provider. In fact, psychologists were penetrating the private sector in larger numbers than ever before. Approximately 40 percent of clinicians were engaged in some private practice, and the number of practitioners available for private practice was fast approaching that of psychiatrists, but with a better geographic spread (Dorken, 1977).

Within psychology, it was necessary to correct the notion that clinical work was more art than science. A positive step in this direction was a shift from all-purpose, a priori based tests to empirically derived, specifically targeted assessments, such as neuropsychological measures and behavior rating scales. In psychotherapy research, close attention was paid to tailoring therapeutic interventions to the specific problems of clients and patients. Another ameliorative change was the turning away from the image of the clinician as a generalist to the image of a specialist, for example, forensic psychologist, child psychologist, marriage and family psychologist, medical psychologist, clinical neuropsychologist.

The penetration of the private sector was facilitated by the rise in third-party payments to psychologists for mental health services. At both federal and state levels, restrictions were being lifted on the public's access to psychologists. By the late seventies, 35 states and Washington, DC (encompassing 78% of the population) had enacted statutes providing access to and free choice of licensed or certified psychologists for covered mental health benefits (Levy, 1981). In addition, efforts were being made to include clinical psychologists in Medicare and Medicaid.

Behind every successful profession is a strong lobby that can promote political, social, and economic advancement. The APA established the Association for the Advancement of Psychology (AAP) in 1974 to foster the interests of professional psychology. Dorken (1979) comments, "as it has been said, the price of success is eternal vigilance—and a damned good lobby" (p. 17). A precedent had been set 40 years earlier by the formation of the Psychologists League, a professional lobby group to assist unemployed psychologists and to prod the Federal Government into greater utilization of psychologists (Machover, 1980).

By the mid-seventies, with the exception of Missouri, all states and Washington, DC had either licensing or certification statutes that covered over 25,000 psychologists (Dorken, 1977). The growth of the private practice model underscored the importance of having professional credentials defined by licensure rather than certification, to be licensed to practice in preference to a certified professional title. Consequently, at the state level the profession began a drive to replace certification with licensure.

The accountability ethic also loomed large during this period. Plans were drawn up to implement the concept of peer reviews of clinical practice in both the public and private sectors. Access to information on qualified psychologists was sorely needed by referral sources and third-party payers. The answer was forthcoming in the publication of the National Register of Health Service Providers, a voluntary, peer-reviewed listing of psychological practitioners. By the 1980s over 13,000 psychologists would be listed (McConnell, 1984). To combat the "half life" of professional knowledge (Dubin, 1972), a strong campaign was started to encourage practitioners to obtain continuing professional education. Finally, the APA Council of Representatives commissioned the Committee on Standards for Providers for Psychological Services to begin work on developing both generic and special standards for training and practice in the applied areas of clinical, counseling, school, and industrial–organizational psychology (Barron, 1977–1978).

An issue of pivotal significance in the seventies was whether a clinical psychologist would continue to be defined as a mental health specialist who dealt exclusively with psychological disorders, or as a primary health-care professional who dealt with both physical and psychological disorders. The issue had strong currency at the time because of several critical trends. First was the shift of medical education and practice from a biological disease model to a comprehensive psychosocial model, in which the focus was on the patient with the illness rather than the illness per se (Schneider, 1980). Second was the anticipated arrival of National Health Insurance (NHI). The uncertainty over whether NHI would include mental health benefits gave a special urgency to broadening the definition of the clinical psychologist as a health care provider. More immediate was the formation of health maintenance organizations (HMOs), an alternative to the private insurer/private practitioner arrangement, that tailored its program to an emphasis on prevention of illness and fostering healthy living habits. With its relatively short history in delivery of professional services, clinical psychology had the flexibility to adapt to the new concept. The third issue was the promotion of a healthy life-style as a significant social movement, supported by the concern of government and industry over the enormous expenditures on medical care, as well as the general public's heightened consciousness of and commitment to healthy living. Fourth was the perception that health maintenance and prevention of illness was an area largely unattended to by other professions, and one that presented psychology with an opportunity to be in the vanguard of the movement through research, education, and service.

Over the years, an increasing number of clinical psychologists had plied their trade within hospitals, medical schools, and family and pediatric medical settings. From this natural base, they could now expand their traditional role to assess the psychological antecedents and consequences of physical illness and disease, and to assist patients to participate in their own recovery by replacing unhealthy living habits with healthy coping behaviors (Schneider, 1980). Schofield (1969) summoned clinical psychologists to the challenge by contrasting their role as mental health professionals in the past, and the opportunity now for a larger role in the health sciences with emphasis on a broader spectrum of human behavior. Following Schofield's summons, the APA Board of Scientific Affairs appointed a task force to study and make recommendations for psychology as a health-care profession (Matarazzo, 1980). Shortly thereafter, a new APA division, the Division of Health Psychology, was established. Several universities began doctoral programs in health psychology or behavioral medicine. Behavioral health internships were soon established. Health psychology was finding a place in the traditional graduate clinically oriented curriculum.

Besides strengthening psychology's long time interface with medicine, health psychology had a unifying impact within psychology. The focus on nonclinical as well as clinical populations, and the need for research and education as well as service, created a common pathway for both the scientists and the professionals. Having overcome much of the earlier opposition from the traditionalists, behavioral clinical psychologists, with their strong suit of helping clients learn and unlearn overt habit patterns, were emerging as the cutting edge of the development of a health care profession.

Psychology's commitment to capture a broader employment market was taking place against a backdrop of shrinking job opportunities in higher education and mental health (APA, 1975) caused by the national recession in the early 1970s. The scarcity of teaching and research positions led many nonclinical Ph.D.s to seek employment in areas of higher demand. Some surveys showed that psychology had succeeded in oversupplying professional manpower needs relative to current societal demand by greater than a twofold margin (Balch and Harper, 1976). Albee (1977) predicted hard times for psychologists, with Ph.D.s entering the armed forces in unprecedented numbers. Graduate students were feeling the economic crunch. Financial support had fallen off sharply, even as the number of applications continued to increase. Although there were 100 APA-approved clinical programs (a fivefold increase in 25 years), the large number of applicants relative to available space produced a selection ratio (3–5 percent for APA-approved programs), more competitive than that of most medical schools (Nyman, 1973).

In spite of the recession in the early 1970s and declining employment, graduate programs continued to turn out as many M.A.-level psychologists as ever. With their lower salary demands, they posed a competitive threat to both Ph.D. clinicians and nonclinical Ph.D.s who were moving into the service area. In addition, opposition from insurance companies and the medical profession to reimbursing psychologists singled out the subdoctoral status of the M.A. psychologist. Some Ph.D. private practitioners perceived the M.A. clinician as a hindrance to their efforts to jockey for a more favorable position in the fee-for-service market (Havens, 1979). Furthermore, with considerable money and prestige at stake if NHI became a reality, many in the profession were willing to jettison the subdoctoral degree if it proved to be a roadblock to psychology's inclusion in NHI. On the state level, M.A. practitioners were encountering concerted opposition to statutory recognition. Both the ABPP and the APA Council of Representatives were on record against continuing the terminal M.A. degree (a consolation prize for those who failed to pass through to subdoctoral status), and the latter argued that only doctoral practitioners could function independently or call themselves "psychologists" (Havens, 1979). Another nail in the M.A.'s coffin was APA Board of Professional Affairs' recommendation to disaffiliate from state psychological organizations that supported M.A. licensing (Havens, 1979). The objections were the familiar ones of limited competency and lack of uniform training standards, and though the objections were usually accompanied by proposals to upgrade M.A.-level training, few were ever acted on.

The APA's Education and Training Board, while acknowledging the economic competition, sustained its support of M.A.-level training. In 1973, the Conference on Levels and Patterns of Professional Training in Psychology took place at Vail, Colorado (Korman, 1974) and singled out the contributions of the subdoctoral psychologist to the nation's mental health manpower force (Dimond, Havens, Rathnow, and Colliver 1977), as had each of the three earlier conferences on professional training. But the Vail Conference went one step further with a proposal of a career lattice for the M.A. practitioner that would provide a framework for horizontal and vertical movement (Dimond et al., 1977).

Besides support from the education and training board and the welcomed affirmation of the Vail Conference, the M.A. group had some strong cards of its own. First, on the state level they were solidly entrenched in the mental health system, largely because they had been available to take up the slack created earlier by the shortage of Ph.D.s. Second, threatened with professional extinction, the M.A. group had begun to organize, and with their sheer numbers they now posed a political threat at the state level.

The ongoing debate to reaffirm or not to reaffirm the

Boulder model of scientist first and practitioner second appeared to be favoring the "negative" team. The 1973 Vail Conference first affirmed the merits of the scientist–practitioner model as exemplified in the traditional Ph.D. degree, and second, recommended a separate professional model to be designated by the Psy.D. degree (McConnell, 1984).

Gordon Derner, a distinguished trainer of clinical psychologists, had used the term *scholar–professional* to describe the model of training that is primarily practitioner oriented (Bellak and Hersen, 1980). This break with the traditional stance of previous conferences did not so much set forth new policy as it made existing policy congruent with reality.

In 1973, the University of Illinois' Psy.D. program received APA accreditation. Before long, five new Psy.D. programs were in place and two additional schools of psychology. By the end of the 1970s, professional programs and schools of psychology were averaging 91 students per program compared to an average of 58 in the APA accredited scientist–practitioner programs (Caddy, 1981).

In 1978, the Virginia Beach Conference was convened to work out the specifics of the professional model endorsed by the Vail Conference, and to address the concerns over the proliferation of free-standing schools of psychology (Caddy, 1981). Internship directors had long faulted graduate programs for turning out inadequately trained clinical psychology interns. Part of the weak preparation could be traced to the traditional academic reward system that placed higher priority on research productivity than on training students. Frank (1984) refers to the lack of professional role models for graduate students because universities wanted scientists and not tradespeople on their faculties. The alternative professional programs would correct the bias by rewarding clinical faculty for time spent on training.

On balance, much had been accomplished in the seventies. The profession had gained considerable credibility with its sister health and human services professions, legislative bodies, and the public at large. The rift between science and the profession showed signs of healing. Between 1970 and 1980, 4 of the 10 presidents of the APA were clinical psychologists (Reisman, 1981). Noteworthy is a statement in 1973 by Donald

Campbell, "relating the practice of Psychology to the science of Psychology will continue to be an organizational [in contrast to philosophical] problem for APA."[2]

A survey of graduates between 1968 and 1980 from 80 accredited clinical psychology doctoral programs (Schneider, 1981) disclosed several sanguine trends: the percentage of minorities, especially women, had increased substantially; children's services were on the upswing; an intrapsychic orientation had given way to other approaches, such as community, marital–family, group, behaviorism, and humanism; there was virtually no unemployment; and the relevant question for graduates "[was] not whether psychology is a profession, but what kind of profession it wants to be" (p. 1445). Certainly, clinical psychology met the definition of a profession as set forth by Peterson (1976); namely, a set of techniques derived from a science or theory and applied differently to different problems, a professional society with membership based mainly on competence, and a code of ethics to safeguard the welfare of society.

However, the profession was guilty of footdragging in its response to advocacy for all types of minorities and the powerless, particularly patients confined to inadequately funded facilities with degrading living conditions and less than adequate treatment programs. Simon (1975) asks for an advocate–professional model as a supplement to the scientist–professional model, and notes that psychologists have been preoccupied with their own professional minority concerns. Albee (1970) calls on the profession to assume some responsibility for developing public awareness and then public support for intervention with the real problems of society; for example, racism, sexism, and economic exploitation.

Another issue that needs resolution is whether clinical psychologists will continue to operate in medicine, law, education, and industry, where they do not have squatters' rights, or build their own "house of business," as Albee had suggested in the 1965 Chicago Conference (McConnell, 1984).

Basically, clinical psychologists had gone where the demand was, and in doing so they frequently incurred an adop-

[2] This statement on issues facing psychology appeared on the APA Election Ballot in 1973 when Campbell was President-Elect.

tive status. Something was clearly wrong when the only human service profession to have its own science of behavior and to offer more innovative concepts and methods than other professions had to spend inordinate time and energy gaining favor and fending off an adjunctive role. Whether clinical psychology can live outside its own sphere and still be recognized as an autonomous profession is a significant part of the unfinished business for the present and future.

CLINICAL PSYCHOLOGY OUTSIDE THE UNITED STATES

Professional psychology has always been (though to a lesser extent today) an American phenomenon. Outside the United States, professional psychology suffered from a lack of numerical strength (especially at the Ph.D. level), political influence, and demand for services (and service rarely meant psychotherapy).

The rate of professionalization has been faster in the industrial nations than in the Communist countries, Latin America, and other third world countries. Approximately one-third of professional psychologists work in the clinical area, with approximately 5 percent in private practice and the rest employed by the government (Ardila, 1982). The number of master and doctoral level training programs in clinical psychology is far below the number in the United States, and clinical internships are required in only a few countries (Fichter and Wittchen, 1980).

CRITICAL ISSUES IN THE EIGHTIES

Training Models and Subdoctoral Education

Strickland (1983a) estimates that practitioner programs now account for over 25 percent of the clinical doctorates. Cummings (1984) predicts that within 10 years the majority of clinical psychologists will be trained in professional schools, and Goldenberg (1983) believes that the professional school movement will be the next major force behind the growth and development of clinical psychology.

For the most part, however, the shift to practitioner-oriented programs has taken place outside the university. The large majority of graduate departments have not seen fit to adopt the recommendations of the Vail conference. Perhaps many have heeded the implicit warning in APA's 1979 official reendorsement of the scientist–practitioner model. APA's pronouncement could be viewed as confirmation that the historical schism between science and the profession is still alive, well, and residing as always in a discipline deeply rooted in scholarly and scientific traditions. However, APA's concern is a pragmatic and urgent one, based largely on the alarming increase of the free-standing schools, close to 20 different ones in Northern California alone.

Basically, the issue is quality control (i.e., control over the quality of clinical student selected, trained, and graduated). Without the safeguards of the university setting, the threat of "counterfeit training" looms large. For many, the question is no longer whether to have practitioner programs, but how to ensure an intimate connection with the scientific base of the profession. Not unexpectedly, the profession remains divided at both the national and state levels over the matter of the training, employment, and statutory credentialing of master's degree clinicians. Sobel (1979) reports that Cummings says there are now 222 APA-approved terminal master's programs. For budgetary reasons (e.g., lower salaries), and manpower needs (e.g., rural locations), universities continue to graduate M.A. psychologists; agencies and institutions continue to hire them; and state licensing boards continue to vacillate between disenfranchising them or "making honest psychologists out of them."

A Delphi poll (to forecast the likelihood and possible time courses of events relevant to a key issue, e.g., subdoctoral training) by Anderson, Parenté, and Gordon (1981) predicted a need for subdoctoral mental health practitioners for at least another decade, and small likelihood that subdoctoral education will be eliminated. In fact, Anderson et al. are betting on a strong trend for M.A. professional training to become highly specialized with mandatory licensing or certification, and resulting competition with Ph.D.s for jobs. In the meantime, like those who seek clinical respecialization, M.A. clinicians may escape from their professional cul de sac by matriculating at one of the free-standing schools for doctoral training. A realistic prediction is for subdoctoral education to continue with the M.A. degree designed for the psychological technician.

Law, Legislation, and Standards

The 1980s have witnessed the struggle of the profession to protect its accomplishments and, at the same time, to overcome the barriers that have excluded or threaten to exclude its participation in a wider sector of the health care delivery system.

Despite recurring opposition to statutory credentialing from the medical profession, nonlicensed professions, excluded M.A.s, and researchers–academicians who oppose it for a variety of motivations, clinical psychology has steadily progressed in this area. The majority of states now define practice over and above the definition and limitations of the title psychologist (Stigall, 1981).

By far the major offensive thrust of the profession has been directed toward the practice of psychology in hospitals and other health care facilities, and inclusion in major third-party legislation. To gain recognition as a primary health care provider for physical and mental health care without having to be authorized or supervised by a physician, the profession has centered its lobbying efforts in three areas (Julius & Handal, 1980). The first effort is to obtain an amendment of existing third-party reimbursement programs at the federal level. The second effort is to facilitate the public's increased access to nonmedical mental health providers via freedom-of-choice legislation in each state. The third effort is to improve the regulation and control of the definition of psychologist through licensing–certification statutes.

So far, 25 of the 50 states and Washington, DC recognize psychologists as reimbursable providers in Medicaid, although there is much variability in covered services and methods of reimbursement (Resnick, 1983). Signal legal and legislative victories have been achieved (e.g., in Virginia) in terms of Blue Shield's reimbursing psychologists for delivery of mental health services, and in modifying the exclusionary stance of the Joint Commission on Accreditation of Hospitals (JCAH) for the practice of psychology in hospitals and other health care facilities (Zaro, Batchelor, Ginsberg, and Pallak, 1982). Wiggins (1984) concludes: "Now the struggle must continue on a state by state, hospital by hospital basis, with the central issue remaining patient need and the qualification, credentials, training and experience of the individual psychological practitioner" (p. 50).

In taking its case to legislatures, courts, and regulatory bodies, the profession has argued that inclusion of psychologists as reimbursed providers in the nation's health care system will not increase the cost burden of the system, and is quite likely to reduce the demand for medical care and hospitalization. A statement by Bersoff (1983) speaks to the blending of public interest, consumer interest, and guild interest: "The rights, privileges, health, and pocketbooks of patients and the public are at stake" (p. 1241).

By being an advocate for the public, the profession has earned the respect and support of legislatures, courts, and other nonmedical professions. What it has learned in the process is the importance of orchestrating a multilevel, multidimensional approach that includes the use of attorney–lobbyists, political action committees, fund-raising support for lengthy legal and legislative battles, data-based presentations, and a national and state organized network of financial and other resources.

Developing a fiduciary relation with the public has always been a critical issue for clinical psychologists. Beginning in the 1970s, the escalating costs of physical and mental health services and the trend for third-party payers to reduce benefits, have underscored the need for accountability. Accountability includes utilization review, which is primarily financial and legal and includes efficient use of resources; quality assurance, which addresses professional and ethical matters and the evaluation of the quality of services offered to the public; and peer review, which is the vehicle for discharging quality assurance (Stricker and Cohen, 1984).

The Committee on Professional Standards of APA's Board of Professional Affairs has been charged with developing and interrelating psychology's quality assurance policies, and has written a casebook for providers of psychological services in order to implement the specific guidelines for delivery of services by the four speciality areas (APA, 1984a). The Professional Standards Review Committee not only monitors and provides guidance to the state review committees, but it also serves as a national policy and coordinating body for all review efforts (Zaro and Kilburg, 1982).

Although the concept of quality assurance by peer review has been endorsed by psychology, the implementation has brought forth many critics. Criticisms are directed at: (1) the issue of confidentiality for clients or patients; (2) the administration of the review process; (3) the threat to the independent judgment of the practitioner; and (4) the validity of judgments made by peers on the basis of selected information (Stricker and Cohen, 1984). At present, APA is moving toward a revision of the association's current peer review system; at the same time it is fending off a minority's clamor to declare an indefinite moratorium on the system (APA, 1984b).

Relations with Other Professions

Cummings and VandenBos (1983) state: "The phrase *relations with other professions* most often translates into *relations with Psychiatry*" (p. 1324). Several professional developments that began in the 1970s and came to fruition in the 1980s (e.g., legislation, hospital practice, insurance reimbursement) have further strained the uneasy truce between clinical psychology and psychiatry. The moderate voices in both professions have sought to soften the conflict points and to turn acrimonious debates into "good faith" negotiations.

One notable step toward interprofessional cooperation is the Joint Commission on Interprofessional Affairs which has been approved by each of the four core mental health professional associations (Cummings and VandenBos, 1983). However, the aggressive expansion of professional psychology into the general health care field in the face of the federal government's retrenchment on funding for domestic programs suggests a guarded prognosis on relations between psychology and the medical profession. The uneasy truce will continue.

Political Consciousness

For psychology to be perceived as a fully legitimate science and a bona fide health care profession, political reality dictates that effective communication evolve between psychologists and the policymakers of the nation's health care and scientific research systems (DeLeon, VandenBos, and Kraut, 1984).

Because psychologists represent only a small proportion of health service providers, they must adopt a proactive rather than a reactive stance in order to increase their visibility with policymakers (Dorken, 1981). There are two strategic considerations. First is to convince policymaking bodies that what is good for psychology is good for society. An optimal balance must be maintained between professional guild interests and the interest of the public at large. The second consideration is to discover politically sensitive methods to increase our credibility and influence.

Hosticka, Hibbard, and Sundberg (1983) describe two roles for psychologists to take in the policymaking arena. One is an advocate position in which psychologists actively support those goals and priorities that will benefit both the profession and the well-being of citizens. As an example, Felipe-Russo (1979) calls upon psychologists to work together in order to overcome the sex bias and sex role stereotypes that have had a devastating effect on women and female children, especially within the minority communities. The second role is one of a technician who learns how policymakers approach decisions and how they translate information into action, and then shares with them knowledge of efficient and effective methods of attaining legislative goals (e.g., national health insurance).

Kempler and Norman (1981) refer to a "political coming-of-age" for psychologists in their appreciation of the importance of presenting a proactive and unified position with an agenda that blends social responsibility, public accountability, and enlightened self-interest. On a nuts-and-bolts level, professional sources have suggested constructive actions to enhance the profession's visibility and to strengthen its credibility on both the state and federal levels. With Sobel (1979), Cummings voiced the hope that more psychologists will seek careers in the public policy field (e.g., specific jobs, lobbying, political candidacy, campaign specialists), not only to compensate for the employment crunch in traditional jobs and to give impetus to the new careers movement, but also to increase the political clout of the profession. Mowbray, Miller, and Schneider (1983) note the impact of the new federalism of the 1980s in which states have a larger and more influential role in funding and policy development. They encourage psychologists to seek careers in state mental health departments, again not only to offset the declining job market, but also to protect and bolster psychology's position at a grassroots level. DeLeon, Frohboese, and Meyers (1984) conclude that many of the content areas in which psychologists have expertise are relevant to a wide range of congressional issues; in addition, the procedural skills that psychologists develop during their scientific and/or practitioner training can help them function effectively on legislative staffs.

There is also professional endorsement for financial support of the American Association for the Advancement of Psychology (AAP), psychology's only national advocacy organization, and the APA's Defense Fund, which was set up to assist with the cost of legislative battles. Founded in 1974 as a nonprofit organization funded by APA donations and individual membership dues, AAP's purposes are to (1) eliminate discrimination in the treatment of mental illness and within the mental health professional community; (2) seek more funding for behavioral and social science research training; and (3) collaborate with other national and state groups in lobbying for professional and scientific goals.

A recent example of AAP's success is a precedent-setting change in the Federal Rules of Criminal Procedure that give psychologists complete parity with psychiatrists through all parts of the Criminal Code (APA, 1985a). This legislative change, for which AAP worked nine years, permits psychologists to examine, report to the court, testify, and treat under provisions relating to the federal criminal court system. Another successful AAP effort has been the Deficit Reduction Act of July 1985, which includes an amendment to allow psychologists to deliver services in risk-sharing health maintenance organizations without the physician supervision and referral that is otherwise required for Medicare-covered services (APA, 1985a). The amendment also represents the first direct mention of psychology in the Medicare statute.

Still other professional sources have made pleas for different factions within psychology to put aside their parochial differences and to present a united front in promoting psychology as a science and a profession. It is important also to form political action groups, to set up public education networks at the state level, and to sensitize the next generation of clinical psychologists to the need for political involvement.

The American Psychological Association has taken action to educate both the public and the profession. A National Policy Studies Unit has been set up to coordinate the gathering and disseminating of information to educate and lobby at the national and state levels. A national publication information committee has also been formed to develop, coordinate, and disseminate information about psychology and psychologists. Finally, the *American Psychologist*, the official publication of the APA, has a public forum section in which legislators, regulatory agency officials, and politically informed psychologists educate the membership about relevant and imminent public policy developments.

Research in Clinical Psychology

The growth of clinical psychology has consistently been subjected to the "parental gaze" of nonclinical psychologists, with concern being voiced about the alleged neglect of research values. The criticism has commonly been that clinical psychologists are too focused on practice techniques and issues, and that neglect of research-based ideas will surely lead to a quasi-professional status for the profession. The dissonance between experimental psychologists and clinical psychologists may be like a generation gap. The predicates for experimental psychology were developed in an era before clinical psychology was in existence. Certainly, clinical psychology needs to understand the importance of research and actively encourage it.

The rise of the practice-oriented programs in professional schools (with the nonresearch Psy.D. degree) and the fall of the research-oriented programs in universities (with the data-based Ph.D. degree) has increased the criticism of clinical training, especially from more experimentally-oriented psychologists. It seems likely, however, that rapprochement will occur, and that clinical psychology will settle on a use of research that adequately accommodates the needs created by practice and the disciplinary preferences of psychology overall.

Lest it seem that clinical psychologists are not self determining—some of the difficulties come from the public policy mandate for human–health services. As Thorne (1961) describes it:

> Clinical psychology and psychiatry have been forced into a premature and overextended application of what little is known by the tremendous pressure exerted by social institutions for answers to pressing questions. At a time when basic science psychology and psychopathology have made only limited progress in supplying adequate basic science foundations for clinical practice, it was inevitable that a flood of untested theories would rush in to fill the void of needed knowledge. The practical result of having so many theories that are unproved, and perhaps unprovable with present basic science resources, has been that there are literally as many schools of clinical practice as there are permutations and combinations of theoretical systems [p. ix].

Regrettably, this societal press to extend poorly researched ideas into virtually all areas of human–health service (not just in clinical psychology) is as true today as it was when Thorne offered the critique a quarter of a century ago.

Thorne's (1961) posture was that: "The ethical justification for making a clinical judgement which does not have complete scientific support and validation is that it only professes to be the best that can be offered at that time and place" (p. 21). While this rationale is pragmatic, it scarcely satisfies the need to advance the research bases of clinical psychology.

The preamble for the APA's (1981b) "Ethical Principles of Psychologists" requires that there be a commitment to "increasing knowledge of human behavior and of people's understanding of themselves and others and to the utilization of such knowledge for the promotion of human welfare" (p. 633). The "Speciality Guidelines for the Delivery of Services" from APA (1981c) support that "Professional clinical psychologists are encouraged to develop innovative theories and procedures and to provide appropriate theoretical and/or empirical support for their innovations" (p. 644). There seems no doubt that present-day and future clinical psychologists must keep research methodologies in the forefront of their services, notwithstanding the trend toward a professional degree program (i.e., the Psy.D. degree).

The public policy dictate for "service now!" cannot be allowed unabashed control. Some clinical psychologists may well feel flattered by such an urgent appeal. But for those of us concerned about the future of clinical psychology there must be a resistance to the seductive nature of flattery. As Cattell (1966) points out:

> If one takes medicine as a model, social experience may argue for a split of the academic-researcher and practitioner degrees, for the skills of a general practitioner are needed in emergencies, and he must be as well drilled to the best practical action as is a soldier. Three considerations throw doubt on this model: (1) The nature of the psychologist's practice does not have life-and-death urgency at any hour of day and night as in general medicine. (2) As a young science, psychology is likely to be transformed almost out of recognition, as in therapeutic procedures in less than a generation by the progress of research. The practitioner who is not also research trained and oriented is going to get badly out of touch, obsolete, and ineffective in his very practice. (3) Medicine is to some extent regretting its own model [p. 13].

While there are certain psychological emergencies where life is at risk (especially now that clinical psychologists have admitting privileges to hospitals and are relied upon to deal with life-threatening conditions), Cattell is quite right that this alone cannot be a justification for forgetting research; the existence of clinical psychology must gain sustenance from research; and the current lackluster state of psychiatry among physicians (it has relatively low priority and low salaries, as compared to other medical specialties) may well be connected to the faulty research patterns endemic to psychiatry.

It seems logical that future research in clinical psychology will have to make methodological adaptations to the public policy mandate for services. At the same time, it must be recognized that clinical psychological research has numerous unique qualities that cannot be neglected. Rotter (1971) points out that, unlike other sciences, clinical psychology does not have much control over the conditions in which the human organism exists, and clinical psychology is a historical science; he states:

> Usually, in order to understand a physical object one has to know its current physical properties. At this time, we have not even the slightest inkling of the physical properties of past experience, but we know that all experience changes the organism. Thus, in order to understand and predict the behavior of a human being, we must know all that it is possible to know about his past experience. Since no two people have exactly the same experiences nor start with the same potential to respond equivalently to the same experiences, each person is unique, and the devising of general laws about behavior is remarkably hard. Not only does the cautious scientist find great difficulty in arriving at generalizations, but he also has even greater difficulty in testing their validity, since he must test the validity on many people but allow for the uniqueness of each at the same time [pp. 106–107].

Clinical psychological research may not be easily advanced to the state expected for other sciences, but it must, none the less, step forward.

The goals of clinical psychological research are varied and complex. Consider the following from Kendall and Norton-Ford (1982):

> Research in clinical psychology is studious inquiry designed for the advancement of our knowledge of human functioning. The purpose of such research is to apply sci-

> entific methods to the gathering of the data necessary to corroborate or reject our tentative theories (i.e., our hypotheses) about how people think, feel, and behave. In addition to this general all-encompassing goal, well-designed clinical research also has more specific *second-level goals* that give collective direction and purpose to subareas of the research efforts in clinical psychology [p. 85].

In considering secondary goals, they point out: "Clinicians involved in psychological assessment want to be able to describe people accurately and make predictions about their future behavior, so their second-level goal is to identify *what sample of data, gathered in what setting, and with what subject and assessor, produced what information?*" (p. 85). Also, they say: "Clinical psychologists involved in clinical intervention research are, as a second-level goal, trying to identify *what intervention, in what settings, and with what client and change-agent produced what effects?*" (p. 86). Rather than trying to pinpoint the ultimate assessment technique, intervention strategy, or theory, the clinical psychologist relies on research to "determine when, and for whom, and for what specific purposes, different assessments, interventions, and theories are most effective in advancing our understanding of human functioning and our ability to help people live full lives" (p. 86).

The research of clinical psychologists has typically followed three approaches (Kogan, 1966). The nomothetic approach holds that human psychology is lawful and may be revealed and measured by empirical methods; that is, there are general principles that apply to everyone. The normative approach relies on standardized tests designed to uncover discrepancies in psychological functioning between the individual and a specific (normative) group; the emphasis is on quantitative measurement, and applied psychometric, differential, or actuarial strategies to interindividual differences. The idiographic approach focuses on the dynamics and development of the individual; the emphasis is on the unique psychological organization and the dynamic–genetic considerations of the individual.

The foregoing three approaches will likely continue to

prevail in clinical psychological research. Historically, the idiographic approach has been a cornerstone, as epitomized by the case studies in psychoanalytically oriented psychology. This approach is still helpful for generating ideas that can be the basis for an experimental research investigation (as well as for helping the clinician gain valuable insights into how to help the person being analyzed), but it typically fails to produce a research result that can be assuredly generalized to other persons. Questionnaires and surveys can, likewise, offer information that will contribute to the formulation of more rigorous investigations, but they too seldom allow for conclusions.

Research in clinical psychology has become increasingly sophisticated and scientific in stature. Therefore, it would appear that the scientific method will be the predominate one in clinical psychological research:

> The scientific method requires that research be *empirical, precise*, and *repeatable*. Empirical means that the researcher gathers data from observation. For precision, the researcher must clearly define (1) the phenomena that are being observed, and (2) exactly how these observations will be conducted. Repeatability requires that scientists document their procedures so that other scientists can check to see that the findings can be reproduced [Kendall and Norton-Ford, 1982, p. 86].

The ultimate goal is to be able to use research data to understand a target individual or group of individuals; this requires that the data attain sufficient stature to accommodate generalization. Stated simply, the objective is to understand what causes a particular behavior on the part of an individual.

Even with a firm commitment to the scientific method and/or pursuing experimentally derived findings, clinical psychology cannot exclude other research strategies, including the clinical case study. Well into the future, the case study will be valuable for ideas, hypotheses, and techniques, albeit that experimental research will be needed to test and evaluate these case-study products. Consequently, there will (and should) be interdependence between the clinical case study and the experimental method, but there will have to be a reasonable balance—one should not overpower the other: "Experimental research, even if sufficiently rigorous, often is far removed from the clinical problems and practice to which the results ultimately need to be generalized" (Kazdin, 1980, p. 30).

This section is included at this point in the book to underscore how critically important research is to the future of clinical psychology. Granted, clinical psychology has made outstanding, noteworthy advances, but it cannot rest on its laurels. The movement toward a professional-practice training model must not be allowed to denigrate the essential nature of research. Instead, clinical psychologists need to be prepared to pursue *meaningful* research. Too often in the past, research training has, in fact, been minimal in relevance to clinical practice, and many of the criticisms leveled at elevating research methods above clinical methods have been justified. But it is shortsighted *and* unprofessional to believe that a clinical psychologist can practice without the benefit of training in research or that the specialty of clinical psychology can continue to exist—not to mention continue to develop, expand, and improve—without a commitment to research on the part of every one of its members–practitioners.

Chapter 2

Becoming Trained as a Clinical Psychologist

Since 1947, the American Psychological Association (APA) has accredited doctoral programs in professional psychology, beginning with the clinical psychology specialty and later counseling psychology, school psychology, and more recently combined professional–scientific programs which meet the minimal criteria in two or more of the other specialties (APA, 1983a). In the APA accreditation handbook, the term *professional psychology* is used in the generic sense to refer to psychologists who provide services to the public (APA, 1983a). The purpose of accreditation is "to promote excellence in doctoral education and training in those specialties of professional psychology designated, so as in turn to provide a service of quality assessment and assurance for the general public, prospective students, and the profession itself" (p. v).

Program accreditation or approval is based on policies and criteria developed by APA's Education and Training Board and implemented by visitation teams. Accreditation policies and criteria have been revised periodically to reflect the changing and expanding field of professional psychology (APA, 1983a). An updated list of APA-approved programs is published annually in the *American Psychologist.* As of 1986 there were 144 approved or provisionally approved clinical psychology programs (compared to 22 in 1947), 46 in counseling psychology, 32 in school psychology, and 5 in combined professional–scientific psychology (Capsule, 1986). Many doctoral programs do not have accreditation status because they are too new, have failed to obtain approval, or the faculty have decided not to seek APA's endorsement. Approved programs must submit an annual report to demonstrate continued compliance with accreditation standards, and will have a reevaluation site visit every five years.

An example of the greater marketability of graduates of APA-approved programs over graduates of nonapproved programs is reported by Walfish and Sumprer (1984). They examined job advertisements in the *APA Monitor* for doctoral-level clinical and/or counseling psychologists, and found nine times as many APA-approved graduates obtained positions, and 95% of the employers listed in the *APA Monitor* stated that they prefer to hire graduates of approved programs. Although approved clinical programs account for the largest number of articles published in major clinical journals, 6 out of 10 articles are published by individuals in nonapproved programs or in other institutional settings (Golden, Kuperman, and Osmon, 1980).

Although the issue of practitioner training programs and the alternative Psy.D. degree continue to be debated in the literature, in reality practitioner and traditional scientist-practioner training programs are more alike than different. Of several conclusions drawn by Peterson (1985) about practitioner-oriented training programs, three stand out: (1) graduates of scientist–practitioner programs and graduates of practitioner programs perform about equally well; (2) curricula of professional schools and scientist–practioner programs are more alike than different; and (3) the main differences between practitioner and scientist–practitioner programs lie in the attitudes and interests of faculty and students.

For a description of graduate programs in professional psychology, students should consult the *Graduate Study in Psychology*, which is published by APA (1986a) at regular intervals. For students who want the traditional model, Section III (Development of Clinical Psychology as an Experimental–Behavioral Science) of APA's Division of Clinical Psychology publishes a directory of scientist–professional programs, which contains considerable descriptive information.

To be eligible for accreditation, training programs must demonstrate a firm commitment to psychology as a science. The traditional program does so by requiring independent research representing a contribution to knowledge, while the practitioner program does so by a scholarly project which addresses some aspect of psychological practice (APA, 1983a). Strupp (1982) captures the spirit of the scholarly commitment in the following statement:

> A great contribution our graduate programs can make to the development of future clinical psychologists is to train thinking clinicians-individuals who question their practice and their techniques, who are capable of entertaining alternative hypotheses to explain clinical phenomena they encounter; individuals who do not accept as a matter of blind faith the teachings of a training institution no matter who the leaders may be [p. 7].

In addition, both training models must demonstrate social responsibility and sensitivity to cultural and individual differences with respect to faculty recruitment and promotions, student recruitment and evaluation, curriculum, and field training. As stated in the *Accreditation Handbook* (APA, 1983a), "programs must develop knowledge and skills in their students relevant to human diversity, such as people with handicapping conditions; of differing ages, genders, ethnic and racial backgrounds, religions, and life-styles; and from differing social and individual backgrounds" (p. 4).

INSTITUTIONAL SETTINGS

There are four types of institutional settings in which accredited professional programs are located: (1) university psychology departments; (2) schools of psychology within universities (e.g., Wright State University, Rutgers University); (3) professional schools within other university administrative units (e.g., medical schools or health centers). At present there are 10 programs awarding the doctoral degree and another 13 planning doctoral programs (Cohen, Lubin, and Nathan, 1979); (4) free-standing schools of psychology (e.g., California School of Professional Psychology).

On the fringes of professional training are numerous external degree programs in which the quality of the education and the financial status are, at best, marginal. The accreditation handbook also states that if it is not a component of an accredited university, a school of professional psychology must be an incorporated, educationally accredited, nonprofit institution with a board of knowledgeable and responsible trustees who have no financial interest in the operation of the school (APA, 1983a).

Further, the training program must: (1) be clearly and publicly identified and labeled as a professional psychology program; (2) allow administrative authority to be vested in a senior-level psychologist; (3) have an identifiable psychology faculty who have clear authority and primary responsibility for all aspects of the program; (4) ensure a breadth of exposure to the field of psychology and include supervised practica and internships; and finally; (5) be affiliated with an institution that provides appropriate financial support for the program.

CURRICULA

Basically, professional preparation in the 1980s calls for an integration of theory, research, and practice in whatever order of importance is determined by the program (Goldenberg, 1983). Students can expect to devote a minimum of three academic years of full-time resident study.

The curriculum must include courses in scientific and professional ethics and standards, research design and methodology, statistics, psychological measurement, and history and systems of psychology. Also, students must demonstrate competence in each of the following content areas: (1) biological bases of behavior; (2) cognitive–affective bases of behavior; (3) social bases of behavior; and (4) individual behavior (e.g., personality theory, abnormal psychology, developmental psychology). Competence may be demonstrated by passing comprehensive examinations in each of the four areas, or by completion of at least one course in each of the four areas (APA, 1983a).

In addition, clinical psychology requires training in individual assessment methods, psychodiagnosis (e.g., familiarity with *The Diagnostic and Statistical Manual of Psychiatric Disorders*, 3rd edition (American Psychiatric Association, 1980), intervention procedures (such as individual, group, marital, family therapy, as well as familiarity with psychotropic medication), and consultation. Training in assessment is particularly important: "Every student must become familiar with major assessment and intervention techniques and their theoretical bases" (APA, 1983a, p. 7). Since the 1960s there has been a decline in emphasis on assessment training and a corresponding increase in emphasis on therapy training. This trend is continuing in the eighties (Kolbe, Shemberg, and Leventhal, 1985). However, Piotrowski and Keller (1984) surveyed 113 APA-approved programs and found that objective assessment measures, such as psychometric instruments and behavioral ratings, were emphasized over projective techniques; assessment was still considered important, and some familiarity with projective techniques was expected.

Practically all training programs require courses in psychotherapy (Kolbe et al., 1985). Although the emphasis on training in various theoretically based individual therapies continues, provision for training in group, marital, and family therapies has been limited. A survey by Zohn and Carmody (1978) indicates that in APA-approved programs training opportunities in group treatment methods are on the rise; however, group training is often left up to the individual student's initiative, and many students must wait until after graduation to obtain supervised experience in conducting group therapy. Similarly, theories and methods of marital and family therapy have been included in training programs in recent years, but the number of programs doing so is small (L'Abate, Berger, Wright, and O'Shea, 1979). Less than 20% of clinical psychology programs offer a minimum of one seminar or one practicum in marital therapy (Prochaska and Prochaska, 1978), and much of the demand for training is met by the proliferation of free-standing institutes (Framo, 1979). Shapiro (1979) observes: "Family therapy is often perceived as complex and threatening to novices [both faculty and students], and institutional support as well as skillful teaching are necessary to ensure a successful training experience" (p. 878).

In addition to instruction in substantive content areas and development of clinical skills, the curriculum must include training in research that is relevant to the professional practice of psychology: "Research training should include the techniques and methods of inquiry appropriate to the professional psychologist, encompassing such procedures as (1) the use of the natural setting, as well as of the laboratory, (2) action research, (3) evaluation and follow-up studies, and (4) demonstration projects" (APA, 1983a, p. 8). Meltzoff (1984) concludes that whether or not a doctoral psychologist does research, research training does provide a respect for the process of knowledge acquisition, a way of thinking about issues, a readiness to evaluate the literature critically, and a willingness to evaluate and modify clinical practice.

The APA policy on training does not object to programs with a strong emphasis in one theoretical orientation, so long as students are exposed to other orientations. Forehand (1985) advises: (1) each program should adopt a middle-of-the-road position between the extremes of no theoretical orientation and only one orientation; (2) a prospective student should be informed as to where a program is on that continuum; and (3) a program with a dominant orientation should ensure that students are well grounded in that orientation.

To safeguard the welfare of the public and to maintain the respect of the professional community, a training program must have explicit procedures for an ongoing evaluation of students' competence in clinical skills. In a survey of APA-approved doctoral programs, Gifford and Lawlis (1978) found that over 90% of the programs require a "rite of passage," analogous to a specialty examination, and that recently a number of programs are tailoring examinations to the needs of individual students.

Along with the trend toward individualizing examinations is an emphasis on performance-based evaluation required for graduation and as preparation for later licensing (Schacht, 1984). Fantuzzo (1984) argues for an objective performance-based evaluation design that defines mandatory skills for insuring minimal competency for practice, and that provides solid evidence that training produces such competency. The APA (1983a) position is: "The specific competencies expected of graduates may vary with the goals of the program. . . . For example, programs training for practitioner roles will have higher requirements for practicing skills while those that emphasize other roles may have higher standards for other skills" (p. 8).

A program's evaluation design must incorporate a policy on student rights and due process procedure. Bernard (1975) surveyed 100 clinical psychology programs to determine how decisions are made and implemented with respect to a student whose progress has been unsatisfactory. Of the 40 programs that responded, 12 had no policy and the remainder had a mishmash of procedures. Meyer (1980) urges the profession to avoid the past trend whereby students were summarily dropped on seemingly arbitrary and/or capricious grounds without allowance for appeal or other avenues of recourse. He points out that the overall market philosophy of higher education has changed, and universities now foster an atmosphere conducive to keeping students enrolled; in addition, students are better organized and more aware of their rights and due process procedures, and courts and legislatures are more responsive to safeguards for students. Several authors (Bernard, 1975; Meyer, 1980; Miller and Rickard, 1983) recommend the following guidelines: (1) an adequate written program description; (2) provision for routine evaluation of all students; (3) written prescriptions for remediation; and (4) a formal due process procedure in which student input is sought. In addition, Meyer recommends that where feasible the problematic student be assessed by a professional psychologist who is independent of the core faculty. One glaring deficiency is that very few departments have written procedures for destroying outdated student evaluation material.

SUBSPECIALTY TRAINING

Although opinion is divided over the wisdom of subspecialty training at the predoctoral level, federal requirements that designate training grants for specific areas or for specific client populations provide strong arguments for the desirability of subspecialty offerings. VandenBos and Stapp (1983) indicate that federal monies are increasingly available for students who are willing to work in rural settings, provide service to particular populations (e.g., elderly, minorities, handicapped), or concentrate on primary prevention and behavioral health.

Rickard and Bernaty (1983) point out that identification and selection of subspecialty offerings are influenced by perception of the need for and the marketability of the specialized service provider, and generic clinical training can add or drop subspecialty offerings as the need changes. The following is an overview of the current status of subspecialty training.

Substance Abuse

Development of skills in assessment, treatment, research, and prevention of substance use disorders are required. Research opportunities in this field are modest and clinical training and coursework are minimal (Selin and Svanum, 1981).

Geropsychology

This area involves the application of clinical skills to the elderly population. Despite federal designation as a high training priority, Cohen and Cooley (1983) found only six formal and 21 informal subspecialty offerings.

Rural Mental Health

Delivery of psychological services in sparsely populated areas: The need is recognized by everyone, but few programs offer systematic coursework and practica.

Forensic Psychology

Provision of consultation and direct clinical service for clients with serious psychological and legal problems is required in this subspecialty. Training opportunities with a joint Ph.D./J.D. degree have increased, but not enough to keep pace with the rapid involvement of practitioners (Lawlor, Siskind, and Brooks, 1981).

Correctional Clinical Psychology

Provision of diagnosis–assessment and therapy to prison inmates: A few programs are in place (e.g., the University of Alabama's psychology department is a leader in the field).

Clinical Neuropsychology

This area involves specialization in the evaluation and rehabilitation of clients with neurologically related disorders. In a survey of doctoral programs Noonberg and Page (1982) found 88% offer preinternship training in neuropsychology, but only 38% of these programs offer practical hands-on clinical experience.

Public Administration and Management

Acquisition of skills in administering, developing, and evaluating mental health programs are required in this subspecialty. Rickard and Clements (1981) surveyed a large number of APA-approved programs and found limited possibilities for a small number of interested students.

Victimology

The APA is promoting training and research regarding recognition and treatment of the consequences of criminal victimization. The outlook is for moderate development in this field in the late eighties.

Clinical Child Psychology/Pediatric Psychology

Specialization in psychological and medically related disorders in children is required. Tuma (1981) reviewed several studies and found 34 formal programs in clinical child psychology, and an additional 52 "informal" subspecialty sequences, but no program at the Ph.D. level in pediatric psychology, which so far is perceived as a special emphasis within clinical child or health psychology. Tuma cites research that projects a serious shortfall in the next decade's need for 10,000 clinical child psychologists.

Medical Psychology/Health Psychology

Medical psychology has been a subspecialty of clinical psychology for some time and in some respects is the precursor of the more recently developing areas of health psychology, behavioral health, and behavioral medicine. Health psychology is clearly the fastest growing subspecialty in clinical psychology.

DeLeon and Pallak (1982) note that health economists, public health professionals, physicians, and others believe that the means to improve the health of the population will be largely behavioral rather than solely medical. The authors also urge psychologists to have a broader focus through a public health perspective that recognizes the role of society in promoting either disability-linked behavior or health-limited behaviors with due attention to public policy issues. Both the University of Hawaii and University of Alabama offer a joint M.P.H. degree in public health psychology, which addresses primary prevention and a psychology's role in improving the health care system.

Community Psychology

Like health psychology, community psychology can be found as a specialty area in its own right or as a subspecialty of clinical psychology. Traditionally its strength lies in program evaluation, consultation with paraprofessionals, and prevention of psychological disorders. Despite a surge in community psychology during the sixties it was in danger of disappearing as a subspecialty due to its amorphous identity and the lukewarm support for its client advocacy role. With the support given to prevention and to service to special populations by federal training funds, community psychology is making a significant comeback in the eighties (e.g., meeting the needs of the homeless/street people, AIDS patients, and victims of abuse).

Minority Service Providers

Despite being one of the targeted areas for federal training grants, growth has been gradual in the area of psychological services to minority populations. A limited number of programs offer one or two courses by one or two faculty to a small number of doctoral students. The outlook for development in the late eighties is favorable.

FACULTY

An APA accredited program is expected to have an experienced and productive faculty who will provide effective leadership, modeling, supervision, and instruction (APA, 1983a). Beyond the normal duties of teaching, research, and supervision, faculty members should be active as licensed practitioners and committed to updating their knowledge and skills through continuing education. The faculty must be large enough to ensure the availability to students of program advisement, teaching, and supervision of the students' practice and research. In order to provide students with knowledge about particular settings and special clinical problems, practitioners are recruited from the local community to serve as adjunct clinical faculty.

In order to retain clinically competent faculty, universities must be willing to give as much recognition to proficiency in training students as they do to research productivity. A statement by Kalinkowitz (1978) is noteworthy: "As academics, we can acknowledge that the professional reputations of our practitioner colleagues represent the same measures of skills and proficiency as our own benchmarks of excellence in teaching and research, and we can help convince our deans and presidents that years of professional expertise merit consideration for professorships and tenure" (p. 5).

ADMISSION PROCESS

In addition to intellectual capability and personal suitability (e.g., self-awareness, interpersonal sensitivity, and tolerance for cultural and individual differences), students are expected to demonstrate a commitment to social justice and to improving the quality of life of those with whom they come in contact. The *Accreditation Handbook* (APA, 1983a) states that students are entitled to receive a full description of the training program. The description should include the following: goals of the program; theoretical orientation; available training resources and facilities; requirements students are expected to fulfill; professional and research interests of faculty members; size of the applicant pool and typical acceptance and attrition rates; percentage of male, female, minority, and handicapped students; opportunities for financial and academic counseling; and requirements for full-time and part-time status.

In an analysis of data from four editions of *The Graduate Study in Psychology* published in the 1970s by APA, Stoup and Benjamin (1982) conclude that the total number of applications to clinical psychology doctoral programs has remained fairly constant. The mean number of applications has declined by 20%, but this was apparently due to an increase in the number of professional programs. They report that during the 1970s the mean acceptance rate for M.A. programs increased from 22 to 33%, and for Ph.D. programs from 4.1 to 6.5 percent. In a comparison of the mean acceptance rate for approved doctoral programs versus nonapproved doctoral programs, Stoup and Benjamin report an increase of 3 to 5 percent for approved programs, and 8 to 14 percent for nonapproved programs. As expected, approved programs receive a higher mean number of applications than do nonapproved programs, but accept a small mean number of students. Based on the Stoup–Benjamin data, for approved programs the Graduate Record Examination (GRE) verbal, quantitative, and psychology advanced test scores average 635, 620, and 635, respectively; the overall Grade Point Average (GPA) and psychology GPA average 3.5 and 3.7, respectively; for nonapproved programs the corresponding GRE averages are 614, 612, and 626, and the corresponding GPAs are 3.4 and 3.6. It should be noted that the above figures are averages rather than cut-off points.

Basically, the admission process has a twofold purpose: first to identify students who display the qualities required of a professional psychologist (intelligence, motivation, social responsiveness, and ethical responsibility), and second to choose from an acceptable pool those students who best match the unique characteristics of a particular program.

Despite the recent emphasis on personal suitability and relevant human services experience, academic criteria still serve as the initial screening basis for admission. Once the initial screening has been completed, admission committees examine nonobjective criteria, such as letters of recommendation, autobiographical material, research, and work experience. In order to determine an appropriate matching between student characteristics and program characteristics, many doctoral programs require an individual or group interview, or at least a telephone interview, as part of the selection procedure. Unfortunately, limited data are available on the effectiveness of the interview or components of the interview other than interrater reliability. In addition, there have been studies showing that letters of recommendation are not weighted heavily.

An example of the current use of interview data is a study by Gluck, Babick, and Price (1979), in which faculty and senior graduate students conducted a one-day group assessment of applicants initially screened on academic criteria. They conclude that the addition of group assessment to the admission procedure produced a more cohesive group of entering students and a smaller program attrition rate.

In a study on student feedback about the interview process, Rickard and Rahaim (1982) surveyed 21 students (9 accepted and 12 rejected). One year following the interview, the accepted students were very positive, and the rejected students were very negative in their appraisal of the interview process.

Berman (1979) compared a combination of academic predictors (GRE, GPA) and nonacademic predictors (age, sex, ratings of autobiographical statements, letters of recommendation, interview ratings) against later ratings of diagnostic and therapeutic competence, graduate GPA, and comprehensive examination scores. Both academic and nonacademic predictors were related to diagnostic competence ratings, but only graduate academic data were related to ratings of therapeutic competence. Sadly, the various nonacademic variables added little to the predictive process.

In general, faculty are still reluctant to make use of peer evaluations even though the literature on personality assessment consistently gives high marks to peer ratings. Noteworthy is a study by Hirschberg and Itkin (1978) in which peer ratings were found to be one of the best predictors of successful completion of a professional psychology program, and one of the best (of the none too good) predictors of which students were likely to publish.

A continuing concern in the admission process is the recruitment of women and minorities (or minorities including women). A survey of graduate departments by Russo, Olmedo, Stapp, and Fulcher (1981) disclosed that approximately half of the students in doctoral programs are women and 10% are minorities, with the expectation of a continued increase in percentages of women and minorities who complete the doctorate. Strickland (1985) reports that close to half of the doctoral graduates now are women. Less optimistic are the findings of Bernal and Padilla (1982) in which less than half of the clinical psychology programs surveyed offer minority-related courses, and a comprehensive multicultural approach to preparing minority and majority culture students to work with minority clients was conspicuously lacking. Surprisingly, there was no significant relationship between whether a program had minority faculty and whether minority-related courses were offered. In a survey of 80 approved clinical doctoral programs, Schneider (1981) points to the success of minority fellowship grants by the National Institute of Mental Health (NIMH) to the APA, as well as the new emphasis on developing minority-staffed and minority-oriented internship centers. On the negative side, Schneider points to a minority student dropout rate in excess of the proportion of minority students in doctoral programs, which probably reflects the reduction in general training grants as well as the limited relevance of training for research on minority populations and for service delivery to minority clients.

Buller, Cervantes, and Brickhouse (1977) list five suggestions to strengthen clinical psychology programs for minority students: (1) graduate level seminars on minority psychological issues; (2) invitations by departments to speakers who are versed on minority issues; (3) in-service training concerning minorities for faculty; (4) research design courses focusing on minority populations; and (5) rotating practica to guarantee exposure to minority peoples. Bernal, Barron, and Leary (1983) present a list of approved clinical psychology programs with minority admission information and minority-related course offerings. Finally, Helms and Giorgis (1982) surveyed directors of approved programs and found that a few programs train the majority of international students, and students from developing countries are less inclined to study professional psychology than are students from developed countries.

FIELD TRAINING

Field training is an integral component of a professional psychology program. Students apply their clinical skills under close supervision in real settings with real clients who have real problems. Field training starts with a series of supervised practica integrated with formal coursework in an on-campus clinic, and culminates in an internship in a broad-spectrum facility, usually off campus. Both the practicum setting and the internship center maintain a close liaison with the graduate program, are reasonably compatible with the training model of the graduate program, and comply with APA standards and guidelines for providers of psychological services.

Practicum training should begin early in the doctoral program and consist of a minimum of 400 hours with a ratio of 1 hour of supervision for every 2 hours of direct service (APA, 1983a). In addition to supervision in assessment, therapy, research, and consultation, students participate in case conferences and prepare clinical notes and treatment plans.

In a survey of 83 approved or provisionally approved doctoral programs, Serafica and Harway (1980) reported the following information. Of the 83 programs, 63 had a clinic affiliated with the graduate department and maintained a balance between service, training, and research activities. The clinic was headed by a senior-level faculty member, had a staff of part-time faculty and graduate students, and relied for its financial support on university funds, clinic income, and to a lesser extent, federal training and research grants. The clinic provided a variety of assessment and therapy services to children and adults who presented a wide range of problems. Primary emphasis was on the education needs of the trainees, and secondarily on community service needs and faculty teaching interests. Surprisingly, students' research interests were ranked as a fourth priority by most respondents. Over half of the clinics conducted informal, in-house evaluation of services and training.

Although private practice has become an attractive work

setting for the professional psychologist (see chapter 3), few departments provide their practicum students with exposure to a private practice setting. Lowe and Ritzler (1980) surveyed directors of approved programs and found that only a few programs offered practicum placement in a private practice setting and a large minority of responding directors did not view such a placement as worthwhile due to the lack of malpractice protection and the absence of the scientist–professional model.

The second stage of field training is the internship which should consist of 2,000 hours of supervised clinical experience in one or more facilities. Kaslow and Rice (1985) refer to the internship year as a transition period from professional adolescence to professional adulthood. The APA *Accreditation Handbook* (APA, 1983a) defines the essential purpose of the internship:

> Internship should provide the trainee with the opportunity to take substantial responsibility for carrying out major professional functions in the context of appropriate supervisory support, professional role modeling, and awareness of administrative structures. The internship is taken after completion of relevant didactic and practicum work and precedes the granting of the doctoral degree [p. 18].

As in the case of graduate programs, the APA accredits internship programs and expects that APA-approved internship programs will select students from APA-approved professional programs. As of 1986, there were 293 approved or provisionally approved internship sites (Capsule, 1986).

Although the large majority of internship centers draw interns from graduate programs across the country, some facilities accept all their interns from one graduate department or professional school. In either case, the internship facility and the graduate program maintain a collaborative relationship in order to facilitate the selection, advisement, and evaluation of interns. In order to provide a broad range of clinical experiences for interns, a group of administratively independent facilities may pool their training resources to develop an internship which then seeks accreditation as a consortium.

Within the facility, responsibility for internship training is generally vested in a senior-level clinical psychologist. All professional psychology staff should be licensed or certified in the state in which they work. Staff who are primarily responsible for supervision should have completed an internship as part of their training. It is assumed that the psychology staff will arrange for interns to have professional contact with staff of other disciplines. The *Accreditation Handbook* (APA, 1983a) sets forth detailed requirements of internship sites, among which are the following:

> Internship settings should develop and distribute descriptive materials in which the goals and content of the training program, including reference to the characteristics of the client population, are accurately and explicitly formulated, so that prospective interns and doctoral training programs may match the program emphasis with intern interest . . . intern recruitment procedures should protect the applicants' rights to make a free choice among internship offers . . . facilities such as office space, clerical support, research equipment, library resources, etc., must be adequate to the needs of the training program . . . opportunities for research in the application of psychology should be available . . . two hours per week for formally scheduled individual supervision is a minimum; more is desirable . . . interns should be kept informed of their progress in the program by means of clearly identified evaluative sessions, with training and content designed to facilitate their change and growth . . . the training program itself should evaluate its own effectiveness in achieving its goals with interns [pp. 22–23].

The *Internship Programs in Professional Psychology*, published yearly by the Association of Psychology Internship Centers (APIC, 1986–87) is an indispensable resource for students planning an internship. The directory provides useful information on the following: accreditation status, number of staff and interns, stipends, distribution of training time, theoretical orientation, opportunities for subspecialty training, and types of doctoral programs from which the internship center will accept students.

Students must begin planning their internship well in advance of the February 10 date for notification of acceptance by an internship program. To cope with the stress of seeking and obtaining an internship, Belar and Orgel (1980) provide a "Survival Guide for Intern Applicants." Among other things, it recommends complying with application procedures described by each internship program, and determining each internship program's policy about submitting nonrequested materials.

In an analysis of the eight editions of the APIC *Directory*, Kurtz, Fuchs, Dabek, Kurtz, and Helfrich (1982) report the following information. Approximately 1,500 students enter internships every year and receive close to $10 million in stipends. Considerable variability exists among internships in terms of staff size, stipends, number of interns accepted, time devoted to assessment and research (psychotherapy receives the major emphasis). Although the predominant orientation is some version of psychodynamic theory, there is considerable variety, and the theoretical orientation is not consistently related to approval status or to the type of facility. Approved sites are larger, offer more training slots, have larger full-time supervisory staff, and devote less time to assessment than do nonapproved sites. Both approved and nonapproved sites clearly prefer students from approved graduate programs over those from nonapproved graduate programs. Sturgis, Verstegen, Randolph, and Garvin (1980) report that on the average nonapproved internships receive only 38 percent of the applications received by approved ones, and the prestigious centers may receive as many as 300 applications each year for 5 to 10 training slots.

In evaluating intern applicants, approved internship sites emphasize clinical experience and personal qualifications over traditional academic courses, and they typically require more supervised practice than the minimum set for accredited graduate programs (Petzel and Berndt, 1980). Shemberg and Leventhal (1981) surveyed directors of 179 APA-approved and nonapproved internship sites, and, consistent with earlier studies, found that there is considerable dissatisfaction with the training which graduate programs provide in assessment–diagnosis and psychotherapy.

Internships vary in providing for subspecialty training. Carmody and Zohn (1980) report that group training opportunities are on the rise, but they generally fall short of providing interns with all of the clinical skills necessary to meet the increasing demands for service in the area of group interventions. Some training in forensic psychology is available in about half of the internship centers, although Lawlor et al. (1981) conclude that psychological training is haphazard, uncoordinated, and unplanned. The number of interns desiring training in clinical neuropsychology is reportedly increasing in internship programs (McCaffrey, Malloy, and Brief, 1985). Golden and Kuperman (1980b) report that of the 98 approved or provisionally approved internship settings, 86 offer training in neuropsychology, and 30 of the 86 admit students who wish to specialize in neuropsychology. Goldberg and McNamara (1984) state that even with the increase in specialized neuropsychology internships, training opportunities have not matched the overall growth of the subspecialty. For the specialties of clinical child psychology and pediatric psychology, Tuma (1981) estimates that approximately 40 percent of clinical practica, internships, and postdoctoral training programs offer some training in pediatric psychology, 40 percent offer training in clinical child psychology, and 17 percent offer some combination of clinical child and pediatric psychology training.

With respect to supervision, Hess and Hess (1983) surveyed 150 approved predoctoral internships and found a ratio of one hour of supervision for every three hours of psychotherapy conducted by the intern. One-to-one supervision is the predominant form, although it is often supplemented by group supervision. Of the 150 sites, approximately one-third provide some supervisory training for the intern, although many internship directors believe that instruction in supervision is best left to graduate departments.

Several studies of supervision are noteworthy. Schmidt (1979) points out that as long as training programs, internships, and licensing laws place emphasis on supervised practice, supervision will be a widely used teaching technique and warrants the research and theoretical attention given to other areas (e.g., psychotherapy). Schaefer (1981) defines three objectives of individual and group supervision: (1) to assist the supervisee in the development of a self-monitoring/self-evaluating mind-set; (2) to train the supervisee for a future supervisory role; and (3) to teach therapeutic skills, ethical behaviors, and skillful interpersonal interactions within the supervisory relationship. Moskowitz and Rupert (1983) surveyed over 150 clinical psychology graduate students and found that nearly 40 percent experienced a major conflict in the supervisory relationship. In most cases conflicts were discussed and resolved effectively, with conflicts over supervisory style being the least difficult to resolve, and conflicts over the trainee's personality style being the most difficult to resolve.

Periodically there are suggestions in the literature to change the title of "intern" to that of "resident" (Sheridan, 1981; Graham, 1984). Sheridan states that over half of the approved internships are in medical schools and hospitals. In such settings, the clinical psychology intern is comparable to a senior-level trainee who is specializing in some area of medical psychology, and therefore the trainee merits a title that is commensurate with the level of training.

EVALUATION OF TRAINING

Kalafat and Neigher (1983) cite eight studies since 1975 that underscore the inadequacy or irrelevancy of clinical training with respect to preparing graduate students to be competent practitioners. Most of the studies are based on retrospective evaluations of training by practicing clinical psychologists.

The consistent recommendation of practitioners is to place more emphasis on the teaching of clinical skills and on the provision of competent supervision for the practice of clinical skills (Garfield and Kurtz, 1976; Norcross and Prochaska, 1982c). Intensive exposure to clinical work also gives trainees a more realistic view of their chosen career. Farber and Heifetz (1981) comment that the career expectations of many graduate students are unrealistically positive (e.g., high status, financial gain, personal growth, autonomy).

Although the APA accreditation policy (APA, 1983a) calls

for an explicit, comprehensive system of evaluation for all approved programs, it is not specific about types of data to be collected and evaluated. Ford (1979) has commented that "research investigating the effects of different training curricula, curriculum content sequences, and curricular materials is, unfortunately, virtually nonexistent in the counselor/clinician training literature" (p. 87). More recently, Norcross and Stevenson (1984) surveyed 62 directors of approved doctoral programs regarding their use of informal and formal training evaluation. Informal, qualitative evaluation measures (e.g., personal impressions, reputations) were used most frequently, while formal quantitative measures (e.g., prepost comparisons) were employed least frequently. Supervisors' written evaluations, APA-accreditation reports, feedback from internship supervisors, and quantitative evaluations of supervisors by supervisees had the most impact in the assessment of the quality of clinical training. Despite the Vail Conference recommendation to seek student input in the evaluation of training models and curriculum, only 2 percent of the programs surveyed by Norcross and Stevenson used a combination of faculty and students to do the evaluation. Stevenson and Norcross (1985) surveyed 131 psychology training clinics to obtain information on the evaluation of clinical training. Of the 74 clinics that returned usable data, 61 percent used quantitative evaluation measures, while the remaining 39 percent reported no systematic evaluation procedure. Stevenson and Norcross conclude that training evaluation is less well developed than treatment evaluation, and for the most part is limited to a combination of supervisors' and supervisees' evaluations.

In a thoughtful analysis of critical issues in program evaluation, Ford (1977) reasons that success in training must be measured in several ways; namely, evaluation by the clients of trainees, by behavior samples and performance outcome measures from trainees, and by supervisors' ratings. In turn, this combination should be matched against follow-up data on the quality of professional performance after graduation. Ford states that training programs cannot remain static and must be responsive to changes taking place in the profession at large. In conclusion, he states the following objective: "In theory and in practice, it is evident that training methods, training objectives, and trainees' personal characteristics are interdependent factors that must be carefully matched with each other in order to produce positive training outcomes" (p. 15).

Overall, graduate programs and training sites are responding constructively to an increased pressure to demonstrate accountability. Stricker and Cohen (1984) and Stricker (1984) report that quality assurance (which addresses professional and ethical issues and the quality of service offered to the public), and peer review (which is the vehicle for discharging quality assurance), are becoming more evident in graduate programs and practicum facilities. They point out that quality assurance and peer review procedures go beyond the traditional supervision of a trainee's caseload in an effort to improve the trainee's clinical skills across clients and over time. Bent (1982) describes a psychology training program in a community-based psychological service center in which doctoral students practice, and participate (serve on peer review panels), in quality assurance programs as part of their training from the time they begin the field placement.

SUBDOCTORAL TRAINING

As noted earlier, both the number of M.A. programs and the acceptance rate have increased during the seventies. Cummings, as reported by Sobel (1979), estimates that there are over 200 APA-accredited terminal M.A. programs (and many times that number of nonaccredited programs).

Traditionally the M.A. degree has served three purposes: (1) as an intermediate stage in the doctoral program in which the student's progress can be reviewed and improvements made; (2) as a practitioner-based program to train students for important jobs that do not require doctoral-level skills —preparation ought to include courses in diagnostic testing, individual and group psychotherapy, and a practicum experience with exposure to crisis intervention and consultation with paraprofessionals; and (3) as a proving ground for bachelor-level graduates who are not accepted directly into a doctoral program.

Although some graduate departments give credit for

courses taken in a terminal M.A. program, many do not, and the more highly rated doctoral programs may be biased against accepting applications from students in terminal M.A. programs. On the other hand, Tucker and Annis (1981) support the notion of a proving ground by pointing out that the M.A. program provides more in-depth experience in psychology than does the undergraduate curriculum, and that the B.A. degree combined with the M.A. degree (with thesis research) is a better predictor of success in doctoral study than the B.A. degree alone. A study by Annis, Tucker, and Baker (1978) disclosed that students with the M.A. degree were more likely to complete the Ph.D. than were students with only a B.A. degree.

Several studies (e.g., Dimond, Havens, Rathnow, and Colliver, 1977; Stevens, Yock, and Perlman, 1979; Erdwins and Buffardi, 1983) have found the M.A.-level psychologist to be either fully employed or employed part-time while working on a doctoral degree; the majority seemed satisfied with their jobs and believed that their training has adequately prepared them to do their jobs responsibly; and psychotherapy was the most frequent professional activity, even though the emphasis in most M.A. programs on coursework was assessment–diagnosis. A less optimistic finding is one by Havens, Colliver, Dimond, and Wesley (1982) in which directors of public mental health settings were surveyed on their perception of the professional capability of Ph.D.s, M.A.s, and M.S.W.s. The M.A.s were at the bottom of the professional hierarchy (e.g., perceived competence, salaries, promotion). Recommendations for training the M.A.-level psychologist surface regularly and range from support for the status quo, collaborative training with another discipline (e.g., social work), to technician training programs separate from doctoral programs and with a job title other than psychologist.

RESPECIALIZATION

Since the midseventies an increasing number of psychologists with Ph.D.s in nonapplied fields have sought training in a practice specialty (e.g., a developmental or educational psychologist who respecializes in clinical child psychology). Chapter 3 deals with several of the relevant issues.

Although APA has always supported the concept of lateral career change, the issues of quality assurance and overall professional accountability have led to a stricter policy (APA, 1976). In 1977, the respecialization principle was written into the generic *Standards for Providers of Psychological Services* (APA, 1977), and three years later it was included in the specific standards for each of the four speciality areas (Hall, 1983). Those who seek respecialization have been advised to train in established university programs, preferably APA-approved programs.

Normally the respecialization training sequence includes two years of coursework and practica plus a one-year internship. Formal admission requirements must be met though less weight is given to academic criteria. The Ph.D. degree must be solid enough to make the respecialization candidate eligible for state licensure, since the respecialization training provides only a certificate or nondegree diploma. Stricker, Hull, and Woodring (1984) surveyed graduate psychology departments and found that 43 were currently involved in respecialization training and 26 of the 43 programs were in clinical psychology.

Although APA has strongly recommended that the profession accommodate respecialization, the response from the training programs has not been encouraging. Each of the approximately 40 university programs or schools of psychology that now accept respecialization students admit less than five per year (APA, 1983b), and only 20 percent of the APA-approved training programs accept respecialization applications. Stricker (1983) reports that typically there are 15 to 20 applications for four or five openings. A listing of respecialization opportunities is available from APA's Education Affairs Office.

CONTINUING EDUCATION

Related to the strong trend toward specialization is the responsibility of clinical psychologists to maintain, enhance, or retool their skills (see chapter 4). Continuing education (CE) started coming on strong during the late 1970s in response to several concerns. Kalafat and Neigher (1983) speculate that the "half life" of professional knowledge may be closer to 5 to

6 years instead of the earlier estimate of 10 to 12 years. They mention also the increased demand for accountability by the public, government regulatory agencies, private third-party reimbursers, legislatures, and consumer groups; in addition, as noted earlier in this chapter, several evaluation surveys have underscored the inadequacy–irrelevancy of traditional graduate training. Patterson (1979) points to a trend among states to require CE credits for relicensure or recertification. Patterson defines the purpose of CE to be one of maintaining previously acquired competencies and/or developing skills in newly relevant areas. In a similar vein, Jensen (1979) stresses the importance of assessing competent professional service that may be obtained through self-directed study (some publications now provide clinical psychologists with the option of obtaining CE credit for their reading by means of self-assessment examinations), workshops–conferences, supervision, or compulsory course work. In 1979, the APA's Council of Representatives addressed the issue by establishing the Sponsor Approval System to provide national standards for CE in psychology, a computerized CE registry, and a CE calendar–clearing house (APA, 1984a).

The need to document one's competency to maintain licensure, combined with the rapidly expanding base of professional knowledge, make it imperative that graduate students begin a continuing education program very soon after graduation. As Vitulano and Copeland (1980) note, lifetime education should be an important goal in training and in practice, and a commitment to continuing education is a sure means of fostering and maintaining public confidence.

CURRENT OUTLOOK

On balance, the outlook for clinical psychology graduates in the 1980s is optimistic. Stapp, Fulcher, and Wicherski (1984) conclude that, compared to the previous decade, doctorate production has leveled off, the employment market has stabilized, unemployment is low, and graduates are finding jobs commensurate with their education and clinical experience. Stapp et al. also note that the percentage who find academic jobs has stopped declining, with an expected increase in available academic positions in the 1990s. Yet the optimism has to be tempered by consideration of economic issues.

Consistent with reduced federal funds for training, there has been a declining percentage of students whose primary support comes from federal funds, as well as a declining percentage of students who receive nonfederal support [e.g., teaching assistantships (Stapp et al., 1984)]. Students have had to rely increasingly on personal resources to finance their professional education, and Stapp et al. find that the trend is more evident for women than for men, and for whites than for minorities, though the differences are small. Strickland (1983c) warns that there are only a handful of clinical psychologists with training and experience to work in geropsychology; there are only four training programs that offer substantial training in rural mental health; with 46 million minority citizens there are only 830 minority licensed psychologists; and there are fewer than ten jails that have any mental health personnel. She warns that with reduction of training funds, the number of low income and minority students may tail off, and clinical psychology students will increasingly incur large loan debts. Instead of taking positions in nursing homes, jails, or rural settings, for financial reasons students will be obliged to work in well-financed health care centers and moonlight in private practice settings to supplement their income.

At best, the prognosis for federal funding of professional education remains guarded. Kraut, Batchelor, Hefferman, Vyeda, and Greenberg (1984) report that the 1985 appropriation for clinical training at the National Institute of Mental Health (NIMH) provides an increase of $1 million over the 1984 appropriation. As expected the funds are targeted to areas of special need rather than to general training support (e.g., psychosocial aspects of health care, minorities, children, the elderly, and prevention services). There is also growing pressure to tie stipends to a "service payback" stipulation in which students work for a designated period in shortage areas or with underserved populations. The Reagan administration wants to eliminate funding for clinical training in its 1986 budget, but Congress has consistently rejected the idea in the past (APA, 1985c). However, the new law that mandates a balanced budget by 1991 threatens funding reductions over the next few years in most programs that are of interest to professional psychology. Funding for clinical training in 1986 is slightly lower than it was in 1985 (APA, 1986b).

Beyond the 1980s professional psychology can be expected to become a generic training label that subsumes both clinical and nonclinical applications of psychological knowledge and principles. As Levy (1984) has recommended, the traditional areas of clinical, counseling, and school psychology should be set aside in favor of a generic professional (or scientist–professional) program within which there would be a human services speciality that offers training in the promotion of human well-being, along with assessment, treatment, and prevention of psychological and physical disorders.

What the foregoing may mean to a would-be clinical psychologist is that instead of the traditional duality of psychologist first, clinical psychologist second, he or she will be a professional psychologist first and a clinician second.

Chapter 3

Gaining Employment as a Clinical Psychologist

INTRODUCTION

As this chapter was being written, an "advisee" sought an appointment and said the following: "You know that I've been a pretty good student. I got an A in both of the classes I've taken from you and my overall grade point average is a 3.5. But I'm in a quandary. My Graduate Record Examination scores were not bad. I've applied to about a dozen APA-accredited clinical psychology training programs and have received rejections from all of them. I remember your lectures about how the quality of the training program influences your future employment, and I don't really care to go to some second-rate university. I'm also becoming aware of the sacrifices that are involved. It would mean going without any real income for at least four more years—my family doesn't have the money, and I don't know if I can borrow it or not. My family and fiancée want me to stay within driving distance of here, and I would prefer that too. On top of it all, my fiancée is threatening to break off our engagement because I believe I should have my graduate studies well underway before we get married. And in last night's paper, I read that the legislature has made cutbacks in the funds for mental health programs and universities. All through college I have wanted to be a clinical psychologist, but I'm beginning to question whether I can afford to make the sacrifices for a field that doesn't seem to be easy to get into nor secure after you arrive. Can you give me some assurances, I really need them!" With such a plaintive tale, it would be satisfying to offer assurances, but that cannot be done. Instead, this chapter is offered to that advisee and to others like him, with the hope that the information will bring about understanding that will be helpful for career planning.

Gaining employment as a clinical psychologist is important both personally and professionally. On a personal level, it is obvious that no one would want to invest the time, money, energy, and identity in a career that would not yield reasonable dividends. On a professional level, the conditions related to employment serve as an index to the status of the discipline and are crucial to assessing the short- and long-term employment potential.

THE CLINICAL PSYCHOLOGIST'S JOB DESCRIPTION

Before reviewing the myriad factors that influence whether or not one gains employment as a clinical psychologist, the basic job description should be considered. As might be expected, there is no single job description. Typically, the duties and functions are determined by the needs of the clientele, the objectives and resources of the employing facility, and the capabilities and preferences of the clinical psychologist. However, a summary job description can be posited. Norcross and Prochaska (1982b) surveyed a sample of members of the American Psychological Association's (APA's) Division of Clinical Psychology. As opposed to surveys of new doctoral degree holders that will be presented later in this chapter (to illustrate where new clinical psychology graduates find employment), this survey included a more senior group of clinical psychologists (the respondents' average age was 47.4 years and amount of experience was 16.7 years).

When queried about particular professional activities, the mean percentage of time spent in involvement with each activity was as follows: psychotherapy, 34.7 percent; diagnosis and assessment, 13.2 percent; teaching, 12.0 percent; supervision (clinical), 8.5 percent; research 7.9 percent; consultation, 7.5 percent; administration, 13.4 percent; and other 2.9 percent. It should be noted that every clinical psychologist was not necessarily involved in all of these activities; the involvement percentages were: psychotherapy, 88.3 percent;

diagnosis and assessment, 73.8 percent; teaching, 61.7 percent; supervision (clinical), 73.7 percent; research, 52.8 percent; consultation, 67.4 percent; administration, 61.6 percent; and other, 12.2 percent.

As will be evident in chapters 5 and 6 on psychotherapy, there are various theoretical definitions of and treatment formats for psychotherapy. Analyzing theoretical orientation, Norcross and Prochaska (1982a) found the following alignments: learning theory–behavior, 14.40 percent; cognitive, 6.26 percent; humanistic, 1.68 percent; psychodynamic, 30.05 percent; Rogerian, 3.14 percent; Sullivanian, 2.29 percent; existential, 1.46 percent; systems, 4.18 percent; eclectic, 30.89 percent; and other, 5.64 percent. When they considered the number of years of experience, they found that there were shifts in the percentage, such as the inexperienced group's being more behaviorally and cognitively and less psychodynamically oriented; they speculate that "it is possible that as clinicians become more experienced, they may gravitate toward a more psychodynamic orientation" (p. 6). The percentage of time devoted to therapy activities according to treatment format were individual therapy, 63.5 percent; group therapy, 7.3 percent; marital–couples therapy, 11.5 percent; family therapy, 9.0 percent; and behavior modification, 7.1 percent (Norcross and Prochaska, 1982b).

When the clinical psychologists were asked about their "primary professional self-view," the percentages were clinical practitioner, 62.8 percent; academician, 17.3 percent; administrator, 8.4 percent; researcher, 5.0 percent; consultant, 3.5 percent; supervisor, 1.0 percent; and other, 1.9 percent (Norcross and Prochaska, 1982a).

As for their primary institutional affiliation, the clinical psychologists were located as follows: none, 0.4 percent; mental hospital, 7.5 percent; general hospital, 7.5 percent; outpatient clinic, 5.4 percent; community mental health center, 6.5 percent; medical school, 7.3 percent; private practice, 31.1 percent; university (psychology), 16.9 percent; university (other), 4.8 percent; and other, 12.5 percent (Norcross and Prochaska, 1982a). When compared to other studies, Norcross and Prochaska note a decrease in employment in academic settings, and an increase in engagement in private practice.

EMPLOYMENT SATISFACTION

The dividends from a career are, of course, far more than only financial. There must be a sense of personal satisfaction derived from one's work, otherwise both the service recipients (e.g., the patients, co-workers, supervisors, and ultimately society itself) and the worker will suffer negative consequences. Lack of job satisfaction results in a poor work product (e.g., lessened quality of service); faulty functioning (e.g., poor motivation to perform or to develop improved skills); and illness (e.g., such mental difficulties as depression, anxiety, and obsessions, and such physical difficulties as stress-related disorders).

Job satisfaction makes much needed contributions to the person's sense of social worthiness, self-esteem, and ego structure. In turn, these intrapersonal qualities influence mightily the qualities that the person experiences interpersonally, such as the degree to which he or she can be a healthy member of a family and a community.

Although money is not the whole story, its importance should not be denied. In this day and age, it is naive (if not ignorant) to assert that a clinical psychologist (or any other professional in the health and human services) should be altruistic to the point of extreme self-sacrifice. There was a time in our societal evolution when a professional could, in fact, experience considerable reward from helping others. The priorities of society were such that there was social recognition and, thus, reward from being dedicated to serving the needs of others and placing this commitment well above such personal needs as income. With the changes in societal values and an economy that mandates concern about income in order to survive (literally and figuratively), the potential benefits from the altruistic element of a profession have been lessened.

To be concerned about profit should not be viewed as greed. Pay is endemic to overall organizational functioning. In other words, the profit dimension of, say, a mental health facility relate in many ways to the services and operations: "At this point, it is sufficient to say that pay systems in organizations are closely linked to the following major aspects of organizations: superior-subordinate relationships, job design, organizational structure, organizational climate, management training and development, information and control systems, performance appraisal, and management philosophy or style" (Lawler, 1981, p. 8). If we consider these organizational aspects as applied to clinical psychology, it is readily apparent that it would be ill-advised to ignore the financial dimension.

Consideration of pay should acknowledge that the number of dollars per se is seldom the whole story. The very nature of pay creates a perceptual set in the minds of the employee. Lawler (1981) tells us:

1. Satisfaction with a reward is a function of how much is received and how much the individual feels should be received (p. 12).
2. People's feelings of satisfaction are influenced by comparisons with what happens to others (p. 12).
3. People often misperceive the rewards of others (p. 14).
4. Overall job satisfaction is influenced by how satisfied employees are with both the intrinsic and extrinsic rewards they receive from their jobs (p. 15).

Thus, the clinical psychologist will be mindful of the amount of income and will evaluate its adequacy according to, among other things, the investment that he or she was required to make in order to become a clinical psychologist. As is clear throughout this book, the investment, such as the number of years of education and training required, is considerable.

If society's priorities change to downgrade the importance of mental health services (as the recent trend indicates)—which results in fewer mental health facilities, fewer job opportunities, and a diminution of intrinsic and extrinsic rewards for being a mental health professional—it is only logical that the clinical psychologist will be dissatisfied with a variety of employment conditions, not the least of which will be the amount of pay. Consequently, a good number of clinical psychologists have, in the recent past, concluded that they should abandon the profession—examples include going to law school, selling real estate, running a campground, and a host of other jobs unrelated to being a psychologist.

Dissatisfaction may relate to the length of time that a

person has been a clinical psychologist. Walfish, Polifka, and Stenmark (1985) found that recent graduates of clinical psychology training programs have a high level of satisfaction, but acknowledge that surveys of older, more experienced clinical psychologists reveal a greater degree of career dissatisfaction.

The negative fallout of job dissatisfaction and of leaving a profession is great. Not only has the person chosen to cut short a career in which he or she has made a substantial personal investment, but our society loses a valuable professional resource, one that will have to be replenished through additional investments of personal and public resources that could otherwise be spent in improving other qualities for life.

CAREER DEVELOPMENT

Employment dissatisfaction underscores the importance of career development, whether it be the person's decision making about what profession to pursue or society's priorities for emphasizing certain services. Schein (1978) captures the essence of a career development perspective:

> (1) the problem of improving human resource planning and development activities in organizations; (2) the problem of improving individual career planning and helping people who are caught in difficult work situations to cope more effectively with those situations; (3) the problem of improving the matching process at all stages of the career so that early-, mid-, and late-career crises can be dealt with more effectively by both the organization and the individuals caught in these crises; (4) the problem of obsolescence, motivation, and leveling off which occurs in mid- and late-career; (5) the problem of balancing family and work concerns at different life stages; and (6) the problem of maintaining the productivity and motivation of all those employees who are individual contributors and/or who are not motivated toward climbing the organizational ladder [p. 2].

Too few students give careful thought to this array of

issues at the time they make their decision to major in psychology, or when they vest so much of their life (and the lives of their family members) in entering graduate studies in clinical psychology. For example, it would be the rare undergraduate student who would give more than a passing thought to what the employment scene would be when he or she has been a clinical psychologist for, say, 20 years. The basic notion is, no doubt, that the longer one is in a career, the wiser one becomes, and the more employment opportunities will be available. This is a logical notion, but it is contradicted by fact. Indeed, discrimination against the worker (including the professional) over the age of 40 has been and continues to be extreme. It is so prevalent that the Age Discrimination in Employment Act was passed in 1974 to offer legal safeguards to persons between the ages of 40 and 70.

Age discrimination comes in many forms. To illustrate how it enters into the employment of clinical psychologists, consider the following two situations.

A clinical psychologist has been employed by the federal government for all of his career, spanning some 25 years. During that time, he has published award-winning research, given leadership within his employing unit (such as serving as director), and achieved prominence (such as through participation on several blue-ribbon committees that charted national and international health policies, and having been elected president of several national mental health organizations). Stated simply, he has given about half of his life to one employer—a mental health unit of our government—and has achieved what most clinical psychologists would consider to be the ultimate career goals. However, the Reagan Administration, presumably because of shifts in public policy priorities, stripped away support for mental health services when this clinical psychologist was 52 years old. According to this individual, an executive branch analysis led to the conclusion that senior mental health professionals in the government should be encouraged to take early retirement, thereby freeing up their salary monies to either hire beginning professionals at lower salaries or to allocate the monies to another governmental sector, say defense. If a senior mental health professional resists the idea of early retirement, reportedly efforts were going to be made to reassign him or her to an undesirable position, a role that might carry the same salary but which would remove previously enjoyed intrinsic benefits (such as status, creativity, and the like) and would inflict new, negative demands (such as performing routine, rigidly scheduled functions). The not so honorable objective is easy to recognize: if the employment conditions produce job dissatisfaction, the senior mental health professional would be pressured toward early retirement, and the administrative goal of freeing up salary monies would be obtained.

As a second example, consider a clinical psychologist employed by a state university as a professor. The professor has been with the university for 25 years, is 52 years old, teaches three classes each semester, publishes regularly in scholarly journals, holds certain honors (such as having been named a diplomate in clinical psychology by the American Board of Professional Psychology), and earns $40,000 per year.

Before going into the example, a couple of side issues would be: if the professor taught at the most esteemed "flagship campus" in the state's university system, it is probable that the salary would be considerably higher (say by $10,000 or more), than if he or she performed the same functions at a secondary campus in the same university system; and if the professor were female, it is probable (at least historically) that her salary would be significantly lower than the salaries of her male counterparts.

Now for the age discrimination example: Suppose that the professor decides that his or her career needs—which would include being more productive professionally—could be better met by seeking employment at another university. Applications are sent out, and despite strong professional credentials, nothing but rejections are received. Why would this be so? Place yourself in the position of the chairperson of the psychology department at the hiring institution. If $40,000 had been allocated to the department to improve the clinical psychology training program, you could afford to hire this particular professor, but for the same amount of money you could afford to hire two beginning professors and thereby double the number of courses that would be taught and double the number of new faculty members in the program (with all the side benefits of having two for the price of one, such as more advisement of students, greater variety of research interests, and so on).

Sometimes the decision to avoid senior professors is for reasons other than money. Like any discipline, psychology has factions of advocacy. For example, a clinical psychology training program might contain several professors who believe that behaviorism is the only approach to use, others who are apostles of psychoanalytic ideas, and others who believe that a community mental health model is more important than a therapy model, and so on. When it comes time to hire a new professor, each faction champions its preferences. While compromises and negotiations usually occur, they may be predicated on the premise that, if I'm going to give in and support hiring your candidate, I want to be sure that he or she is potentially open to my preferences. Age discrimination enters in because senior professors are perceived, probably rightly so, as having established their postures on professional issues and as being less malleable than a younger professor who is still formulating his or her postures.

The message here has to do with more than the student's considering the possibility of becoming a clinical psychologist. The student should also give thought to his or her *long-range* needs and *the employment issues that are likely to be encountered* (of course such long-range forecasts would have to be tenuously made). The message further supports that at some point, say 10 years into one's career, there will likely have to be recognition that the possibility of moving to another position in later life will be difficult (assuming that societal priorities for mental health services remain somewhat like they are today).

A clear-cut example of unpredictable trends in employment of clinical psychologists is found in the community mental health movement. During the administrations of John F. Kennedy and Lyndon B. Johnson, there was great public support for mental health services. The Joint Commission on Mental Illness and Health (1961) gave impetus to the establishment of many community-based facilities, and employment of all types of mental health professionals was readily available. Clinical psychology training programs added courses in community concepts, particularly mental health consultation. Some training programs changed their designations from "clinical" to "community-clinical" psychology. Then came a change in political orientation, and the years of the Nixon administration introduced the continuing trend away from publicly-supported mental health services. Today's economic priorities do not give great favor to mental health funding. Consequently, employment opportunities have diminished, at least in the community mental health arena.

There is an even more critical message that the student of psychology should heed; that is, often our society shifts its priorities, whether they be witnessed in decisions made by the executive branch of the federal government or the persons involved in the recruitment of faculty members for a university. Many of these shifts will fulfill the old adage of robbing Peter to pay Paul. A priority will perhaps shift away from mental health services and toward lower taxes for reasons that may be of dubious long-range benefit. Not only will this inflict unpredicted, unjust, and hurtful conditions on the individual, such as depriving a clinical psychologist of employment opportunities, it will have an equally hurtful effect on society itself. That is the nature of a democratic society, however; public policy does shift, and often the shifts may not be in the best interest of anything but short-term gains.

PREREQUISITES FOR EMPLOYMENT

As a profession, clinical psychology adheres to a set of ethics, known as the "Ethical Principles of Psychologists" (APA, Committee on Scientific and Professional Ethics and Conduct, 1981b). Ethics serve many purposes, such as promulgating standards for professional conduct that will: (1) safeguard the public, namely, those who are served by psychologists, and (2) advance the profession. Even the latter purpose has a public-service core. A strong profession will lead to an upgrading of standards for the members, and will lead to higher quality for the services that they provide. Chapter 4 will present a detailed coverage of the ethical and legal considerations for the practice of clinical psychology. It will suffice for now to acknowledge that entry into employment as a clinical psychologist is predicated on fulfilling ethical principles.

A set of ethics, including the "Ethical Principles of Psychologists," represents the views of a professional association, the American Psychological Association (APA). The ethics apply to the members of the APA, but there are other psychologists who are not members and who are, technically, not held accountable to those ethics.

Does this mean that the entry into employment will have different ethical prerequisites for those who are APA members as opposed to those who are not APA members? It is possible, but not likely because the APA's ethics are generally recognized as creating a general framework for practice. Consequently, it is not uncommon for a state licensing board, which is totally independent of the APA, to incorporate the APA "Ethical Principles of Psychologists" into its licensing statute or into the board's rules. In this way, the APA ethics become applicable to all who would practice as a psychologist in that state, be he or she an APA member or not.

On the issue of competence for employment as a psychologist, the APA ethics prescribe as follows:

> Principle 2—COMPETENCE: . . . Psychologists recognize the boundaries of their competence and the limitations of their techniques. They only provide services and only use techniques for which they are qualified by training and experience. In those areas in which recognized standards do not yet exist, psychologists take whatever precautions are necessary to protect the welfare of their clients. They maintain knowledge of current scientific and professional information related to the services they render [p. 634].

Principle 2—COMPETENCE, goes on to require that psychologists accurately represent their competence, education, training, and experience; perform their duties on the basis of careful preparation; recognize the need for continuing education; and meet other conditions that protect the welfare of their clients.

This ethical posture spawns several prerequisites for employment as a clinical psychologist; let us consider three examples.

First, the would-be clinical psychologist must have the qualifications endorsed by the profession. He or she cannot self-ordain readiness for employment.

Second, even when the prerequisite of academic training has been met, the would-be clinical psychologist is restrained from seeking employment that might involve techniques or skills that are not adequately mastered. For example, there are certain types of patients who require highly specialized therapeutic interventions that few trainees emerging from a Ph.D. program would be prepared to provide (particularly without the wisdom of a more experienced supervisor), yet some employers (e.g., those more concerned with expenditures than for quality of service) might be open to hiring a new Ph.D. holder. Ethically, the new Ph.D. clinical psychologist cannot accept such a decision by the employer.

Third, the matter of competence is never fulfilled, it is much like seeking self-actualization: great progress can be made with clear-cut evidence of accomplishments, but this only opens the potential for new vistas. In employment, remaining in the same position carries the responsibility of growing with the position—if the employment is to be ethical, there can be no stagnation.

The starting point for employment is academic training. While Woods (1976) reports that career opportunities for students with an undergraduate major in psychology but not a graduate psychology degree are expanding (such as in business, schools. the military, and community health and welfare programs), the term *clinical psychologist* is reserved for those with advanced and specialized graduate training (note that the volume edited by Woods contains a number of essays which discuss ideas for identifying a psychological career). About 80% of clinical psychologists hold doctorates (Kiesler, 1979). Nondoctoral clinical psychologists tend to have more restricted job roles, but do engage in psychological testing and therapy, and are generally satisfied with their duties (Erdwins and Buffardi, 1983). Perlman's (1985) survey of master's-level clinical psychologists reveals: (1) they maintain a strong identity with clinical practice (about 50% of their time is spent providing psychotherapy); (2) they have noteworthy dissatisfaction with their training (over one-fourth express some dissatisfaction with their overall graduate training); and (3) "The doctoral psychologist engages in a wider array of activities (greater role variety) . . ." (p. 563).

Basic membership in the APA (1985b) requires:

> The minimum standard for election to Member status is receipt of the doctoral degree based in part upon a psychological dissertation, or the doctoral degree based upon other evidence of proficiency in psychological scholarship. The doctoral degree must be received from a program primarily psychological in content and must be conferred by a graduate or professional school that is regionally accredited, or that has achieved such accreditation within five years of the year the doctorate was granted, or is a school of equivalent standing outside of the United States [p. x].

Among other things, this would mean that: (1) a Ph.D. degree from a program that was not primarily psychological in content, no matter what the recipient's personal qualities nor how prestigious the university, would not suffice for membership; and (2) the fast-track or "store bought" Ph.D. degree, such as from one of the commercial purveyors of doctorates, would not fulfill the degree requirement. To be legitimate, the academic psychological training must be through a university, college, or professional school that is accredited by the U.S. Office of Education and a recognized regional accreditation board (note that being licensed by the state department of education to be a training program, as is the case with many of the "store bought" degree sources, is insufficient).

It is feasible that a legitimate doctoral degree in one area of psychology can be used to gain employment in another area of psychology. For example, a psychologist who was a member of the APA and who held a Ph.D. degree in experimental psychology from the psychology department of a highly respected university found that he could not obtain employment. Finally, he was hired by a state hospital for the mentally ill as a clinical psychologist. Although this was legal it was probably not ethical because he had no specialized training in such areas as psychological testing and psychotherapy, and had never received supervision for the clinical services he provided. Fortunately, he recognized the dilemma that the financial press to support his family had created, and he immediately arranged for a senior professor of clinical psychology to supervise his work (at his own expense!) and enrolled in clinical psychology courses.

This attempted remedy, often referred to as "back dooring" into clinical psychology, is not recommended. The specialty of clinical psychology has carefully established standards.

However, there are appropriate ways for someone with training in a nonclinical area of psychology to capitalize on the previous preparation and to move into clinical psychology, as might be necessitated by the shifting priorities of public policy that dictate employment opportunities. This "retreading" approach, however, does not allow for after-the-fact supervision and coursework. Rather, it means having a clinical trainer tailor a sequence of training experiences which will, for all practical purposes, provide the psychologist with a "second major"; that is, he or she will have comprehensive training, say, in both experimental psychology and clinical psychology.

THE APA'S GUIDELINES FOR SPECIALIZATION

In 1977, the APA's Council of Representatives adopted the first generic set of guidelines for psychological service delivery. In 1980, the Council adopted specialty guidelines. These are set forth by the APA's Committee on Professional Standards (1981c) as the "Specialty Guidelines for the Delivery of Service," which contain separate sets of detailed standards for each of the following four specialties: (1) clinical psychology; (2) counseling psychology; (3) industrial–organizational psychology; and (4) school psychology.

The guidelines hold that the practices in these four specialties necessitate particular skills and competencies:

> Traditionally, all learned disciplines have treated the designation of specialty practice as a reflection of preparation in greater depth in a particular subject matter, together with a voluntary limiting of focus to a more restricted area of practice by the professional. Lack of specialty designation does not preclude general providers of psycho-

> logical services from using the methods or dealing with the populations of any specialty, except insofar as psychologists voluntarily refrain from providing services they are not trained to render. It is the intent of these Guidelines, however, that after the grandparenting period, psychologists not put themselves forward as *specialists* in a given area of practice unless they meet the qualifications noted in the Guidelines . . ." (p. 640).

The specialty guidelines were structured to recognize legal authority (e.g., statutory licensure), govern the quality of services in both the private and public sectors, endorse levels of training and experience, and foster accountability.

In considering employment, the would-be clinical psychologist would need to acknowledge the service scope of the specialty guidelines: "*Clinical psychological services* refers to the application of principles, methods, and procedures for understanding, predicting, and alleviating intellectual, emotional, psychological, and behavioral disability and discomfort. Direct services are provided in a variety of health settings, and direct and supportive services are provided in the entire range of social, organizational, and academic institutions and agencies" (APA, 1981c, p. 642). The clinical psychology services include psychodiagnostics, therapeutic interventions, professional consultation, program development, supervision, and evaluation, as would be relevant to the clinical context.

The specialty guidelines for clinical psychology promulgate many proscriptions and prescriptions. For example, they specify the organizational elements necessary for clinical psychology service, such as how long records should be kept, when and how supervision should be provided, and so on.

It is possible that an employer might maintain a clinical organization that would satisfy the standards of another profession, say psychiatry, but would fail to uphold the standards for clinical psychology. For example, known incidents include a non-psychologist administrator's wanting a psychologist to prepare a diagnostic report with data that were inadequate by the accepted psychological standards; attempting to denigrate the confidentiality of psychological records; and offering a psychologist a pad of medical prescriptions already signed by a physician, to be issued at the discretion of the psychologist. Here the clinical psychologist considering employment in that organization is confronted with the reality of disciplinary identity, and the action is clear: a clinical psychologist must not subvert the professional standards of his or her discipline or specialty in deference to those of another profession.

Analysis of the standards for specialization in clinical psychology has not stopped with the 1981 guidelines, it is a continuing task. The APA's Board of Professional Affairs (1984d) has sponsored a Subcommittee on Specialization, and its draft predicates all specialization on a scientific core: "i.e., competence or formal coursework in research methodology, statistics and measurement, history and systems, regulatory standards and ethics, and the biological, cognitive, affective, social and individual bases of behavior" (p. 6). From this foundation, applied generic cores of proficiencies, knowledge, and skills for a specialty can emerge. While there will likely be some overlap of the applied generic cores for different specialties, there will be uniqueness; that is: "Beyond this core, each Specialty then further defines additional elements of the knowledge and skills in each parameter which then describes the Specialty Core. These additional elements (Specialty Core) provide the basis upon which Specialties and Proficiencies can be differentiated while acknowledging the commonalities between these applied areas in psychology which then describe the Specialty Core" (p. 8). The subcommittee posits a number of principles for formulating a specialty.

The important message to the psychology student considering employment possibilities is that the specialty of clinical psychology is not in a permanent form. For the student who will not enter the job market for several more years, the specific prerequisites for employment as a clinical psychologist may not yet be available. Also, there may be other specialties available by that time, and employment as a clinical psychologist may not be the number one preference.

TRAINING PROGRAMS ACCREDITED BY THE APA

The APA's Committee on Accreditation accredits training programs, namely, in clinical psychology, counseling psychology, industrial–organizational psychology, and school psychology. Many employers, particularly those who honor high standards for the provision of clinical psychology services, seek employees who are graduates of fully or provisionally approved training programs. Being from an APA-approved training program is a status symbol, based on the proven quality of the training, that will facilitate employment.

It has long been difficult to be admitted to doctoral study in psychology, particularly in clinical psychology. Nyman (1973) found that the odds were greater against admission to a clinical psychology program than for admission to medical school. It seems likely that today the odds against admission are at least as great or even greater than in 1973, particularly if admission is sought to an APA-accredited program.

Accreditation has direct relevance to employment. As already stated, some employers (especially now that the job market is shrinking) give preference to psychologists from APA-accredited programs. Moreover, there is reason to believe that state licensing boards are moving in the direction of requiring that applicants for licensure be from APA-accredited programs or their equivalent (with the equivalency having to be documented by a university dean).

There are, of course, many fine clinical psychology training programs, including those in prestigious universities, that do not have APA accreditation. The odds of being admitted to a training program that does not hold APA accreditation may or may not be better. The training may be excellent, and job opportunities may be plentiful for the graduates. The only message is that having a degree from an APA-accredited school is a positive attainment.

INTERDISCIPLINARY "COMPETITION" FOR EMPLOYMENT

Clinical psychologists enter a job market that is also open to psychiatrists, clinical social workers, marriage and family therapists, mental health counselors, and other types of psychologists, most notably counseling psychologists. While each of these disciplines or specialties has specialized skills, each has many skills in common with those possessed by the clinical psychologist. Since admission and graduation requirements are different, some of the other types of professionals, such as social workers and mental health counselors, may be able to offer a potential employer most if not all of the same skills that could be offered by the clinical psychologist, and they can do so along with other benefits to the employer (such as being willing and able to work for a lesser salary).

Professional Similarities

Fiedler (1950) found that therapists of different theoretical schools did not differ in their descriptions of the concepts for an ideal therapeutic relationship (their degree of expertise, not their theoretical allegiance, was thought to be the significant factor). Strupp (1955) compared the psychotherapeutic technique of psychiatrists, psychologists, and psychiatric social workers, and concluded that the disciplinary affiliation exerted, at the most, only a relatively minor influence (when theoretical orientation was held constant).

Clinical Psychology Versus Counseling Psychology and School Psychology: Clinical psychology has always been closely akin to counseling psychology and school psychology. From its early days, clinical psychology was believed to emphasize psychopathology, whereas counseling psychology was believed to emphasize normality or hygiology—the condition of health or absence of clinically defined illness (Super, 1955). The training programs in the two specialties were and are highly similar in content, except perhaps for the site of the internship and a difference in the amount of coursework in abnormal behavior (i.e., more for clinical psychology) and vocational development (i.e., more for counseling psychology). The eminent clinical psychology trainer at Purdue University, the late John M. Hadley (1961), chose to consider clinical and counseling psychology together, which seemed to be the harbinger of the contemporary "professional psychology" stance of many psychologists in health care. School psychology received much of its impetus from clinical psychologists who had an interest in serving children [the schools afforded an access route, and some training programs have joined clinical psychology and school psychology together (Vane, 1985)]. Furthermore, Lightner Witmer worked with educationally related problems, and is considered to be a "founding father" of school psychology.

As for employment, Tipton (1983) studied the roles and functions that could distinguish clinical psychologists from counseling psychologists. He found the normality (or hygiology) to pathology continuum, with the counseling psychologists being [as Super (1955) posited nearly three decades earlier] more aligned with normality, and clinical psychologists more aligned with pathology. There were, however, many similarities, but (1) clinical psychologists maintained an assessment–diagnostic component, with minimal reference to therapy for a relatively normal population; (2) clinical psychologists gave more support than counseling psychologists to providing marital interventions and other consultation; and (3) "Particularly notable among the discrepancies between how the two specialties rated the relevance of the activities for counseling psychology were the following four activities that were given significantly lower ratings by the clinical group: counseling/therapy with adults, counseling/therapy with the mild to moderately disturbed, preventative treatment, and outreach programs" (p. 844).

Clinical Psychology Versus Psychiatry: Even though the psychiatrist may treat pathological patients, he or she is not qualified to administer and interpret psychological tests. Of course, the clinical psychologist is not qualified to prescribe medication, and this provides for a logical teamwork effort for the clinical psychologist and the psychiatrist.

It is a reality that clinical psychologists have more extensive training and greater depth to their understanding of normal and abnormal human behavior than representatives from certain other disciplines. More extensive training is particularly manifest in research methods and psychotherapy such as comparative analyses; these combine to produce a clear-cut scientific basis for the practice of psychology, something that may or may not be present in psychiatric training. The best strategy, however, is to sell the qualifications of the clinical psychologist for expertise, as opposed to denigrating another discipline. There has been far too much warring among mental health professionals for what can only be deemed ego gratification, and which can be interpreted only as being fueled by a faulty professional self-identity.

Clinical psychology has matured to the point where it is in no way second to any other profession or discipline. Clinical psychology need not be in "competition" with other psychological specialties, such as counseling psychology and school psychology, or with psychiatry.

SPECIALIZED CREDENTIALS

In keeping with the earlier comments about specialty guidelines, obtaining employment as a clinical psychologist is increasingly reliant upon skills that will separate one applicant from another applicant. In other words, it is recognized that clinical psychology is a complex specialty, one that possesses so many possible areas of expertise that it is impossible for every clinical psychologist to possess equal competence in each of them. Consequently, specialized credentials have been developed (and more are on the way) that will provide distinction.

Today, there is a proliferation of specialty credentials, and while this presumably helps safeguard standards for the consumer, it is not without problems. As President of the APA's Division of Clinical Psychology, Lee B. Sechrest (1985) states: "Psychology, and clinical psychology which is at the crux of the matter, appears to be headed toward the creation of 'specialties' at a frightful rate"; and he notes that "there are now about 30 (!) different groups proposing themselves as specialties" (p. 1). While acknowledging the "to protect the public" rationale, Sechrest critically asserts that there are two other motives: (1) specialty diplomas accommodate advertising that will increase income; for example, "Specialists expect to charge higher fees, and the evidence from medicine is certainly that they do" (p. 1); and (2):

> One suspects also that just sheer ego has something to do with the problem of specialization. Most diplomas, at least in psychology, are probably of very little material value; they may serve no greater purpose than persuading their possessors that they are in some way special. Presumably some warm feeling flows through the practitioner who can gaze upon the large array of neatly framed documents

> decorating his or her office wall. One of my colleagues has suggested that we go into business manufacturing diploma wallpaper that could simplify the whole thing [p. 1].

Although it may sound as though Sechrest is a heretic regarding his clinical psychology specialty, such is not the case. He goes on to encourage assembling evidence to support standards, arrangements, and a specialty that will "truly protect the public and preserve the honorable practice of psychology" (p. 3).

Diplomating Boards

There are, of course, some boards that award specialty diplomas that are worth little more than a "buy your diploma" operation, and nothing good can be said for those boards that are in business to collect application fees and award (read "sell") the diploma simply for payment.

There are, however, two other types of specialty diploma boards that are more legitimate. The first type has several members of the board review the applicant's credentials, and those candidates endorsed receive the diploma without an examination. The second type of board does, in fact, require a credential review, a work sample for analysis, and an examination—surely an honorable peer-review process.

As noted in the Sechrest comments, there are many specialty boards, and it would be inappropriate to try to list them all or to pass judgment on them. Suffice it to say, that a specialty credential is possible in behavioral medicine, biofeedback, hypnosis, psychotherapy, marriage and sex therapy, family psychology, and so on.

The American Board of Professional Psychology

The American Board of Professional Psychology (ABPP) had its inception in 1947, and since that time, it has awarded about 3,660 diplomas, with about 3,000 of those diplomates still being active or only recently retired (Palo, 1984), and it is a specialty program that deserves applause. In brief, the

ABPP sponsors an examination program whereby psychologists with high-quality training and experience can submit work samples for peer review, and if they pass muster, move on to an examination. The examination typically includes working with an actual patient while being observed through a one-way window by several examiners. Successful completion of the examination leads to award of the diplomate status. One can become diplomated in clinical psychology, counseling psychology, school psychology, clinical neuropsychology, forensic psychology, and industrial–organizational psychology.

A clinical psychologist can become a diplomate in more than one specialty, but only if an examination is successfully completed for each specialization. For example, a clinical psychologist might initially become a diplomate in clinical psychology, reflecting his or her overall professional identity and competency, but because of involvement in legal cases (e.g., giving expert testimony), he or she could potentially also become a diplomate in forensic psychology. The American Board of Forensic Psychology (ABFP) and the American Board of Clinical Neuropsychology (ABCN) have affiliated with ABPP.

The APA, while independent of the ABPP, recognizes the diplomates created by ABPP and its affiliates, as well as those psychologists who have been named diplomates of psychological hypnosis by the American Board of Psychological Hypnosis (ABPH). This recognition is somewhat nominal, but the aforementioned diplomates are listed in the *APA Directory* (1985b), and it is common to have the diplomate status from these sources listed in the directories of state-level psychological associations. To date, the APA has not accorded recognition, even in a nominal manner, to any of the many other specialty boards that exist.

Among psychologists, holding ABPP diplomate status is an honor. It signifies that the psychologist's credentials have been inspected and approved of by peers, that his or her work product has been scrutinized and endorsed as supporting the potential for effectiveness, and that he or she has satisfied the standards of a professional examination that is both academic and clinical in nature; that is, deemed an exceptional clinical psychologist by the profession.

It is commonplace for certain positions, particularly those

at a more senior level, to specify that applicants should hold the ABPP diploma. In addition, an ABPP diplomate might also justify a higher salary or fee for service. For example, Senator Daniel K. Inouye (1984) spearheaded the passage of the Veterans Health Care and Facilities Improvement Act of 1984, which was ratified by the 98th Congress, and provided authority to give a pay bonus of up to $10,000 for those clinical or counseling psychologists who were ABPP diplomates.

Professional Memberships

A clinical psychologist's claim to specialization can also gain credence through membership in certain professional organizations. There are some professional organizations that admit virtually any professional who pays the dues and which may provide a handsome certificate to display on the office wall. This type of membership does little, if anything, to document training, competency, or expertise. On the other hand, there are certain other professional organizations which have stringent requirements for membership; that is, being a psychologist, expressing interest, filling out an application form, and paying the dues are not enough to gain membership.

When membership in a professional organization is restricted to those who can document having had, as a minimum, specialized coursework, it seems reasonable to deem the membership a form of certification of competency, albeit less rigorous and less esteemed than having obtained certification through a peer-administered examination process. Some organizations of this type go beyond coursework, such as: in psychotherapy, having personally received some therapylike experience that would presumably equip the psychologist with insight about his or her personal–professional self-concept (as might be critical to the transference–countertransference issue); in group psychotherapy, having conducted a certain number of therapy groups of a particular duration; or in sex therapy, having treated a certain number of patients with sexual problems.

In most of these specialties, it is common also to require a certain amount of clinical supervision of one's services, with the supervision being provided by a more senior professional in the specialty. For example, the American Association for Marriage and Family Therapy (AAMFT), which predicates Clinical Member status on a number of qualifications, requires that some of the supervision be provided by an approved supervisor, a marriage and family therapist previously approved by the organization for its roster of supervisors (or an equivalent professional).

As with the ABPP diplomate status, it is not unusual for an announcement of a position in, say, marriage and family therapy to specify that preference is for a psychologist who is, for example, a clinical member of the AAMFT, or if the position is in training, such as with a university, to prefer an AAMFT approved supervisor. If the position involves conducting group psychotherapy, it would be a plus (if not a prerequisite) to be a member of the American Group Psychotherapy Association (AGPA), since it specifies a number of qualities relevant to training and experience before membership is granted.

Although not a certification of competency per se, achieving fellow status within a professional organization can complement employment potential. By being active in, say, the committee work of a professional organization and becoming an elected officer, or in some other manner making a distinguished contribution, a psychologist can become a fellow. Being named a Fellow of the APA would be an asset in the job market; it would signify that the individual had made an outstanding contribution to his or her professional discipline.

Specialized Training Experiences

Distinctive training in a specialization can be a noteworthy credential. For example, having one's Ph.D. internship in a unique context, say a neuropsychology facility, would afford a benefit when a position involving neuropsychology was sought. Grace (1985) offers guidelines for evaluating prospective clinical internships. Many clinical psychologists do a postdoctoral fellowship in order to gain advanced specialization. On a more modest level, completion of continuing education seminars, which is consonant with the ethical responsibility for every psychologist, can serve to form a specialization.

It should be noted that certain continuing education experiences will be better than others for this purpose. For example, there have been a number of training programs in hypnosis that could actually taint a professional's reputation (e.g., the training was conducted by laypersons with a "stage hypnotism" flare), whereas training in hypnosis from a reputable source could be an important aid in seeking a position in, say, a health psychology context.

EMPLOYMENT OPPORTUNITIES AND INCOME

It should be emphasized that there is a tight job market for clinical psychologists in the mid-1980s. In part this is due to the large number of psychologists that have been trained [e.g., from 1966 to 1976, there was a 153 percent increase in the number of psychology doctorates awarded (Syverson, 1982)]. The job market has also been influenced by the shift in public policy priorities away from publicly supported mental health programs. So, no matter what the applicant's qualifications, the job market for clinical psychologists is difficult at best.

The condition of the job market means that it will be the exception rather than the rule to be able to target a particular type of employment, select a desired geographical locale, readily obtain a job there, work in it for a while, and then move eventually to a position that will represent an advancement. Steinhauser (1985) discusses his experiences when seeking employment as a new Ph.D. holder. Even though he recognized before he started that the job market was crowded, that he could not restrict himself to a dream job, and that he could not choose a geographical location, he made 122 job applications, had 10 interviews, and received two job offers.

The message, therefore, is that obtaining employment is a challenge. It requires cultivating professional and personal qualities; the candidate must earn academic credentials that will be equal to or greater than those possessed by other candidates. Personally, the candidate must not place his or her ego in jeopardy by expecting immediate endorsement—it is not a sign of failure to be denied a job in this day and age, it is merely the product of a complex array of political, financial, and social factors.

Since 1975, the APA has assessed the employment status of those with new psychology doctorates [there are now about 3,000 psychology doctorates awarded each year (Syverson, 1983)].

From their survey of 1981 and 1982 recipients of psychology doctorates, Stapp, Fulcher, and Wicherski (1984) found for the clinical psychologists: 80.0 percent were employed full time; 9.9 percent were employed part time; 7.1 percent were postdoctoral fellows; 1.0 percent were unemployed but seeking employment; and 1.2 percent were unemployed and not seeking employment. For clinical psychologists, the employment settings and percentages were: university, 9.8 percent; four-year college, 1.3 percent; medical school, 4.9 percent; other academic, 1.0 percent; schools and other educational, 4.1 percent; independent practice, 8.6 percent; hospital, 26.1 percent; clinic, 25.2 percent; other human service, 8.8 percent; business, government, and other, 10.0 percent; and not specified, 0.2 percent.

In a preliminary report of the 1983 survey of new psychology doctorates, Fulcher, Pion, and Stapp (1985) note that "a higher percentage of new doctorates of clinical psychology are employed part time, most likely due to the availability of private practice as an employment option" (p. 2). Only 56.9 percent of all employed respondents had a single (full-time) position. For clinical psychologists, 77.2 percent were employed full time; 11.0 percent were employed part time; 9.0 percent were postdoctoral fellows; 1.6 percent were unemployed but seeking employment; and 1.3 percent were unemployed and not seeking employment. Note that data on the employment settings and percentages therein were not provided.

Salaries are always of interest. Table 3.1 provides the findings of the Fulcher et al. (1985) survey.

As might be expected, demographic characteristics enter into the selection process, it is hoped in a nondiscriminatory manner. While data are not available for all possible employment situations, the Stapp et al. (1984) survey considers employment status by sex and ethnicity, as well as the degree subfield. In brief, this survey seemed to reveal less pronounced differences between Caucasian and minority psychologists in the matter of full-time versus part-time employment; and more men (84–85%) than women (70–71%) were employed full time, and there were a number of gender differences among the various employment settings. In their study of employment in academia, Klesges, Sanchez, and Stanton (1982) found: "The data related to the characteristics of the hired faculty members suggest that the 'typical' successful job applicant hired for the 1980–81 year in clinical departments was young, white, behavioral, and female; whereas the 'typical' faculty member in experimental departments was young, white, behavioral, and male" (p. 585). Regional differences also enter into the salary issue, as might be due to local or regional economic conditions; for example, Stapp et al. (1985) provide a survey of 1984–1985 faculty salaries in graduate departments of psychology that reveal differences according to geographic region, whether the department is a public or private institution, and type of department, such as being labeled psychology, educational psychology, and so on.

CONTINUING EDUCATION

Employment will be influenced by the strong trend toward specialization. Specialization, among other things, has created the responsibility of clinical psychologists to maintain, enhance, or retool their skills (see chapter 2). Continuing education (CE) started coming on strong during the late 1970s in response to several concerns. Kalafat and Neigher (1983) speculate that the "half life" of professional knowledge may be closer to five to six years instead of the earlier estimate of ten to twelve years. They mention also the increased demand for accountability by the public, government regulatory agencies, private third-party reimbursers, legislatures and consumer groups; in addition, several surveys have underscored the inadequacy/irrelevancy of traditional graduate training. Patterson (1979) points to a trend among states to require CE credits for relicensure or recertification. Patterson defines the purpose of CE to be one of maintaining previously acquired competencies and/or developing skills in newly relevant areas. In a similar vein, Jensen (1979) stresses the importance of assessing competent professional service that may be obtained

TABLE 3.1
Full-time Salaries of 1983 Doctorate Recipients in Selected Positions and Settings[a]

Position Type	Employment Setting	Median	Mean	S.D.	*N*
Assistant professor[b]	All settings	21,000	22,401	4,584	242
	University psychology department	21,000	21,672	3,501	116
	University education department	20,000	21,176	2,481	17
	University business school or department	29,000	29,400	5,275	10
	University, other academic department	23,000	24,688	4,729	16
	Four year college psychology department	19,500	19,694	3,560	36
	Medical School, psychiatry department	26,000	25,353	4,061	17
Research position	All settings	25,000	26,505	6,882	107
	University research center or institute	23,000	22,100	3,542	10
	Private research organization	27,000	29,250	8,625	12
	Government research organization	26,000	27,250	4,250	16
	Business or Industry	32,000	33,846	8,726	13
Direct human services—Clinical psychology	All settings	26,000	27,009	7,475	436
	University/college counseling center	24,000	24,067	2,890	15
	Elementary or secondary school	26,000	27,308	4,803	13
	Public general hospital	30,000	30,190	4,976	21
	Private general hospital	25,500	25,583	3,798	24
	Public mental hospital	27,000	27,333	5,110	54
	Private mental hospital	26,000	28,375	6,908	16
	Veteran's Administration hospital	30,000	28,350	2,477	20
	Individual private practice	40,000	41,238	18,036	21
	Group psychological practice	30,000	31,769	11,606	13

	Medical/psychological group practice	29,500	27,600	6,159	20
	Outpatient clinic	24,000	25,200	8,446	25
	Community mental health center	23,000	23,505	4,136	97
	Health maintenance organization	26,500	27,833	6,088	12
Direct human services—Counseling psychology	All settings	25,000	26,661	9,697	109
	University/college counseling center	21,000	21,542	2,734	24
	Community mental health center	24,000	24,500	4,501	20
Direct human services—School psychology	All settings	26,000	27,573	6,009	75
	Elementary of secondary school	26,500	28,429	6,309	28
	School system district office	25,000	26,471	5,113	17
	Other educational setting	27,000	26,250	4,920	12
Direct human services—Other psychology	All settings	26,000	28,100	8,209	89
	Community mental health center	24,500	25,500	6,836	14
Administration of human services	All settings	26,000	27,461	6,246	128
	Public mental hospital	27,000	28,125	3,344	16
	Community mental health center	23,500	25,167	5,136	18
	Special health services	25,000	26,385	6,318	13
	Other human service setting	27,500	30,000	7,958	10
Applied psychology Industrial/organizational	All settings	33,000	36,130	9,097	23
	Business or industry	33,500	35,750	6,758	16

[a]From Fulcher et al. 1985, reproduced with permission.
[b]Salaries for these types of positions are typically paid on a 9-10 month (academic year) basis. The statistics given here may be converted to their 11–12 month (calendar year) equivalents by multiplying by 11/9.

through self-directed study (some publications now provide clinical psychologists with the option of obtaining CE credit for their reading by means of self-assessment examinations), workshop/conferences, supervision, or compulsory course work. In 1979, the APA's Council of Representatives addressed the issue by establishing the Sponsor Approval System to provide national standards for CE in psychology, a computerized CE registry, and a CE calendar/clearing house (APA, 1984a). To assure optimum employability, clinical psychologists must maintain a commitment to continuing education throughout their career.

EMPLOYMENT PROGNOSIS

Predicting employment opportunities is highly speculative. There are always too many unknown and unpredictable conditions that can alter the employment trend to allow for sure predictions. This was certainly witnessed over the past two decades. Given the surge of public policy support for mental health in the 1960s, the allocation of governmental funding to develop training programs, and the proliferation of graduates in psychology, few soothsayers would or could have predicted the radical shift away from human services, and the concomitant underemployment and unemployment of clinical psychologists that has occurred.

For now, it can be said that there is likely to be a continuing decline in employment in academic settings: "in 1975, almost 50% of the 1975 doctorate recipients were employed full time in academic settings as compared to only about 27% of their 1983 counterparts" (Fulcher et al., 1985, p. 4). Since doctoral production in psychology has leveled off and public policy has stabilized (at least tentatively), it appears that the employment market is steady; but the fact that more women are being awarded doctorates, the reduction in federal sources of support for graduate training, and an increasing emphasis on applied research and nonacademic career roles, all combine to create a substantial press on the job market for clinical psychologists (Stapp et al., 1984).

It seems likely that the private practice of clinical psychology will become even more widely accepted by the public and will, therefore, create new employment possibilities. But this will lead more practitioners into the market, and private practice, like other contexts, could soon be overcrowded and highly competitive.

Public policy supports the private practice of clinical psychology, but there is a push for a unification of clinical psychologists with other health care providers—a unification that could threaten professional autonomy and remuneration (Martin, 1983). Reorganization into health care organizations is a double-edged sword: it promises employment for clinical psychologists, but it relies on greater patient cost sharing, which is known to deter the use of health services: "Experience has indicated that people who pay more of the cost at the time of use are less likely to use any mental health services and have lower expenditures when they do. It is also to be expected that over time people subject to greater cost sharing would increasingly consider price when deciding which mental health or general medical provider to choose" (Sisk and Langenbrunner, 1985, p. 92). Thus, it is difficult to forecast the effects of the health care movement. It is feasible that it could either enhance or undermine the practice of clinical psychology.

As clinical psychologists come out from under the protective cloak of employment by an institution, their declaration of independence brings new personal exposure to stress. Nash, Norcross, and Prochaska (1984) found that independent practitioners cited satisfaction from professional independence, promoting patient growth, autonomy, and professional success, but acknowledged their major sources of stress to be time pressures, economic uncertainty, caseload uncertainty, business aspects, and excessive workloads. Norcross, Nash, and Prochaska (1985) found that "part-timers rated the opportunities for independent practice in their locale as less favorable than did the full-time practitioners" (p. 572). This means that, even if there is employment possible in private practice, it may take its toll in terms of personal satisfaction, security, and health. Thus, some clinical psychologists will likely find independent practice to be an undesirable alternative.

Having issued cautions, a note of optimism is in order. It seems that clinical psychology has developed in a professionally unprecedented manner. From modest roots at the turn of the century, clinical psychology has blossomed into a mature discipline that is nourished by an impeccable, scientifically derived energy. Public policy has acknowledged this stature, and recognized the fact that clinical psychology has accomplished much good for society.

Among all of the psychological specialties, clinical psychology seems to have one of the most solid curricular frameworks for its graduates. Consequently, the clinical psychologist, in keeping with the scientist–practitioner model, is capable of changing with the times. Few of the other psychological specialties can boast of the generalizability of academic foundations and the adaptability of practice competencies of clinical psychology.

The endorsement by public policy and the scientist–practitioner composition generate optimism about the employment potential of the clinical psychologist. Stated differently, even if there are rough spots in the employment road ahead for psychologists, clinical psychologists are apt to have a relatively smooth passage.

Chapter 4

The Regulation of Clinical Psychology

It just did not seem right, so the clinical psychologist called his attorney for legal counsel: "I have this dilemma. I have an affiliation with the local school system, and was referred a 13-year-old girl named Cassie. I've been treating her, and her test data support that she has some major problems. In therapy, she tells me about using marijuana and drinking beer with a couple of her girl friends, and having had sexual relations with several of the guys she's dated. She has insisted that I not tell any of these things to her parents. So far, I've been comfortable with not telling them any details—I believe Cassie and I have a strong therapeutic connection, and that she would turn to me before doing something really foolish. Now, however, I find out that her parents are divorcing, and are going to fight over who gets custody of the children. Today I received a *subpoena duces tecum* that says I have to turn over all of my records about Cassie to the parents' attorneys, and I was told they want to take my deposition in two weeks. The problem, obviously, is that I promised Cassie that I wouldn't reveal any of the details—she still wants me to keep my promise, and suggested I just lie about it. Well, I'm not going to lie, but I really don't want to turn my records over to anybody and I don't want to tell attorneys things that will put me into the middle of the parents' custody fight. For one thing, if I don't keep my promise to Cassie, it will certainly screw up our therapeutic relationship—if you can't trust your therapist to keep confidentiality, you can't trust anyone. Also, if she tells other students about my breaking a promise of confidentiality, as she would likely do, it will probably lessen my credibility and my referrals will drop. I'm a member of the American Psychological Association, and our ethical principles clearly state—here let me read a line to you, 'They reveal such information to others only with the consent of the person or the person's legal representative.' Cassie hasn't consented, and neither of the attorneys is her legal representative. Of course I'm a licensed psychologist here in the state, and there is a statute that says my communications with my patients are privileged. My question is, can you as my attorney do something so I can keep my promise of confidentiality?"

At first glance, it might seem that the professional ethics and the privileged communication statute would surely combine to justify the clinical psychologist's avoidance of a breach of the patient's confidentiality because of the subpoena and the notice to take a deposition. While the attorney for the clinical psychologist would have an opportunity to try to get the court to set aside the *subpoena duces tecum* and/or to deny or restrict depositions, there is no automatic assurance. Indeed, as will be presented in this chapter, there is a strong likelihood—for several reasons—why the court would be apt to require a clinical psychologist in this kind of case to reveal any and all information about the girl. More will be said about this case example in the final section of this chapter.

INTRODUCTION

In considering the regulation of clinical psychology, it could be asserted that clinical psychologists should have the prerogative of relying on self-determination for their professional functioning. After all, every clinical psychologist has survived countless challenges in graduate school and has proven to a distinguished faculty of clinical psychology trainers that he or she merits wearing the mantle of professionalism—otherwise, the doctoral degree would not have been awarded.

Typically, a clinical psychologist has also been subjected to extensive evaluation on the postdoctoral level, such as through taking a national standardized (objective) examination and/or a state-created essay and/or oral examination, in order to obtain licensure to practice psychology. Of course, many clinical psychologists voluntarily subject themselves to additional evaluations, such as seeking diplomate status from the American Board of Professional Psychology (ABPP).

The rationale for self-determination would be that since the clinical psychologist has successfully passed so many assessments, it would seem reasonable to allow autonomous decision making about professional practices.

For the skeptic of autonomous decision making, there would be the alternative of letting clinical psychologists, as a group, regulate themselves. That is, given the uniqueness of the clinical psychologist, only clinical psychologists would have the knowledge necessary for establishing professional practices. This would be termed the *peer review* approach.

As logical as these two alternatives might seem, neither prevails today. There is, of course, a large amount of autonomous decision making virtually every moment in the practice of clinical psychology, and peer review (i.e., a determination made by clinical psychologists as a group) fulfills an important role—but there are other sources of control and regulation.

According to Claiborn (1982), there are seven organizational contexts that constitute a primary means for ensuring competence in professional psychology: standards for providers; ethical codes; professional standards review committees; third-party payer quality assurance; state licensing and certification boards; the National Register; and diplomate status. Each of these seven contexts has been either explicitly discussed or implicitly referred to at other points in this book, but this chapter will unite them in a framework for professional regulation.

STANDARDS FOR PROVIDERS

Foremost in this category are the specialty guidelines prepared by the American Psychological Association's (APA's) Committee on Professional Standards (1981c), hereafter referred to as the "specialty guidelines." There are four sets of specialty guidelines; namely, for clinical psychology, counseling psychology, industrial–organizational psychology, and school psychology. This discussion will be restricted to the specialty guidelines for clinical psychology.

The primary purpose of the specialty guidelines is to promote the best interests and welfare of the consumer of the clinical psychologist's services (note that the guidelines refer to the clinical psychologist as the "provider" and the patient or recipient of services as the "user"). The intention is to provide assurance that the clinical psychologist is accountable for the nature and quality of services (but not to the point that new methods or innovative procedures are negated).

The specialty guidelines seek to: (1) "provide a foundation for mutual understanding between provider and user and facilitate more effective evaluation of services provided and outcomes achieved" (p. 641); (2) foster uniformity for the credentialing of clinical psychologists; (3) "give specific content to the profession's concept of ethical practice as it applies to the functions of clinical psychologists" (p. 641); (4) have an impact on future education and training models for clinical psychologists (and their support personnel); (5) "influence the determination of acceptable structure, budgeting, and staffing patterns" (p. 641) in the health service facilities that employ clinical psychologists; and (6) obtain continual review and revision of the guidelines applied to clinical psychology. Thus, the specialty guidelines are for improving the quality and delivery of clinical psychological services: "Systematically applied, these Guidelines serve to establish a more effective and consistent basis for evaluating the performance of individual service providers as well as to guide the organization of clinical psychological service units in human service settings" (p. 641).

Guideline 1: Providers specifies standards for: (1) establishing the availability of clinical psychologists within a service unit; (2) supervising minimally qualified providers; (3) involving a clinical psychologist in planning, directing, and reviewing services; (4) influencing overall organizational goals, planning, and development; (5) maintaining up-to-date knowledge of scientific and professional developments; (6) limiting practice to areas of demonstrated competence; (7) having consonance between practice and education-training standards; and (8) encouraging innovative theories and procedures.

Guideline 2: Programs deals with the composition and organization of clinical psychological services, such as: (1) being responsive to the needs of persons or settings served; (2) delineating lines of responsibility (including for supervision and accountability); (3) having sufficient numbers of professional and support personnel; (4) protecting the legal and civil rights of users; (5) adhering to standards and ethical principles promulgated by the APA; (6) conforming to statutory laws; (7) being informed about and linked to the community network of human services; (8) maintaining collegiality to meet the best interests of users; and (9) having proper procedural guidelines within the service unit for the delivery of clinical psychological services (e.g., effective records, a system for confidentiality).

Guideline 3: Accountability is devoted to promoting human welfare, and holds that: "Clinical psychologists pursue their activities as members of the independent, autonomous profession of psychology" (p. 647); that is, no other profession or discipline can govern the profession of psychology. The latter, while not stated per se, supports that clinical psychology will not be subservient to another discipline, such as medicine, and any service unit that creates conditions for employment that would require such subservience is unacceptable to the standards of clinical psychology. This guideline also promotes "periodic, systematic, and effective evaluations of clinical psychological services" (p. 648).

Guideline 4: Environment sets forth the promotion of facilitative physical, organizational, and social environments for the unit offering clinical psychological services. This would include meeting legal requirements for safety, health, and sanitation, and being concerned about any condition that could potentially have an adverse effect on the quality of services; for example, "Physical arrangements and organizational policies and procedures are conducive to the human dignity, self-respect, and optimal functioning of users and to the effective delivery of service" (p. 648).

From this synopsis of the specialty guidelines, it is evident that quality control and consumer protection are critical dimensions. Certainly, the clinical psychologist has directions for professional functioning. Moreover, and where the real challenge may be encountered, the clinical psychologist cannot allow any source, such as another profession–discipline or an administrative policy, to denigrate the standards for the specialty of clinical psychology.

ETHICAL PRINCIPLES

As discussed in chapter 3, ethics emanate from a professional organization and apply only to the members of that organization. Therefore, if a clinical psychologist chose not to be a member of the APA, its ethical principles would not apply to that particular person. There are, however, two exceptions to the notion that ethical principles are without legal clout. Let us consider the exceptions in detail.

First, while a set of ethics has no legal authority per se, ethics can be incorporated into a state statute. This may be found in the statutes of certain states that incorporate the APA's (1981b) "Ethical Principles of Psychologists" into the law for licensing psychologists. Or, if the ethical principles are not incorporated into the statute by legislative action, the board of examiners can incorporate them into their rules via their administrative authority.

Second, certain civil law cases, such as those that involve an alleged tort (a wrong done to another person), can hinge upon the standard of care that should have been exercised by the alleged tortfeasor, and can rely upon ethical principles for defining (at least to some extent) what should or should not have occurred under the circumstances (malpractice is a good example). Any presumably therapeutic action that was not predicated on protecting the welfare of the patient would seemingly be counter to ethical principles, and it is likely that such unethical conduct would carry substantial weight in determining, say, negligence on the part of the therapist.

As these two exceptions illustrate, ethical principles have far-reaching effects. An ethical violation could lead to such detriments as professional censure or loss of one's license to practice, thereby lessening career potential. An ethical violation can also be part of a litigation judgment that imposes a great financial burden, as well as the penalty of having been found guilty of harming a patient.

The "Ethical Principles of Psychologists" (APA, 1981b), hereafter referred to as the ethical principles, are the primary source of ethical governance for clinical psychologists. However, there may be other ethical sources. For example, if a clinical psychologist was a member of the American Association for Marriage and Family Therapy (AAMFT) or the American Association of Sex Educators, Counselors, and Therapists (AASECT), his or her practice in the areas of marriage, family, and/or sex therapy would fall under the governance of the ethics promulgated by those two organizations. Consequently, if there were a malpractice suit based on alleged faulty provision of marriage and family or sex therapy, there could be multiple sets of ethics embraced in the establishment of the standard of care that should have been maintained.

The ethical principles of the APA have a preamble that is dedicated to the protection and welfare of the individual and society:

> Psychologists respect the dignity and worth of the individual and strive for the preservation and protection of fundamental human rights. They are committed to increasing knowledge of human behavior and of people's understanding of themselves and others and to the utilization of such knowledge for the promotion of human welfare. While pursuing these objectives, they make every effort to protect the welfare of those who seek their services and of the research participants that may be the object of study. They use their skills only for purposes consistent with these values and do not knowingly permit their misuse by others. While demanding for themselves freedom of inquiry and communication, psychologists accept the responsibility this freedom requires: competence, objectivity in the application of skills, and concern for the best interest of clients, colleagues, students, research participants, and society [p. 633].

Beyond the protection of others, it should be noted that there is a personal verve required, as reflected in such words as *committed to, pursuing*, and *demanding*. The affirmative duty to enhance professional functioning must permeate into the core of the clinical psychologist's personal identity.

There are 10 ethical principles. Each of these receives elaboration, but for purposes of this chapter, it will suffice to state the fundamental or basic segment of each principle:

Principle 1: Responsibility. In providing services, psychologists maintain the highest standards of their profession. They accept responsibility for the consequences of their acts and make every effort to ensure that their services are used appropriately (p. 633).

Principle 2: Competence. The maintenance of high standards of competence is a responsibility shared by all psychologists in the interest of the public and the profession as a whole. Psychologists recognize the boundaries of their competence and the limitations of their techniques. They only provide services and only use techniques for which they are qualified by training and experience. In those areas in which recognized standards do not yet exist, psychologists take whatever precautions are necessary to protect the welfare of their clients. They maintain knowledge of current scientific and professional information related to the services they render (p. 634).

Principle 3: Moral and Legal Standards. Psychologists' moral and ethical standards of behavior are a personal matter to the same degree as they are for any other citizen, except as these may compromise the fulfillment of their professional responsibilities or reduce the public trust in psychology and psychologists. Regarding their own behavior, psychologists are sensitive to prevailing community standards and to the possible impact that conformity to or deviation from these standards may have upon the quality of their performance as psychologists. Psychologists are also aware of the possible impact of their public behavior upon the ability of colleagues to perform their professional duties (p. 634).

Principle 4: Public Statements. Public statements, announcements of services, advertising, and promotional activities of psychologists serve the purpose of helping the public make informed judgments and choices. Psychologists represent accurately and objectively their professional qualifications, affiliations, and functions, as well as those of the institutions or organizations with which they or the statements may be associated. In public statements providing psychological information or professional opinions or providing information about the availability of psychological products, publications, and services, psychologists base their statements on scientifically acceptable psychological findings and techniques with full recognition of the limits and uncertainties of such evidence (pp. 634–635).

Principle 5: Confidentiality. Psychologists have a primary obligation to respect the confidentiality of information obtained from persons in the course of their work as psychologists. They reveal such information to others only with the consent of the person or the person's legal representative, except in those unusual circumstances in which not to do so would result in a clear danger to the person or to others. Where appropriate, psychologists inform their clients of the legal limits of confidentiality (pp. 635–636).

Principle 6: Welfare of the Consumer. Psychologists respect the integrity and protect the welfare of the people and groups with whom they work. When conflicts of interest arise between clients and institutions that employ psychologists, psychologists clarify the nature and direction of their loyalties and responsibilities and keep all parties informed of their commitments. Psychologists fully inform consumers as to the purpose and nature of an evaluative, treatment, educational, or training procedure and they freely acknowledge that clients, students, or participants in research have freedom of choice with regard to participation (p. 636).

Principle 7: Professional Relationships. Psychologists act with due regard for the needs, special competencies, and obligations of their colleagues in psychology and other professions. They respect the prerogatives and obligations of the institutions or organizations with which these other colleagues are associated (p. 636).

Principle 8: Assessment Techniques. In the development, publication, and utilization of psychological assessment techniques, psychologists make every effort to promote the welfare and best interests of the client. They guard against the misuse of assessment results. They respect the client's right to know the results, the interpretations made, and the bases for their conclusions and recommendations. Psychologists make every effort to maintain the

> security of tests and other assessment techniques within limits of legal mandates. They strive to ensure the appropriate use of assessment techniques by others (p. 637).
>
> *Principle 9: Research With Human Participants.* The decision to undertake research rests upon a considered judgment by the individual psychologist about how best to contribute to psychological science and human welfare. Having made the decision to conduct research, the psychologist considers alternative directions in which research energies and resources might be invested. On the basis of this consideration, the psychologist carries out the investigation with respect and concern for the dignity and welfare of the people who participate and with cognizance of federal and state regulations and professional standards governing the conduct of research with human participants (p. 637).
>
> *Principle 10: Care and Use of Animals.* An investigator of animal behavior strives to advance understanding of basic behavioral principles and/or to contribute to the improvement of human health and welfare. In seeking these ends, the investigator ensures the welfare of animals and treats them humanely. Laws and regulations notwithstanding, an animal's immediate protection depends upon the scientist's own conscience (p. 638).

As mentioned, the foregoing quotations represent only the basic segments of the ethical principles. Although each ethical principle has a number of subsections, as would clarify a variety of issues, even so, the individual clinical psychologist is always left with the need to interpret.

If there is an alleged ethical violation, tradition has it that the complaining psychologist should talk to the colleague who is believed to have been in violation of the ethical code. The word *tradition* is used because in this litigious era, such confrontations carry a risk. For example, the psychologist whose performance is being questioned may be indignant toward or even threaten legal action against the complaining psychologist. In any event, it now seems best to carry all complaints, whether between two professionals or between a layperson and a professional, to a professional ethics committee.

As long as a complaint is processed formally within an established professional grievance process, it is likely that those involved will receive legal support.

The exact route for an ethics complaint depends, to some degree, on the nature of the complaint and the place where the psychologist is located. There are other types of ethical violations that could potentially be cleared up, to the advantage of all concerned, by informal communications. Certain locales have local or regional ethics committees, from which a decision could possibly be appealed to a state-level ethics committee, which in turn could possibly be appealed to a national-level ethics committee—and there are many other feasible committee routes. Moreover, there are some ethical violations which might best be handled by bypassing ethics committees altogether, and be transformed into a criminal and/or civil lawsuit.

PROFESSIONAL STANDARDS REVIEW COMMITTEES

Some state associations sponsor a professional standards review committee (PSRC). Such a committee receives complaints about a psychologist's practice, and provides mediation or arbitration to resolve the matter. Informal or formal hearings may be held. Any opinion issued is commonly considered advisory, such as stating what might be deemed "usual and customary" for the practice that is in question (Claiborn, 1982).

THIRD-PARTY PAYER QUALITY ASSURANCE

Major health plans, such as those available through the federal government or through insurance companies, can potentially include third-party reimbursement to the patient–policyholder for the services provided by clinical psychologists. Ostensibly, in order to maintain control of the quality of services that will reimburse (and perhaps to lessen the number of practitioners who will qualify for third-party payments), health plans have implemented several rules.

An insurance policy could exclude mental health services, unless the policyholder paid a premium for such special coverage. Or an insurance policy could restrict payment to those services provided by psychiatrists and psychologists (thereby excluding, say, clinical social workers). Note that many states have so-called "freedom of choice" legislation that specifies, for example, that if a medical physician is eligible for reimbursement, so shall a licensed psychologist be eligible for reimbursement. In other words, the policyholder has a right to seek treatment from any health care provider licensed by the state. Or an insurance policy may provide payment only for those psychologists who have been designated "clinical" psychologists, such as by special certification through the state board of psychology examiners or by the American Board of Professional Psychology (ABPP) or by the National Register of Health Care Providers in Psychology.

Even after the services of a clinical psychologist have been deemed eligible for coverage, the insurance carrier may maintain a review of the treatment program. By careful review of the treatment program, fraud can be avoided, and the treatment approach can be monitored for appropriateness and quality. These evaluative judgments are made by clinical psychologists or other mental health professionals employed as reviewers. It is interesting to note that: "Even when utilization review leads to the conclusion that incompetent treatment has occurred, the usual disposition is to deny reimbursement for the individual case alone and to take no further action against the incompetent provider" (Claiborn, 1982, p. 154).

Some wags have asserted that third-party reimbursement will create too much use of mental health service. Contrary to other findings, DeMuth and Kamis (1980) obtained data that contradicted the belief that third-party insurance payments encouraged overutilization. They found use was not dependent on economic or provider variables: "Availability of public third-party reimbursement did not lead to excessive service utilization by needy, severely disturbed clients" (p. 795). The amount of the fee, the patient's sociodemographic profile, and the provider's characteristics offered little explanation for the service utilization patterns that were found.

At the risk of sounding crass, there is no doubt that third-party payments have enhanced the financial aspects of clinical psychology practice. At the same time, it is believed that it has had a constructive regulatory impact on the profession, for the benefit of the client/patient and of society.

With the elimination of a stigma regarding psychotherapy, the provision of mental health services constitutes a sizable industry. Magaro, Gripp, and McDowell (1978) offer a historicoeconomic analysis of the mental health industry. They conclude that the best system is one in which there would be "the cessation of automatic funding of all publicly maintained mental institutions" (p. 220). Instead, they endorse "a return of competitive capitalism in the mental health industry" (p. 218). This free enterprise economic arena would mean that "the funds would be reserved for disbursal to treaters according to the degree of rehabilitation, improvement, or 'success' they facilitate in their clients" (p. 220). The Magaro, Gripp, and McDowell stance supports the view that the quality assurance efforts of the third-party payer should have a positive effect for all concerned.

STATE LICENSING AND CERTIFICATION BOARDS

Through legislation, a state controls employment in its jurisdiction via the granting of licenses and permits. Sometimes there is similar regulation by other governmental entities, such as at the country or municipality level. This regulatory function is intended to assure quality and safeguard the citizenry, but it may also generate financial revenue for the governmental entity.

A state board of examiners of psychologists administers the licensing program. This board is typically comprised of psychologists and one or more laypersons (the latter is intended to keep the profession aware of the public voice). The board may be under the administrative aegis of a larger state department, such as the department of professional regulation. Such an umbrella department generally oversees a number of disciplinary boards.

The authority of the board is stated by statute. Certain qualifications for practice are specified, usually in terms of academic training and employment experience. The area of practice is defined, and the procedures for examination are set forth. Misconduct, violations, penalties, exemptions, and renewal matters may be delineated.

An interesting dovetailing of regulatory efforts can be found when a state licensing board restricts those psychologists deemed eligible to sit for the examination to those who have graduated from an APA-accredited training program (or the equivalent). This APA–statutory combination could effectively regulate the standards of a university.

Another important trend is continuing education. More and more states are predicating the renewal of a license upon the psychologist's having completed a certain number of continuing education hours.

Keeping up to date in one's profession has long been and remains an ethical matter. Ethical Principle 2: Competence, states: "They maintain knowledge of current scientific and professional information related to the services they render" (APA, 1981b, p. 634).

Nowadays, staying current is also a legal matter. Unless there is documentation of continuing education, the assumption (in some states) is that the psychologist's knowledge of current scientific and professional information has become outdated to the point that the public welfare would best be served by denying the renewal of his or her license to practice.

NATIONAL REGISTER

Another form of regulation of clinical psychologists emanates from the *National Register of Health Service Providers in Psychologists* (Council for the National Register of Health Service Providers in Psychology, 1983), hereafter referred to as the National Register. The National Register appears in the form of a directory of approximately 13,500 psychologists who have voluntarily submitted their credentials for evaluation according to criteria intended to assure competency in providing health services.

The threshold criteria are: (1) the applicant holds a doctoral degree in psychology from a regionally accredited educational institution (there are over 800 doctoral programs that have been listed as approved sources of training); and (2) the applicant has received licensure and/or certification from a state board of examiners of psychologists. For approval, the applicant must have at least two years of supervised experience in health service in psychology; at least one of these years must be in an organized health service training program, and one year must be postdoctoral.

The Council offers the following definition: "A Health Service Provider in Psychology is defined as a psychologist, certified/licensed at the independent practice level in his/her state, who is duly trained and experienced in the delivery of direct, preventive, assessment and therapeutic intervention services to individuals whose growth, adjustment, or functioning is actually impaired or is demonstrably at high risk of impairment" (p. xiii).

The National Register has come to be recognized as a source for sorting out the qualified independent practitioners from the self-proclaimed practitioners. That is, the National Register evaluates an applicant's credentials to assure consonance with the established standards for health care providers.

Other professional sources turn to the National Register for guidance. For example, an insurance company might require that the clinical psychologist be a member of the National Register in order for his patients to qualify for third-party reimbursement. Or a clinical psychologist who has a patient moving to another state might refer to the National Register to locate the name of a clinical psychologist in the new locale to whom the patient can be referred for continued treatment.

DIPLOMATE STATUS

Since diplomate status was discussed in detail in chapter 3, the subject will be briefly summarized here.

As will be recalled, becoming "diplomated" refers to a clinical psychologist's having passed a peer review for expertise in a specialty. This review might be based only on an analysis of the "paper credentials" of the candidate, or—as would be the case with the more prestigious diplomating boards—it could include an analysis of the credentials and a work sample, as a prerequisite for a written and/or oral examination.

At the present time, there are numerous specialties that have a relevant diplomating program. The most honorific source is the American Board of Professional Psychology (ABPP), which has an examination process for becoming a diplomate in the following specialties: clinical psychology; counseling psychology; school psychology; clinical neuropsychology; forensic psychology; and industrial–organizational psychology. At this writing, there are negotiations underway for possibly adding other specialties.

The status of diplomate creates a press for competency: "The American Board of Professional Psychology (ABPP) diploma is seen by some as a means to encourage a higher level of ability by defining a higher 'floor' of competence, which may prove helpful to the public in assessing competence" (Claiborn, 1982, p. 155).

Much like a listing in the National Register, the ABPP diplomate status might be expected for third-party reimbursement from an insurance company (although some states have statutes that could limit the type of qualifying restrictions that an insurance company could maintain), or might lead a clinical psychologist to give preference to a practitioner in another part of the country to which one of his patients is moving. Moreover, some states recognize the ABPP diplomate in the licensing–certification requirements. For example, an examination might be waived if the applicant were an ABPP diplomate.

While the foregoing seven regulatory sources might seem like a plethora of safeguards, there are weaknesses in the system. As Claiborn (1982) summarizes:

> There are no centralized, standardized, organized means to define or detect incompetence; no accepted mechanisms to define it; few mechanisms for adjudication in cases of suspected incompetence; and few sanctions available for cases of proven incompetence. None of the contextual definitions of incompetence . . . include consideration of the following as bases for determining professional competencies: treatment outcomes; relative efficiency of treatments; safety and efficacy of treatments; or treatment plan, that is, did the plan have a reasonable, conceptual,

> and empirical linking of goal, method, and outcome [p. 155].

There is, however, a final source of regulation of clinical psychology that steps in when peer-review regulation fails, namely the legal system.

LEGAL JUDGMENT OF CLINICAL PSYCHOLOGY

The American legal system is devoted to maintaining social order: "It is a dynamic process by which rules are constantly being adopted and changed to fit the complex situations of a developing society" (Grilliot, 1975, p. 3). As reflected throughout this book, clinical psychology has moved rapidly and is very much a part of contemporary society's development and complexity. Consequently, society has expanded its legal umbrella over the practice of clinical psychology:

> As society recognizes a profession, it imposes upon that discipline a concomitant responsibility or duty—a set of expectations as to what should and should not occur in professional practice. In other words, the *quid pro quo* for societal recognition of professionalism is professional accountability to society. When society judges professional practice to be substandard, it attaches legal liability. It is this interface between public policy and professionalism which creates the legal framework for malpractice [Woody, 1985, pp. 509–510].

In other words, society has an expectation of high quality care from those to whom it gives a virtual monopoly for a service via its professional licensing. When the professional breaches the standard, society asks its legal arm to reach out and impose sanctions, such as by withdrawing professional status (e.g., eliminating the license) or seeking compensation for the injured person (e.g., imposing a court-ordered judgment for damages emanating from the malpractice).

Clinical psychology can have the bitter-sweet satisfaction of knowing that its professionalism is well established, as documented by the number of lawsuits that are filed against its practitioners. According to Fisher (1985), from 1955–1965 (the first 10 years that the APA offered malpractice coverage), no claims were filed against psychologists; from 1976–1981, there were 266 claims (an average of 44 per year); from 1982–1984, the annual rate more than tripled (an average of 153 claims per year); "the number of claims against psychologists have risen faster in the past three years than for any other mental health profession" (p. 6); and "In the past two years, the number of sexual malpractice suits against psychologists have multiplied by five, so that they represent 20 to 30 percent of all suits, and cost insurers twice as much as all other causes combined" (p. 7).

Psychologists are sued for many reasons. Hogan (1979) analyzed legal allegations against psychotherapists (not just clinical psychologists), and found: "In the 300 cases collected here, more than twenty-five types of actions were brought, including involuntary serviture, false arrest, trespass, malicious infliction of emotional distress, abuse of process, loss of liberty, misrepresentation, libel, assault and battery, malicious prosecution, and false imprisonment. Outnumbering all actions put together, however, is the simple negligence or malpractice suit, which occurs in more than two-thirds of the cases" (p. 7). Stated differently, this analysis reveals that: (1) psychotherapists are not exempt from sociobehavioral frailty; and (2) the legal system imposes a standard of care for professional practice.

Malpractice is predicated on a standard of care: "The quality of professional care is required legally to meet the standard of minimum knowledge, skill, and intelligence common to members of the profession" (Woody, 1983b, p. 1435); and "As for professional standards of conduct, the practitioner need not be superior but must possess and exercise the knowledge and skill of a member of the profession in good standing" (Woody, 1984, p. 393).

For the conscientious clinical psychologist, there are safeguards for avoiding malpractice (Woody, 1983a). On the other hand, the litigious era is such that even the conscientious practitioner is not immune from a lawsuit. Indeed, there is reason to believe that many lawsuits are filed by patients who are dissatisfied for dubious reasons, such as suddenly deciding that the clinical psychologist did not exercise an adequate standard of care only when an attempt is made to make the patient pay an overdue treatment bill (Wright, 1981a, b).

As a defensive strategy:

> The prudent human services professional should (1) have a clear delineation of the standard of care that would be applied to his or her services; (2) adopt assessment procedures to ensure that the services were reasonably tailored to the needs of the client and were consonant with the standard of care; (3) maintain a system by which clients are informed about and consent to the professional interventions; and (4) consistently exercise safeguards against any knowing or inadvertent deviations from or any real or imagined breaches of the established standard of care (Woody, 1984, p. 400).

It should be readily evident that, if peer-review regulatory functions fail, the legal system affords society a final means for regulating professional practices. Given the mushrooming number of lawsuits against professionals of every ilk, it would appear that the legal system is keenly sensitive to societal concerns about regulation, as would be applied to clinical psychology (along with many other professional disciplines). From the standpoint of social theory: "It is unprofessional to attempt to deny, consciously or unconsciously, that these public policy legal sanctions are justified" (Woody, 1984, p. 401).

Aside from malpractice, the legal system can also regulate the specific practices within a profession. As a cogent example, clinical psychologists predicate many of their interventions, particularly psychotherapy, on maintaining confidentiality. Going further, state statutes typically extend confidentiality into privileged communication between the clinical psychologist and his or her patient. That is, public policy endorses, through its laws, that the relationship between, say, a clinical psychologist and a patient is so sacrosanct that others cannot have access to its contents.

Refer back to the "Ethical Principles" section of this chapter. Principle 5: Confidentiality, indicates that confidentiality (or even privileged communication) may be breached if there is a "clear danger to the person or to others" and that it is acknowledged that there are "legal limits of confidentiality" (APA, 1981b, p. 636).

Even though a privileged communication statute might deem the clinical psychologist–patient relationship sacrosanct, the legal system may sanction exceptions. For example, the court's subpoena power can be used to obtain a clinical psychologist's records or testimony about a patient embroiled in a legal controversy. In other words, public policy supports that sometimes the right to social justice supersedes the right to confidentiality or privileged communication.

While the focus of this section is on the regulation of clinical psychology, it should be noted that patients are often unable to differentiate between privacy as an ethical versus a legal concept (McGuire, Toal, and Blau, 1985). The complexity of the law and the characteristics of patients combine to construct a difficult problem: "The challenge to practitioners . . . is how to provide accurate, impartial, and comprehensive information to clients who vary so widely in their ability to understand" (Muehleman, Pickens, and Robinson, 1985, p. 396). The inconsistencies, contradictions, and exceptions within the law governing privileged communication led Knapp and VandeCreek (1985) to assert: "Until these laws are changed, psychologists will practice under the current patchwork of existing laws" (p. 405). Needless to say, any thing that is "patchwork" does not give a solid composition. There are many ambiguities inherent to the clinical psychologist's allegiance to confidentiality and privileged communication.

CASE ANALYSIS

At the beginning of this chapter, a brief case was presented. In this section, that case will be dissected, with the objective being to clarify the regulatory principles that enter into the decision making of a clinical psychologist.

Point One: The clinical psychologist realizes that there is a conflict of interest between his duty to society, to the employer (the school system), to the parents, and to the patient. The psychologist wants to be sure that the rights of the patient are safeguarded. Since he is unsure, the advice of an attorney is obtained. This is consonant with the APA's Principle 1 regarding responsibility.

Point Two: The clinical psychologist recognizes that the girl has major problems, including behaviors that run counter to the law and to her best interests. Since she is an unemancipated minor, technically she has few legal rights—she is still under the total custody, care, and control of her parents, and legal duties and rights relevant to her welfare are vested in her parents. The clinical psychologist reveals that the promise of confidentiality is being strained. Ethically and legally, the psychologist may reveal the confidential information to the parents; this is consonant with Principle 3 regarding moral and legal standards, and with Principle 5 regarding confidentiality. The psychologist will logically be tactful in presenting any confidential information to the parents, with the goals being to: (1) maintain as much confidentiality for the girl as possible; (2) retain the girl's trust, notwithstanding the breach of confidentiality; and (3) maximize the parental cooperation with the treatment plan.

Point Three: The court has the power to override professional ethics. As mentioned in an earlier section, even statute-based privileged communication can become secondary to the legal process. Thus, the *subpoena duces tecum*, which mandates that the clinical psychologist relinquish any and all records to the court (i.e., to the attorneys for the custody dispute), may very well have to be honored, even if it is over the personal opposition of the girl and the clinical psychologist. If a motion to quash the subpoena is denied, the clinical psychologist could potentially be held in contempt of court if he refuses to comply with the court-endorsed subpoena. The same would hold true for subpoenaed testimony by the clinical psychologist.

It should be remembered that the parents are the source of vested legal rights for the minor girl, unless there has been a legal termination of those rights by the court. To be sure, there are certain situations where the court would probably support a minor child's preferences (perhaps even in a case like this), but it would be necessary to establish legally that it was in the child's best interest and that preservation of this interest yielded a benefit that justified the loss of evidence.

Given these analytic points, the clinical psychologist's question "can you as my attorney do something so I can keep my promise of confidentiality" cannot be given a definitive answer. It would, as explained, have to be submitted to the court for an answer.

PERSONAL CONSIDERATIONS

The message in the foregoing example is clear-cut: a clinical psychologist cannot be self-determining. Even with the best interests of the patient in mind, the clinical psychologist must submit to the regulatory power of many sources. Standards for providers, ethical codes, professional standards review committees, third-party payer quality assurance efforts, state licensing and certification boards, the National Register, diplomate status, and, perhaps foremost, the legal system exert unyielding pressure on virtually every element of the practice of clinical psychology. The pressure never ceases, as exemplified by the renewal of a license to practice being predicated (in more and more states) on the psychologist's fulfilling a continuing education requirement. Lest this seem inappropriate, it must be remembered that *professionalism is a product of society*, and regulatory sources are society's servants for maintaining public welfare.

PART II

THEORIES AND METHODS FOR PRACTICE

Chapter 5

Being a Psychotherapist, Part I: An Introduction to Theories and Strategies

> Psychotherapy, in its broadest sense, originated with the beginning of mankind—when the first two people formed a relationship, each offering the other solace, comfort and encouragement. . . . The ancient Greeks utilized specific psychotherapeutic techniques in their healing temples, where the ailing person was exposed to music, soothing environments, as well as having the opportunity to express his troubled thoughts and feelings to the priest [Barron, Fabrikant, and Krasner, 1971, p. 1].

> What good is psychotherapy? As good as man's faith in his humanity. Men have always believed in their ability to change for the better and to help each other so to change—through mutual assistance, love, religion, and art. Conceived in the broadest terms psychotherapy derives from the same faith and, employing of necessity some of the same means, attempts to formulate these more precisely [Rosenzweig, 1954, p. 303].

As the first quotation suggests, the essence of psychotherapy is a helping relationship in which one human being ministers to another through the healing power of words. And, as the second quotation suggests, faith in one's ability to change and to help others change is fundamental to the generic meaning of psychotherapy.

As a professional specialty psychotherapy has four defining characteristics (Ford and Urban, 1963): (1) two or more persons engaged in a highly confidential interaction in which one or more is required to be self-revealing; (2) the mode of interaction is usually limited to verbal exchange; (3) the interaction is relatively prolonged; and (4) the agreed-upon purpose is to achieve change; that is, to foster appropriate and realistic thought–feeling–action patterns that are consistent with one's values, and that lead to responsible and satisfying interpersonal relationships. Three critical assumptions are that change is desired, that life circumstances and environment do not rule out change, and that change can be brought about by psychological procedures.

The terms, *psychotherapy, counseling, treatment*, and *therapy* are often used interchangeably. However, the term *counseling* ordinarily excludes serious psychopathology; *treatment* is often synonymous with medical interventions; and *therapy* does not differentiate psychological from nonpsychological interventions.

Although psychotherapy differs from other therapeutic interventions, such as educational, medical, sociological, environmental, it may be used in conjunction with the latter methods. Although similar in some respects to therapeutically beneficial friendships, psychotherapy differs in having formally designated roles of therapist and client, and in the absence of the social consequences that often follow from personal relationships.

Psychotherapy can be conducted with one client (child or adult), with a group of unrelated clients, with a couple, or with a family. The length of psychotherapy varies depending upon the goal (e.g., personality reorganization, resolution of specified problems, crisis intervention); the adjustment level of the client (e.g., mild, moderate, or severe dysfunction); the orientation of the therapist, and financial resources of the client. Psychotherapy may be long term (usually 20 or more sessions), short term (generally 10–20 sessions), or brief (less than 10 sessions). Two therapists may work as a cotherapy team, and a client may be in one or more modalities (individual, group, couple, or family) at the same time with the same or different therapists.

At least three stages of psychotherapeutic work can be

identified. The first stage is developing a collaborative relationship, specifying problems, and prioritizing goals. The second stage consists of the therapist's application of specific interventions to implement therapeutic goals. The third stage is designed to generalize and maintain therapeutic gains.

For both clients and therapists the psychotherapy process is sometimes tedious and exhausting, sometimes exciting and energizing, always challenging, and never quite finished. During the course of psychotherapy a therapist plays many roles: interpersonal model, conceptualizer of information, change agent, and "professional" friend.

Being a psychotherapist is a complex personal, as well as professional undertaking. For those who aspire to be psychotherapists, Strupp (1978) has this to say: "I would place a good deal of emphasis on the prerequisite of native talent. Given such endowment, the rest is prolonged hard work, patience, and extensive experience . . . a fine therapist closely resembles a painter, novelist, or composer. As is true in all the sciences and the arts, few reach the summit" (p. 317).

Although the assertion can be debated, psychotherapy as a unique blend of science and art originated with Freud's theory of psychoanalysis. Freud formulated a complex theory and a painstaking method to explore and explicate a person's past life with the goal of producing an insight-based catharsis of unconscious conflicts. Although Freud's psychoanalysis had to make room for inevitable splinter groups and rival factions, the theory and method maintained a proprietary claim on psychotherapy for nearly half a century.

The first nonpsychoanalytic theory to mount a serious and permanent challenge was the client centered approach developed by Carl Rogers in the 1940s. Basically, Rogers (1942) made it intellectually respectable to deal with the conscious; therapeutically relevant to focus on the present; professionally permissible for the therapist to disclose his personhood; and scientifically responsible to open both the process and the outcome of one's psychotherapy sessions to professional scrutiny.

Following Rogers's lead several learning theorists, notably John Dollard and Neal Miller (1950), demonstrated that Freudian concepts and principles were not theory-specific, but could be translated into theoretical language that allowed greater conceptual clarity and empirical confirmation or disconfirmation. For example, global psychoanalytic concepts, such as repression, displacement, conflict, were translated into the specific and empirically derived terms of *drive, cue, response*, and *reward*.

During the past 25 years there has been a mind-boggling proliferation of psychotherapies. Goldfried (1980) cites a figure of 130 different therapeutic approaches, and Corsini (1981) estimates there are 250 alternative approaches. Even the conservative Civilian Health and Medical Programs of the Uniformed Services (CHAMPUS) includes over 40 different psychotherapeutic procedures in its approved list for reimbursement (APA, 1980).

Clearly, *psychotherapy* has become a generic term that subsumes a bewildering array of competing claims to better serve the psychological health needs of the public. In general, most current psychotherapy systems can be compared and contrasted on six theoretical dimensions: (1) conscious versus unconscious determinants of behavior; (2) insight versus behavior change as the therapeutic goal; (3) a focus on the present–future versus the past; (4) a scientific versus aesthetic attitude; (5) the therapeutic relationship versus the therapist's techniques as a basis for change; and (6) diagnosis versus assessment. As others have noted, what theorists choose to exclude or deemphasize is as significant personally and professionally as what they choose to include or emphasize.

CURRENT PSYCHOTHERAPEUTIC SYSTEMS

Psychodynamic Orientation

This section presents an overview of Freudian psychoanalytic psychotherapy, Adlerian individual psychotherapy, Jungian analytic psychotherapy, the sociopsychological theories of Karen Horney, Erich Fromm, Harry Stack Sullivan, and the ego analysts, such as Heinz Hartmann, Anna Freud, Erik Erikson, and Heinz Kohut.

Underlying psychodynamic theories is the postulate that within each person there are opposing forces that make painful intrapsychic conflicts inevitable, and that these conflicts, of which the person may or may not be aware, often originate in childhood, and have a powerful influence on personality development and the ability to cope with current life stresses (Goldenberg, 1983). Although strongly influenced by Freud's theory of psychoanalysis, the neopsychoanalytic theorists (Adler, Jung, the social-psychological theorists, and the ego analysts) rejected parts of Freud's theory, modified other aspects, and made significant additions (Corey, 1982). Other theoretical contributions to the psychoanalytic literature have been Otto Fenichel's theory of neurosis, Otto Rank's will therapy, and Wilhelm Reich's body-oriented theory.

Freudian Psychoanalysis. Although Freud developed a comprehensive theory of personality development, only the psychoanalytic theory of psychotherapy is described. Psychoanalytic psychotherapy is primarily a method of treating neurotic disorders, and usually involves a commitment of two or more years of four to five sessions per week.

Unconscious intrapsychic conflicts are considered to be a major cause of psychological disorder, and to result from unsuccessful mastery of the psychosexual stages of development in infancy and early childhood. The overall goal is: (1) to relieve psychic distress; (2) to strengthen the conscious, adaptive part of the personality (ego) in coping with the pressures of instinctual drives (id), and the demands of conscience (superego); and (3) to improve psychosexual maturity. A key assumption is that current problems of living cannot be successfully resolved without a thorough understanding of the unconscious basis of the early conflictual relationships with parents or parent surrogates.

The central focus of the therapy sessions is on the interplay between the patient's unconscious impulses and unconscious efforts to cope with the impulses by various defense mechanisms. The primary intervention strategy is to resolve unconscious intrapsychic conflicts by gaining insight into the causes and by applying this insight to current behavior. To accomplish this strategy, several techniques are used. The foremost technique, free association, involves the person's free verbal expression of every thought, feeling, or impulse which serves to reduce inhibitions, to establish meaningful connections between his or her statements, and to bring unconscious material into consciousness (Goldenberg, 1983). The analyst remains silent and neutral, except to intercede when the patient is experiencing temporary resistance.

Another technique is dream analysis, in which the patient verbalizes the manifest (conscious) content of a dream, and then free associates to the manifest content so that the analyst can discern the latent (unconscious) meaning. Freud postulated that dreams represent a disguised compromise between unconscious wish fulfillment and unconscious fear of wish fulfillment.

Another technique, analysis of transference, is used to identify and resolve patients' "unfinished business" with significant others, by allowing them to react to the analyst as they did (and may still do) to significant persons in their early life (Corey, 1982). The abnormal effect of early parent–child interactions on the patient's current interpersonal relationships is counteracted by working through similar problems in the relationship with the analyst (Corey, 1982).

The purpose of resistance is to defend oneself from acute anxiety that would occur if the unconscious suddenly became conscious. Thus, analysis of resistance is a potent technique. The analyst directs attention to any aspect of the therapeutic relationship that the patient is attempting to avoid, as well as to anything that is blocking the process of uncovering unconscious material, so that therapy can progress and the patient can begin to understand how resistance interferes with his or her daily life (Corey, 1982). Once patients have overcome resistance, they can then deal directly with the conflicts that underlie the resistance.

Finally, interpretation is an important technique that is combined with the ones outlined above. Interpretation consists of the analyst pointing out, describing, explaining, even teaching clients the meaning of their behavior, as manifested by free associations, dreams, transferential reactions, and resistances (Corey, 1982). Interpretations need to be well timed; that is, made at a point when unconscious material is close to awareness and the patient is ready to assimilate painful insights.

The following excerpt shows an analyst's use of analysis of transference, followed by the use of free association.

Patient: I don't understand why you're holding back on telling me if this step is the right one for me at this time in my life.

Analyst: This has come up before. You want my approval before taking some action. What seems to be happening here is that one of the conflicts you have with your wife is trying to get her approval of what you have decided you want to do, and that conflict is occurring now between us.

Patient: I suppose so. Other people's approval has always been very important to me.

Analyst: Let's stay with that for a few minutes. Would you free associate to that idea of getting approval from others. Just let the associations come spontaneously—don't force them.

The patient–analyst relationship can be characterized as very professional and businesslike, the purpose of which is to resolve the client's "there and then" interpersonal problems by working through the problems in the "here and now" interaction with the analyst. The role of the analyst is that of a neutral observer whose task is to encourage, examine, and interpret the meaning of the patient's verbalizations. The role of the patient is that of a passive participant whose task is to disclose his innermost reactions to the therapist.

Three strengths of the psychoanalytic theory are: (1) close attention to the way in which patients replicate in the therapy session the problems experienced outside the session; (2) thorough understanding of unconscious determinants of current behavior; and (3) detailed examination of critical events in the patient's past life. Three weaknesses are: (1) too little attention to the present and immediate future; (2) insufficient emphasis on the patient's personal strengths and assets; and (3) preoccupation with hidden or unconscious meanings, or as Arnold Lazarus, a leading behavior therapist, once remarked, "sometimes a cigar is just a cigar."

Many psychodynamic therapists use psychoanalytic theory to conceptualize problems and therapeutic goals, although they may use techniques other than or in addition to the orthodox ones. An extended discussion of Freud's theory can be found in Brenner (1973) and Arlow (1984). The reader is also referred to Freud's (1915–1917) *The Introductory Lectures on Psychoanalysis*.

Adlerian Individual Psychotherapy. Developed by Alfred Adler, a one-time colleague of Freud, this theory, in contrast to Freudian theory, emphasizes conscious processes and social determinants of personality.

A major cause of psychological disorder is thought to be self-centered and unrealistic goals that individuals develop early in life to overcome real or imagined inferiorities. The overall goal is to overcome inferiority feelings by setting aside egocentric motivations and values in favor of a socially responsible and individually productive life-style. A key assumption is that human beings develop a life goal that centers their existence and toward which their life-style is directed, and an individual patient can be understood through knowledge of conscious goals and subsequent goal-directed behavior (Goldenberg, 1983). The central focus of therapeutic work is the present and future thrust of the patient's conscious memories, needs, values, beliefs, feelings, and actions.

The primary intervention strategy is an examination of early childhood recollections, birth order, the family constellation, parental practices, from which the therapist constructs a picture of the patient's life-style, shows him or her how the life-style is creating current problems of living, and what positive changes need to be undertaken. The therapist uses the techniques of interpretation, confrontation, and instruction to assist the patient to live more productively and responsibly in the present, which then forms a solid foundation for the future. Adlerian therapists may also use Freudian methods, such as dream analysis, transference, and analysis of resistance, but the emphasis is on the present rather than the past.

The following illustrates the methods of early memories.

Patient: Many times I act as if I believe what someone is telling me, but inwardly I have strong reservations about believing them.

Therapist: Let's digress for a moment. I'd like for you to identify and describe one of your earliest memories.

Patient: Well, I was about four or five. I was standing in my backyard. Two neighborhood kids were there and they were standing over a pail. They asked me to come over and look at what they had in the pail. I went over, and they told me to bend down and look into the pail. When I did, they pushed my head into the pail of water. I remember how scared I was—I thought they were going to drown me. I remember them laughing as they did it to me.

The patient–therapist relationship is similar to a teacher–student interaction, in which the role of the therapist is to be energetic, directive, and instructive, and the patient is expected to be a receptive, motivated learner who seeks to understand and correct in the present, and for the future, the mistakes of the past.

A strength of the Adlerian approach is the perception of problems as an expression of life-style. A limitation is reliance on reeducative methods. For additional information on this approach the reader is referred to Mosak (1984), and for an original source, Adler's (1929) *Problems of Neurosis: A Book of Case Histories*.

Jungian Analytic Psychotherapy. Developed by Carl Jung, who like Adler was a one-time colleague of Freud, this theory offers a model of human experience that is broader than Freud's conception of human beings engaged in an unremitting struggle between instinctual forces and sociocultural taboos.

A major cause of psychological disorder is held to be an unbalanced and opposing relation between conscious and unconscious processes. The overall goal is to assist the patient to understand the unconscious, to respect its power, and to utilize its positive, creative elements in order to live a fully developed and evenly balanced life.

A key assumption is that in order to live a life free of disabling symptoms, a patient must develop a constructive coupling of conscious and unconscious processes. Jung's concept of the unconscious is more inclusive than Freud's concept insofar as it includes collective–societal elements as well as personal–individual elements, and it is more balanced insofar as it allows for growth-producing as well as growth-inhibiting possibilities.

The central focus of the therapy sessions is the patient's inner world of dreams, daydreams, fantasies, and other symbolic expressions.

The primary intervention strategy is to achieve a balance between the conscious and unconscious so that the two complement rather than conflict (Goldenberg, 1983). To this end, the therapist uses interpretation of the unconscious as expressed in the patient's waking life. Dream analysis is a major technique which takes into consideration the patient's dream history rather than single, isolated dreams (Corey, 1982). Jung believed that dreams were not only a reaction to the past, but also a statement of current life and a portent of the future.

The patient–therapist relationship can be likened to that of two persons who join together for a journey into territory unknown to both, in which the therapist as a guide uses his or her training to chart their course.

A strength of the Jungian approach is the conception of the unconscious as a source of growth and creativity. A limitation is the heavy emphasis on the patient's inner world of symbolic experiences. For an extended discussion of Jung's theory, the reader is referred to Kaufmann (1984) and Jung's (1956) *Two Essays on Analytical Psychology.*

Social Psychological Theorists. Karen Horney, Erich Fromm, and Harry Stack Sullivan are among the best known of the social psychological theorists, all of whom assigned a major role to social and cultural determinants of normal and abnormal behavior.

The recurrently conflictual relationship between the patient and those who transmit the values and beliefs of society (primarily parents and parent surrogates) is considered to be a major cause of psychological disorder. The overall goal is to revise the patient's self-image so that it is congruent with potentialities and realistically based goals (Horney), to develop a "productive" orientation to life; that is, to actualize the patient's potentials (Fromm); or for the patient to understand who he or she is, and could be, in relation to significant others (Sullivan). A key assumption is that there are strong formative influences (positive and negative) beyond those of early childhood, and that psychotherapy has the potential to restore the patient's capability to make substantial personality changes. The central focus of the therapy sessions is past and current relationships with significant others.

The primary intervention strategy is to help patients understand their role and the role of significant others in the development and perpetuation of relationship problems. Horney and Fromm relied on the Freudian techniques of free association and dream analysis, supplemented by whatever techniques seem appropriate at a particular stage of therapy, while Sullivan relied on an interview-based exchange of information.

The patient–therapist relationship is one characterized by a genuine respect for the individuality and latent capabilities of the patient. Especially for Sullivan, the therapist's sharing of his or her personhood was believed to be therapeutic for the patient.

A strength of the social–psychological approach is the interpersonal focus. A limitation is the lack of a systematic strategy for changing behavior. For additional material the reader is referred to Hall and Lindzey (1978).

Ego Analysts. The contribution of the ego analysts, notably Erik Erikson, Heinz Kohut, Heinz Hartmann, and Anna Freud, to psychoanalytic theory is primarily a revised and expanded conceptualization of the structure and functions of the ego.

The unresolved problems of one or more stages of ego development are felt to be a major cause of psychological disorder. The overall goal is to strengthen the autonomous, nonconflictual functions of the ego in order to better organize behavior and to deal constructively with the current personal and social environment. A key assumption of ego analysis is that human beings "are capable of organizing their behavior and directing their activities to deal constructively with their environment" (Goldenberg, 1983, p. 217).

The central focus of therapeutic work is on the reactive functions of the ego (i.e., to reduce conflict between the id or instinctual drives and the superego or conscience), and the proactive functions of the ego, which involve nonconflictual, productive interactions with the environment.

The primary intervention strategy is to give the patient

insight into how the past continues to influence the present, and to develop the patient's awareness of what can be done in the present to correct the harmful effects of the past. The usual techniques are interpretation and constructive suggestions, and where applicable, orthodox psychoanalytic methods.

An important focus of Erikson's (1963) developmental theory is the relationship between a patient's current developmental problem and success or failure with an earlier developmental problem. For example, a male patient in his late twenties was seeking help with difficulties in forming intimate relationships. The therapist soon discovered that the patient had never resolved the identity confusion and conflict of adolescence. Before the patient could develop and maintain an intimate relationship with another adult, he first had to clarify and gain confidence in his own identity.

The patient–therapist relationship is a collaborative one in which the patient is an active change agent who makes constructive use of the therapist's shared knowledge of developmental stages and developmental crises.

A strength of this approach is the attention given to the adaptive functions of the ego. A limitation is insufficient emphasis on changing behavior. Erik Erikson (1963) and Blanck and Blanck (1974) provide additional information.

Phenomenological–Humanistic Orientation

This orientation includes person-centered, gestalt, and existential psychotherapies. The phenomenological designation stresses the importance of understanding the client's frame of reference by ascertaining how the client perceives reality and the personal meaning given to reality. The humanistic designation underscores the value placed on freedom and self-determination, and the positive role of life-affirming emotions (love, joy, hope, excitement) in coping with life's problems.

Person-Centered Psychotherapy. The theory was developed and later modified and expanded by Carl Rogers with important contributions by Eugene Gendlin, Robert Carkhuff, and Gerrard Egan.

A major cause of psychological disorder is a failure in the normal growth process. As a result of frustrating interactions with the interpersonal environment, the normal drive to develop oneself fully becomes blocked. Symptoms are manifestations of the discrepancy between one's current level of personal–social functioning and one's capabilities.

The overall goal of person-centered psychotherapy is to assist a client to become more fully the person he is capable of becoming. A key assumption is that the relationship which the therapist develops with the client is the primary curative factor. The central focus of the therapy is on the conscious experiences of the client in the present, although the therapist assists him to verbalize implicit or unspoken awarenesses.

The primary intervention strategy is to create a therapeutic relationship by being genuine, by showing unconditional positive regard for the personhood of the client, and by conveying respect for his inherent ability to make intelligent and responsible choices about how to live his life. Specific techniques are: (1) empathic reflection of explicit and implicit feelings, needs, values, and goals; (2) the therapist's self-disclosure of relevant personal and professional experiences, as well as perceptions about the immediate relationship with the client; and (3) nonjudgmental confrontation of discrepancies between clients' self-statements on the one hand, and statements of who they wish to be, their report of what others say about them, or the therapist's perception of them.

Below are three pairs of client and therapist statements. The first pair illustrates empathic reflection, the second, self-disclosure, and the third, confrontation.

Client: I guess I'm feeling bitter right now.

Therapist: You feel bitter because you were misled. I also sense you feel lonely because right now there is no one else to take her place.

Client: I really resent what happened.

Therapist: If that were me, I'd not only feel angry, but also hurt because of having my confidence betrayed.

Client: I suppose I want them to do it.

Therapist: Your need to be a follower is strong; yet you have said that you value taking the initiative and asserting yourself.

The client–therapist relationship is an egalitarian, psychologically intimate one, in which the client is viewed as the change agent, and the therapist as a facilitator of and a participant in the client's change process.

A strength of person-centered psychotherapy lies in the importance given to the therapist's interpersonal skills in developing a therapeutic relationship, while a limitation is the lack of technical or structured interventions. Rogers (1961) and Meador and Rogers (1984) provide additional information.

Gestalt Psychotherapy. Fritz Perls was the originator of gestalt psychotherapy, with contributions by James Simkin, E. Polster, M. Polster, Walter Kempler, and others.

The client's dissociation of important parts of self from awareness and acceptance is considered to be a major cause of psychological disorder. The overall goal is to assist the client to become aware of and take responsibility for the previously dissociated aspects of self, and to reintegrate into consciousness the disowned parts of self. A key assumption is that the client's psychological resources are sufficient to cope with problems successfully, once the resources can be activated and utilized with conscious purpose. Stated otherwise, increased self-awareness leads to improved self-direction (Goldenberg, 1983). The central focus of each session is on the ongoing, give-and-take interaction between the client's self-awareness and the therapist's awareness of the client.

The primary intervention strategy is to reintegrate into conscious awareness the disowned parts of self. The therapist confronts the discrepancy between what clients say they are doing at the moment, and how the therapist perceives their behavior at that moment. Three commonly used techniques are: (1) two-chair dialogue, in which two chairs represent two sides of a conflict, and the client moves back and forth between the chairs in creating a dialogue between conflicting aspects of self; (2) dream analysis, in which the client assumes the role of each element in the dream, and creates a dialogue between two or more conflictual dream elements (the assumption is that each dream element is either a conscious or a dissociated aspect of self); (3) awareness exercises, in which the client in a free associative manner reports a sequence of physical and psychological awarenesses, such as sensations, images, thoughts, memories.

The following is an example of a therapist conducting a two-chair dialogue.

Client: Sometimes I feel it's better just to go along with what they say—other times I want to take a stand.
Therapist: There's a part of you that wants to play it safe, and another part of you that would like to stand up for what you believe is right. Which part are you more in touch with now?
Client: The part of me that wants to go along with others.
Therapist: OK. Then let's put the part of you that wants to take a stand over there in that other chair. Now I'd like for you to have a conversation between these two parts of you. Let's start with the chair you're in, the part of you that wants to play it safe, and let that part express itself. Afterwards, I want you to switch to the other chair and be that part of you that wants to take a stand, and express that part as fully as you can. After you get going with the conversation, I'll just let you decide when you want to switch chairs in order to be the part of you that you're in touch with at the moment.

The client–therapist relationship in gestalt psychotherapy is one in which the therapist's role is to facilitate clients' awareness of how they use their capabilities ineffectively, and what they do to block self-fulfillment (Goldenberg, 1983). The clients' role is to: (1) center their attention on the here-and-now moment; (2) enter fully into the interventions which the therapist suggests; and (3) be receptive to what the therapist says he sees, hears, senses, or intuits. Explanations and interpretations are left to the client. In the end, the client makes a commitment to be aware of self now rather than then, here rather than there, and to rely on self rather than on others.

A strength of this approach is the belief in the client's "response-ability," or the ability to respond differently. A limitation is the emphasis on immediate and often minute awarenesses. Polster and Polster (1973) and Simkin and Yontef (1984) provide further information.

Existential Psychotherapy. Several psychologists and psychiatrists have contributed to the formulation and applications of existential psychotherapy, notably Rollo May, Irvin Yalom, Viktor Frankl, and James Bugental. Rather than being a theory of psychotherapy with a repertoire of interventions, existential psychotherapy is a set of values and attitudes (i.e., a philosophy), which a psychotherapist applies to self and clients.

The failure to be aware of, accept, and act on one's personal freedom and responsibility is regarded as being a major cause of psychological disorder; the failure is expressed symptomatically in anxiety, guilt, alienation from important aspects of self and others, and despair over the lack of meaning, purpose, and direction in life. In the existential view, clients have problems of living rather than sickness or psychopathology.

The overall goal of psychotherapy is to help clients expand self-awareness, recognize the freedom they have, accept responsibility for setting the direction of their life, and actualize their potential to make critical life choices (Corey, 1982). A key assumption is that the therapeutic relationship is both a stimulus for and an ongoing response to therapeutic changes. The central focus in existential psychotherapy sessions is on the client's choices, decisions, values, and personal meanings in the context of the present and the immediate future.

The therapist's communication of an empathic and compassionate understanding of the client's present subjective world is the primary intervention strategy. By sharing his personhood with passion and conviction, the therapist creates an interpersonal environment in which clients confront who they have been and are now in relation to the person they might become, and reclaim the freedom and responsibility to make decisions that validate their self-chosen values. Although techniques are secondary to the therapeutic use of the relationship, therapists may choose specific techniques from other theories to facilitate particular changes (Corey, 1982).

Below is a brief excerpt of an existential therapist responding to a client statement.

Client: I know it's probably the right thing for me to do, but somehow I don't feel right when I do it.

Therapist: My hunch is that you're trying to live up to someone else's values, and in doing so, you're not living up to your values. It doesn't feel right because you're being untrue to yourself.

The client–therapist relationship is an egalitarian, I–thou, interpersonal encounter in which the therapist's growth and the client's growth are mutually facilitative. The role of the therapist is to: (1) stimulate the client's self-confrontation; (2) support the client's letting go of unauthentic aspects of self; and (3) encourage the clients to make choices, however painful they may be, and to take responsibility for their choices, however fearful that responsibility may be.

A strength of this approach is the view that negative emotions are natural responses to one's existential problems rather than symptoms to be eliminated. A limitation is reliance on an I–thou encounter as the primary basis for therapeutic change. Bugental (1978) and May and Yalom (1984) offer extended discussions of existential psychotherapy.

Cognitive and Behavioral Orientation

This orientation includes rational–emotive, transactional analysis, behavioral, and cognitive–behavioral psychotherapies. It is characterized by (1) an emphasis on the present and immediate future rather than on the past; (2) a concentration on cognitions and overt behavior; and (3) attention to conscious rather than to unconscious determinants of behavior. The therapist is viewed as a change agent who uses her professional knowledge and methods to assist the client in coping with current problems in living.

Rational–Emotive Psychotherapy. This theory, developed by Albert Ellis, is a cognitive–philosophical one insofar as the client is helped to develop a realistic and pragmatic philosophy of living.

Irrational thinking that leads to emotional distress, self-defeating actions, and an attitude of blaming self and others for lack of self-fulfillment is considered to be a major cause of psychological disorder. Although clients have been conditioned by their interpersonal environment to think irrationally, they are responsible for maintaining and perpetuating unrealistic beliefs that underlie irrational thinking. The overall goal of this form of psychotherapy is to deemphasize emotionality and to eliminate self-defeating behavior by adopting rational, realistic, and tolerant beliefs about self and others. A key assumption is that clients can change their actions and feelings by rational thought processes based on realistic beliefs and values. The central focus of the sessions is primarily on thoughts, attitudes, and beliefs, and secondarily on feelings and actions.

The primary intervention strategy is one in which clients are taught that it is not the problem situation (interpersonal or otherwise) that causes emotional and behavioral problems, but rather the incorrect way they interpret the problem situation—their interpretation, in turn, is the result of one or more irrational beliefs. Next, the therapist teaches clients how to dispute and challenge their beliefs, and to think about problem situations in a way that facilitates appropriate feelings and constructive actions. Finally, the therapist must monitor and evaluate the client's thinking, feeling, and acting so that the client can maintain and perpetuate the new beliefs, just as they maintained and perpetuated the irrational ones.

The therapist may use a variety of therapeutic techniques, including explanation, confrontation, activity oriented assignments, and selected behavioral techniques.

However, central to the practice of rational–emotive therapy is the A-B-C-D paradigm. *A* refers to the stressful event or person; *C* is the emotional reaction to the event or person; *B* is the client's interpretation of or belief about *A* that causes the negative emotional reaction at *C*; and *D* means to dispute the belief or interpretation at point *B*. To change the negative emotional reaction, the client, assisted by the therapist, challenges and corrects the interpretation or belief that causes the negative emotional reaction. Consider this exchange between a therapist and client.

Client: Everytime my boss corrects me at work, I feel enraged.

Therapist: Okay, this is a good place to try out the A-B-C-D method I explained at our last session. *A* is the situation, your boss correcting you. *C* is your feeling of rage. Now *A* cannot directly cause *C*. You have to be saying something to yourself about that situation that causes you to feel rage, and what you're saying to yourself is the point we call *B*.

Client: Like no one should ever criticize me? Like I think I have to be perfect?

Therapist: You could be making one or both of those statements. Now I'd like for you to take a different approach and see if you can challenge the validity of those statements—point out the flaws in each one. Afterwards, we'll look at some alternative ways for you to interpret the boss's criticism.

The client–therapist relationship is not considered the primary therapeutic ingredient. It can be likened to a mentor–"mentee" relationship based on mutual respect. The role of the client is similar to that of a student who learns how to apply rationality to the problems of living, and how to exercise reasonable tolerance for human nature. As mentor, the therapist explains, challenges, confronts, models, and persuades the client, all for the purpose of stimulating the client to formulate a more realistic, and eventually more satisfying set of beliefs for conducting his life.

A strength of rational–emotive psychotherapy is the clearly formulated procedure for restructuring self-defeating beliefs; a limitation is the secondary role assigned to emotions. Ellis and Grieger (1977) and Ellis and Whitely (1979) offer worthwhile treatises on this approach.

Transactional Analysis. Originated by Eric Berne with contributions by Thomas Harris, Robert and Mary Goulding, Muriel James, Dorothy Jongeward, and John and Katherine Dusay, transactional analysis can be classified as cognitive–decisional insofar as it is designed to replace old life-negating decisions with new, life-affirming ones.

A major cause of psychological disorder is considered to be recurring, dysfunctional behavior patterns that are based on decisions that a person made at a time of life when he was dependent and easily influenced by significant others. The overall goal of psychotherapy is to replace anachronistic decisions about what to expect of self and others with appropriate and realistic decisions about how to think, feel, and act. A key assumption is that at an early age human beings make important and enduring decisions about how to cope with life; yet, they can overcome the past by redeciding how they will live their life.

The central focus of the therapeutic work is the identification of current thoughts, feelings, and actions that are derived from earlier, and now anachronistic decisions about how to cope with intrapersonal and interpersonal conflicts.

The primary intervention strategy is to assist the client to develop more effective thought–feeling–action patterns based on current knowledge and experience. Commonly used techniques are: (1) structural analysis, in which clients identify their ego states (critical parent, nurturant parent, adult, adapted child, and natural child), and correct faulty interaction between the ego states; (2) analysis of transactions, in which clients identify and correct self-defeating interactions between their ego states and the ego states of significant others; (3) multiple chair technique, in which each chair represents an ego state of the client, and the client moves back and forth between the chairs in creating a dialogue to resolve intrapersonal conflict; (4) script analysis, in which the client's life plan is examined in terms of parent messages that led to decisions about how to think and feel about oneself, and how to think, feel, and act toward authority figures and peers; and (5) selected gestalt and behavioral techniques to overcome therapeutic impasses within and between sessions.

In the following excerpt, the therapist uses analysis of ego states to intervene in a client's procrastination.

Client: And I keep going round and round on what I should do first.

Therapist: Okay. Let me hear how you go round and round with the decision.

Client: Well, I know that this is the time to send in the applications for grad school . . . but then you should take care of the term papers first because . . . well, I just can't do everything at once. I'm afraid I won't get anything done the way I'm going.

Therapist: That's an instance of what I meant by getting bogged down in a conflict between your different ego states. Your *adult* ego state says something pretty straight: I know this is the time to send in the applications. But then your *critical parent* ego state comes up with the stopper: you should take care of these other things. Then your *adapted child* ego state expresses the fear of the consequences of not doing anything. So let's start again with your *adult* ego state.

Client: I know this is the time to take care of the applications.

Therapist: What does your *natural child* ego state want?

Client: I want to go to grad school.

Therapist: From your *adult* ego state, tell me what you will do, and what you won't do.

Client: I will set aside the next three Sunday afternoons to work on the applications. And I will set aside the next three Saturday mornings to work on the term papers. And I won't spend those times hassling myself about it.

The client–therapist relationship is a partnership based on a mutually agreed-upon contract between therapist and client that spells out joint responsibilities for achieving the client's specific goals. The role of the client is to identify specific goals, prioritize them, and implement them, by experimenting with new ways of behaving within and between therapy sessions. The role of the therapist is to restore the client's belief in self-change; that is, to make more appropriate decisions now, as opposed to living by archaic decisions of the past (Corey, 1982).

A strength of this approach is the conviction that clients have the power to redecide the course of their lives. A limitation is undue emphasis on decisions as the cause and solution of problems. Dusay and Dusay (1984) and Goulding and Goulding (1979) offer additional information on transactional analysis.

Behavioral Psychotherapy. Although several major learning theorists have made significant contributions to the formulation of behavioral psychotherapy, the pioneering work was conducted by first-generation behaviorists, notably Joseph Wolpe, Arnold Lazarus, Leonard Krasner, Hans Eysenck, and Albert Bandura. Behavioral theory can be characterized as an action-oriented, directive, time-limited, structured approach to correct overt dysfunctional behavior.

Learned maladaptive behavior is considered to be a major cause of psychological disorder. The problem is seen as being the overt behavior rather than the behavior being a manifestation of an underlying disorder or illness. The overall goal of psychotherapy is for the therapist, in collaboration with the client, to develop a plan to replace maladaptive behavior patterns with adaptive behavior patterns (Goldenberg, 1983). A key assumption is that abnormal behavior, having been learned in the same way that normal behavior has been learned, can be unlearned and replaced by new learned patterns [i.e., eliminate the abnormal behavior and the client's disorder is eliminated (Goldenberg, 1983)]. The central focus of the sessions is on the ways in which the client and the client's interpersonal environment maintain the maladaptive behavior, and what the client can do to change his behavior. The primary intervention strategy is to stop reinforcement of undesired behavior and to begin reinforcement of alternative behaviors. The following are widely used techniques:

Systematic desensitization is designed to diminish or eliminate negative emotional responses that are inhibiting adaptive responses to currently stressful situations. To counteract negative emotional reactions, the client uses deep muscle relaxation (often in conjunction with positive imagery) in response to visualization of a stressful situation, beginning with the least stressful aspect and proceeding to the most stressful aspect. Once the client can imagine the problem situation without negative emotional reactions, he then visualizes how to cope with the situation in an adaptive manner. At this point the client moves from imaginal desensitization to in vivo desensitization by practicing the new learning in the actual problem situation. A variation, implosion or flooding, is to extinguish negative emotional reactions by prolonged imaginal exposure without the counteracting effect of relaxation and positive imagery.

Another technique is behavior rehearsal in which the therapist first instructs the client in adaptive actions to a problem situation, then models the adaptive actions, followed by the client rehearsing and practicing the actions, and finally by planning how to transfer the adaptive actions to the actual problem situation.

Still another technique is based on aversion procedures that are used to eliminate maladaptive behaviors, such as substance abuse or sexual deviation, by associating the undesirable behavior with actual unpleasant consequences (e.g., electric shock) or imagined unpleasant consequences (e.g., aversive images).

Contingency contracting is a frequently used technique in which the client receives a specific reward if he or she performs the mutually agreed-upon behaviors, and a specific penalty if the behaviors are not performed.

A therapist may use a client's statement of a problem as a cue to introduce an intervention, such as behavior rehearsal.

Client: I plan ahead just how I'm going to ask a girl for a date, but I think there's something wrong with the way I approach it.

Therapist: Perhaps you're saying all the right things, but it's how you're saying it. I think it would be helpful if you and I role-play it. I'll be the girl, and you say what you typically say. Then, I'll react as I think she might. Afterwards, we can rehearse some different ways of broaching the subject of a date.

The client–therapist relationship is basically an educative one in which the role of therapist is to teach clients how to replace maladaptive with adaptive behaviors, as well as to model adaptive behaviors within the therapy session for clients to acquire by imitation. The client's role is to be actively involved by cooperating with the interventions suggested by the therapist, and by making a genuine effort to transfer and generalize the learning acquired within the sessions to problem situations outside the sessions (Corey, 1982). Mutual respect and interpersonal compatibility between therapist and client are important in order to strengthen and sustain the client's motivation to relinquish familiar behavior patterns and to experiment with new ones.

A strength of behavioral psychotherapy lies in the notion of learning by doing; a limitation is the failure to use the therapeutic relationship to resolve clients' interpersonal problems. Supplemental information on behavioral interventions may be found in Goldfried and Davison (1976), Rimm and Masters (1979), and Wilson and O'Leary (1980).

Cognitive-Behavioral Psychotherapy. This approach, a variation of the behavioral theory of psychotherapy, places primary emphasis on the clients' cognitions rather than on overt behaviors.

A major cause of psychological disorder (as in rational–emotive psychotherapy) is considered to be the client's thoughts about and interpretations of stressful events and interpersonal problems.

The overall goal of this type of psychotherapy is to help the client identify and correct dysfunctional thoughts and images in response to problems he encounters. A key assumption is that reorganization and improvement of self-statements and internal dialogue will lead to a corresponding reorganization and improvement of overt behavior (Corey, 1982). The central focus of the therapy sessions is on identification and examination of the dysfunctional elements in the client's self-dialogue or self-talk, which lead to distressing feelings and maladaptive actions.

The primary intervention strategy is cognitive restructuring, in which clients are trained first to listen to their subvocal talking, both what they say to themselves, and how they say it; and second, to examine how subvocal talking arouses unwanted feelings, activates maladaptive responses, and inhibits adaptive responses. In the second step, the therapist helps clients to make specific changes in their self-talk and to practice these changes until a connection is formed with positive feelings, sensations, images, and adaptive actions. The cognitive–behavioral psychotherapist may also use traditional behavioral techniques (behavior rehearsal, contingency contracting) to supplement cognitive restructuring.

The client–therapist relationship is similar to that of behavioral psychotherapy.

A strength of cognitive–behavioral psychotherapy lies in its underscoring of the importance of the client's self-dialogue; a limitation is the failure to use the therapeutic relationship to resolve the client's interpersonal problems. Detailed discussions of cognitive–behavioral psychotherapy can be found in Beck (1976) and Meichenbaum (1977).

Comparative Analysis

Before continuing with a description of the fourth major orientation, eclectic psychotherapy, some comparative statements about the first three orientations are in order.

With respect to the six dimensions listed earlier (see p. 124), the three psychotherapy orientations can be characterized as follows. Unconscious determinants of psychological disorder are (1) emphasized in the psychodynamic orientation; (2) minimized in the phenomenological–humanistic orientation; and (3) barely acknowledged in the cognitive and behavioral orientation.

Psychodynamic therapists view insight into unconscious conflicts as a prerequisite for change; phenomenological–humanistic therapists value present-centered awareness, with the emphasis on what one does and how one does it rather than why one does it, and for that reason prefer the term *self-awareness* to the term *insight*. Behavioral therapists are likely to view overt behavior change as a way to change thoughts and feelings, and may even consider overt behavior change as a prerequisite for insight or self-awareness. Cognitive therapists and the cognitive–behavioral therapists stress insight into or awareness of self-statements as a basis for changing thoughts, feelings, and actions.

With respect to the time dimension, psychodynamic therapists emphasize the client's past. Phenomenological–humanistic therapists stress the present, even the present moment, and to some degree the immediate future. Cognitive and behavioral therapists focus on the current context of the client's life, with some attention to the past and future.

In the phenomenological–humanistic orientation, the client–therapist relationship has a primary role in facilitating therapeutic change. In the cognitive and behavioral orientation the relationship has an adjunctive role; that is, it facilitates a positive response to the interventions. In the psychodynamic orientation, both formal interventions and analysis of the transferential relationship are potent factors in fostering therapeutic change. In the psychodynamic orientation, diagnostic evaluation of the client's problems is crucial and precedes psychotherapy.

In the behavioral and cognitive orientation, assessment of the ways in which both the client and his or her interpersonal environment maintain the problems provides the basis for planning the therapy sessions. In the phenomenological–humanistic orientation, formal diagnosis is considered intrusive and unnecessary; assessment and change are interactive processes in psychotherapy.

Finally, in the psychodynamic orientation, the practice of psychotherapy is viewed as both art and science. An aesthetic rather than scientific attitude characterizes the practice of the phenomenological–humanistic orientation. In the cognitive and behavioral orientation, the practice of psychotherapy involves the application of scientific principles to problems of living.

Integrative or Eclectic Orientation

Brammer and Shostrom (1982, p. 35) define eclectic psychotherapy as "the process of selecting concepts, methods, and strategies from a variety of current theories which work." At present, eclectic psychotherapy is not a formal system in which goals, assumptions, interventions, and client and therapist roles are conceptualized within a single theoretical framework. However, since the mid-1970s an increasing number of psychotherapists have developed therapeutic approaches that are based on concepts and interventions from two or more current theories.

Between one-third and one-half of practicing psychologists choose some form of eclecticism (Garfield and Kurtz, 1976; Norcross and Prochaska, 1982a). A representative panel of psychotherapy practitioners, trainers, and researchers predicted that an eclectic system of psychotherapy would increase in popularity more than any other system in the 1980s–1990s (Prochaska and Norcross, 1982). Norcross (1986a) reviews a variety of studies that show eclecticism as the preferred therapeutic orientation for 30 percent of academic clinical psychologists, 40 percent of counseling psychologists, 30–32 percent of psychologists conducting psychotherapy, 35 percent of independent practitioners, 36 percent of M.A.-level psychologists, and 37 percent of M.A.-degree counselors. Indicative of the expanding interest in eclectic psychotherapy are publications (e.g., *International Journal for Eclectic Psychotherapy, Comprehensive Psychotherapy*) and professional organizations (e.g., Society for Psychotherapy Research, Society for the Exploration of Psychotherapy Integration).

Norcross (1986a) cites six reasons for the rapid rise of eclectic approaches to psychotherapy: (1) the unwieldy proliferation of psychotherapies; (2) the inadequacies and insufficiencies of any single approach; (3) the absence of differential effectiveness among competing systems; (4) a growing recognition that client–patient characteristics and the therapeutic relationship are the most potent contributors to successful outcome; (5) a major research thrust toward delineating the common change factors in a variety of psychotherapeutic systems; (6) socioeconomic–political forces (e.g., shrinking job market, increased competition for clients, and pressures from third-party payers and the public for psychotherapy that is short term and has pragmatic goals).

Currently, four subtypes of eclectic psychotherapy are practiced: (1) synthetic eclecticism, which combines two or more major theories (e.g., gestalt and transactional analysis); (2) integrative eclecticism, which blends concepts, change strategies, and specific interventions from several theories within a new conceptual framework; (3) technical eclecticism, which brings together a variety of interventions within a single theory (e.g., cognitive–behavioral theory); and (4) atheoretical eclecticism, which utilizes varied interventions (e.g., behavioral rehearsal, dream analysis, two-chair dialogue) without the underpinning of a formal theoretical system. Recent surveys of eclectic therapists disclose a strong preference for synthetic eclecticism, followed by technical eclecticism, and a small percentage who choose atheoretical eclecticism (Norcross and Prochaska, 1982a; Prochaska and Norcross, 1983). Preference for integrative eclecticism has not yet been established in published surveys of eclectic therapists.

Two examples of integrative eclecticism are transtheoretical eclecticism (Prochaska and DiClemente, 1984), and systematic eclectic psychotherapy (Beutler, 1983). Transtheoretical eclecticism is a multilevel approach in which the first level consists of a set of theoretical assumptions about psychotherapy, the middle level consists of 10 change processes or strategies common to several theories (e.g., counterconditioning, self-reevaluation), and the third level consists of specific interventions derived from each of the 10 change strategies. The specific interventions for each of the 10 change strategies are applied differentially, depending on the level of the client's problem (symptom–situational, maladaptive cognitions, current interpersonal conflict, family–system conflict, and intrapersonal conflict); and the specific stage of therapy in which the client is working, such as precontemplation (resistance or weak commitment to change), contemplation (willing to consider specific changes), action (experimenting with specific changes), and maintenance (consolidating and perpetuating therapeutic gains).

Like transtheoretical eclecticism, systematic eclectic psychotherapy is an integration of various change strategies or change procedures, such as emotional awareness and escalation procedures (e.g., empathy, relational immediacy); evocative procedures (e.g., interpretation, confrontation); or behavioral procedures (e.g., desensitization, implosion). The theoretical underpinning for the integration of change procedures is a "superordinate theory" of human functioning (e.g., theory of interpersonal influence and persuasion), that provides the therapist with a general rationale and direction for the application of the change procedures. The application of change procedures is preceded by a thorough assessment of the client's problems, personal strengths, and environmental resources. From the assessment, decisions are then made on four factors: (1) symptom severity–complexity, which in turn determines one or more of six categories of goals (e.g., resolution of underlying conflict, symptomatic relief); (2) client's defensive style of coping; (3) reactance, or the strength of the client's need for personal control; (4) therapist–client compatibility, or the type of therapist interpersonal style most likely to facilitate the client's motivation and ability to change. From these four factors a treatment plan is formulated and implemented.

A well-known example of technical eclecticism is multimodal therapy developed by Lazarus (1981) who coined the term *technical eclecticism*. Multimodal therapy uses an array of specific interventions within a framework of social learning theory supplemented by systems theory and communications theory. Client problems, such as anxiety, depression, interpersonal conflict, intrapersonal conflict, are assessed and conceptualized in terms of planned changes in seven modalities: (1) overt actions; (2) emotions; (3) sensations; (4) imagery; (5) cognitions; (6) interpersonal relationships; (7) biology, which includes use or abuse of drugs–medications, sleep, diet, and exercise. Specific interventions are selected for the problem(s) in each modality, and the modalities are sequentially addressed in terms of most to least amenable to intervention. The manner in which the interventions are introduced, and the number of modalities addressed within a particular therapy session, depend on the client's receptiveness and the therapist's level of intervention skill and clinical experience.

Below is an example of a client's multimodal profile.

Behavior: withdrawal
Affect: feeling rejected
Sensation: lethargic
Imagery: fantasies of future rejections
Cognition: self-statements about being unlovable
Interpersonal: trying to please
Biology: difficulty in sleeping and eating

For each modality, the therapist would plan one or more methods to produce a positive change, and then decide on an optimal sequence for implementing the positive changes.

Radical eclecticism is an example of atheoretical eclecticism (Robertson, 1979, 1986). This therapeutic approach can be described as (1) experientially oriented (present-centered with an emphasis on emotions); (2) radically eclectic (specific interventions, rather than general change strategies or theoretical concepts, are selected from current psychotherapy theories); (3) flexibly structured (session agenda tailored to client, problem, and stage of psychotherapy, e.g., early, middle, late); (4) time-adjusted (tentative time limits correlated with periodic progress reviews); (5) contractually based (between session assignments); and (6) thematically focused (problems conceptualized as recurring affective-cognitive-behavioral patterns for which goals are derived and interventions are chosen). The choice of an intervention is dictated by the client's personality, nature of the problem, and stage of therapy, rather than being derived from a theoretical system or from an integration of two or more theories. Although there is no explicitly stated theory, the therapist is guided by assumptions based on research findings and clinical experience. One important assumption is that clients: (1) learn by doing (i.e., they become aware of alternative patterns of thinking, feeling, and acting); (2) decide which alternatives to implement and how best to implement them; and (3) rehearse the alternatives in sessions and practice them between sessions.

Following is an excerpt of a session with a male client in his early thirties.

Client: Well, instead of thinking it's all up to me, and then doing the whole job myself, and feeling taken advantage of, I could ask the others to share the work with me, do what I do best, and then feel only partly responsible for the outcome.

Therapist: Okay. It starts with your asking others to help you, listening to their ideas and negotiating a division of labor. Let's rehearse it. I'll be one of your fellow workers. We'll work it out here in the session, so that you'll feel ready to do it tomorrow at the office. If it goes okay, fine. If not, next week we'll troubleshoot it and perhaps explore other possibilities.

The following statements are consistent with an eclectic orientation to psychotherapy, though not all apply to each eclectic theorist's approach.

The major cause of psychological disorder is recurring, maladaptive patterns of thinking–feeling–acting, which result from faulty socialization experiences, and create intrapersonal distress, dysfunctional marital–family and social relationships, and impaired educational and vocational adjustment. The overall goal of eclectic psychotherapy is similar to that of other approaches (i.e., relief of personal distress, improved interpersonal relationships, and increased ability to cope with problems of living). A key assumption is that from different systems theoretical concepts and postulates, general change strategies, and specific techniques or interventions can be selected and integrated in a form that is theoretically and empirically defensible. The central focus of the sessions is the client's perceptual, cognitive, emotional, and behavioral interactions with his or her interpersonal environment.

The primary intervention strategy consists of change processes which are common to most psychotherapy theories, and from which specific interventions of known effectiveness are used to implement agreed-upon therapeutic goals.

The client–therapist relationship is a collaborative partnership. With input and feedback from the client, the therapist develops and implements a service plan that is relevant to the client's goals, realistic in terms of the client's psychological adjustment and environmental resources, and ethically responsible with respect to the welfare of the client and society at large.

For the six theoretical dimensions which were used to summarize psychodynamic, phenomenological–humanistic, and cognitive and behavioral orientations (see p. 124), the eclectic orientation: (1) stresses conscious more than unconscious determinants; (2) focuses more on the present and the immediate future than on the past; (3) gives equal weight to interpersonal skills needed to form a therapeutic alliance and to intervention skills to facilitate specific changes; (4) clearly acknowledges the importance of assessment–diagnosis before and during psychotherapy; (5) conceptualizes insight–awareness and therapeutic change as mutually facilitative processes; and (6) endorses scientific rather than aesthetic values.

A strength of the eclectic approach is the commitment to seek a rapprochement of current psychotherapy systems. A limitation is the lack of consistent rationale for clinical decision making (Dryden, 1986). Additional material on eclectic approaches to psychotherapy can be found in Thorne (1973), one of the earliest proponents of eclecticism and in Norcross, *Handbook of Eclectic Psychotherapy* (1986a) and *Casebook of Eclectic Psychotherapy* (1986b).

CONCLUSION

The purpose of the chapter has been to give an introduction to the state-of-the-art, or the state-of-the-science of psychotherapy, and an overview of current psychotherapy orientations. The choice of a psychotherapy orientation is a significant decision in the process of becoming a therapist. A theory may be selected for professional and/or personal reasons; for example, sustained contact with the theory of a professional mentor, selective exposure to research favoring a specific theory, compatibility with one's cognitive style, closeness to one's philosophical values, a positive experience as a client with a particular theory.

Chapter 6

Being a Psychotherapist, Part II: Effectiveness and Special Modalities

EFFECTIVENESS OF PSYCHOTHERAPY

Outcome Research

Research on the effectiveness of psychotherapy has always been fraught with conceptual and methodological obstacles, and definitive and unequivocal findings continue to be elusive. Persistent problems include: failure to use a control or no-treatment group to assess improvement due to therapeutic life experiences and environmental changes; absence of long-term follow-up to assess durability of improvement; vague specification of in-session therapist behaviors, client behaviors, and therapist–client interactions; the "uniformity myth" of assuming that all clients, all treatment strategies, and all therapists are comparable; lack of clearly defined, nonbiased outcome measures; and limited progress on differentiating common or nonspecific treatment effects from specific, planned treatment effects. For a recent, comprehensive coverage of psychotherapy effectiveness and related issues, the reader is referred to Hariman (1984).

Eysenck's (1952) indictment of psychotherapy jolted the field out of its feelings of competency by declaring that effectiveness was at best a moot point, at worst a nonproductive enterprise. Although Eysenck's position has been ably refuted (Meltzoff and Kornreich, 1970; Bergin, 1971), the issue of effectiveness has surfaced again, this time from outside the field (e.g., third-party payers, consumer–advocate groups, the federal government, the courts). However, as many have noted, the field continues to benefit from periodic doses of conflict and challenge.

Despite shortcomings in research design and in interpretation of outcome data, there is a strong consensus that psychotherapy does benefit the consumer as indicated by outcome measures, such as reports of clients, therapists, significant others, professional observers, or psychological test data (Luborsky, Singer, and Luborsky, 1975; Bergin and Lambert, 1978; Lambert, 1979; Parloff, 1979; Smith, Glass, and Miller, 1980; Imber, Pilkonis, and Glanz, 1983). In a meta-analysis (statistical analysis of the analyses of individual studies), Smith et al. (1980) conclude that the typical or average person receiving psychotherapy is better off than 75–80 percent of those who might benefit but who do not receive therapy. Although reports of spontaneous remission of symptoms vary according to the type and severity of disorder, the figure of one-third is a reasonable estimate (Garfield, 1981), which leaves a large number of distressed persons for whom nature cannot be expected to take a benevolent course.

Long-term maintenance of therapeutic gains is another matter; many studies show an attrition of gains with the passage of time (Imber et al., 1983). Especially in substance use disorders, improvement is neither robust nor very durable. For major cognitive and affective disorders, a combination of psychotherapy and medication is critical for both improvement and stability of improvement. Stability of therapeutic changes does not occur automatically or spontaneously, and appears to be a function of the individual client and his life circumstances (Lieberman, Yalom, and Miles, 1973; Goldstein, Lopez, and Greenleaf, 1979). In addition to resolution of current problems, psychotherapy must help clients acquire self-coping strategies for unexpected problems in the future.

A review of studies that compare different psychotherapy systems shows minimal evidence for the differential effectiveness of competing theories for most specific disorders (Sloane, Staples, Cristol, Yorkston, and Whipple, 1975; Bergin and Lambert, 1978; Frank, 1979; Parloff, 1980; Smith et al., 1980; Landman and Dawes, 1982). The conclusion that all therapies seem to work, without any one theory holding a consistent edge over the others, has been immortalized in the statement (borrowed from Alice In Wonderland) by Luborsky et al. (1975): "all have won and all must have prizes."

Even the staunchest supporters of psychotherapy concede that some clients become worse during and/or after psychotherapy (Strupp, Hadley, and Gomes-Schwartz, 1977; Imber et al., 1983). Anecdotal reports suggest a typical deterioration rate of 3–10 percent. Research on types of negative effects and their occurrence in different therapy modalities, as well as therapist and client variables associated with negative outcome, have been summarized by Lambert, Bergin, and Collins (1977). Examples of therapist errors associated with negative outcome are: failure to structure and focus therapy sessions, failure to address client's negative attitudes toward the therapist or therapy, and poorly timed or inappropriate interventions (Lambert and Bergin, 1983). Imber et al. (1983) conclude that until more systematic research is conducted, therapists must continually monitor and evaluate the impact of their therapeutic procedures on clients.

Process Research

Whereas outcome research focuses on the amount and durability of therapeutic change, process research studies in-therapy variables that are believed to be associated with improvement. Greenberg (1983) states that "therapeutic change (or its cause) clearly occurs in the transaction between therapist and client, and process research is an attempt to catch, by various measuring devices, the crucial aspects of the transaction" (p. 193).

More so than technique variables, the personal characteristics of the therapist, the client, and the quality of their relationship, have been singled out as the critical variables in the positive outcome of psychotherapy (Bergin and Lambert, 1978; Frank, 1979; Strupp and Hadley, 1979; Smith et al., 1980; Lambert and Bergin, 1983). Less than 10% of outcome variance is accounted for by technique variables (Lambert, 1979; Smith et al., 1980). In a "review of reviews" of the essential therapist characteristics that facilitate an effective relationship, Patterson (1984) states emphatically: "the evidence for the necessity, if not sufficiency, of the therapist conditions of accurate empathy, respect or worth, and therapeutic genuineness is incontrovertible" (p. 437).

Patterson's conclusion is consistent with reports that clients frequently attribute their success to the personal qualities of the therapist, and that these personal qualities are similar across different therapeutic orientations and different research methodologies (Lambert and Bergin, 1983). On the other hand, Strupp (1980) points out that clients must not only perceive these personal qualities, but also be ready to use them appropriately. Bergin and Lambert (1978) sum up: "The largest variation in therapy outcome is accounted for by pre-existing client factors, such as motivation for change, and the like. Therapist personal factors account for the second largest proportion of change, with technique variables coming in a distant third" (p. 180).

Greenberg (1983) concludes that the quality of the therapist–client interaction, combined with the client's active participation in the therapy tasks, are consistently related to positive outcome. Greenberg adds the proviso that a therapist's interventions are an integral part of the interaction, and that a client must perceive the therapist's actions as relevant and helpful, and must respond positively to the interventions.

Not everyone agrees that the primary determinant of therapy outcome is the quality of the therapist–client interaction. An example is Telch (1981) who argues strongly that techniques or interventions are more potent than the relationship or the therapist's interpersonal skills. Polemics aside, an important thrust of current research is the identification and development of problem-focused interventions. Lambert and Bergin (1983) report that interventions positively related to therapy outcome are those that facilitate therapist–client communication, maintain a current time focus, and enable the client to talk freely about feelings and life experiences. Korchin and Sands (1983) identify several effective interventions which are used in varying degrees by all therapy systems: persuasion, suggestion, affective arousal, different forms of learning, promoting self-exploration and self-understanding, constructive feedback, practice–rehearsal, and creating opportunities for success within and outside therapy sessions.

Garfield (1981) caps the debate over technical skill versus interpersonal skill by stating: "both skill and personality variables are important and so nothing is gained by emphasizing one over the other" (p. 183). Overall, psychotherapy is more likely to be helpful than unhelpful, and far more likely to be helpful than harmful. The critical variables associated with outcome are: (1) the client's motivation for and positive expectations of therapy; (2) the client's pretherapy adjustment level; (3) the therapist's interpersonal and technical skills; and (4) the quality of the client–therapist interaction.

A continuing challenge for psychotherapy research is to achieve a degree of specificity that will answer the question posed frequently by researchers, for example Parloff (1979), "what kinds of changes are effected by what kinds of techniques applied to what kinds of patients by what kinds of therapists under what kinds of conditions" (p. 303). All of us who teach, do research, or practice (or do all three) would be well-advised to heed Benjamin's (1984) statement: "There is no shortcut for a science of psychotherapy. We may have to go as slowly and as tortuously as the hard sciences" (p. 24).

GROUP PSYCHOTHERAPY

Overview

The proliferation of therapy approaches, which was noted in the preceding chapter, has been accompanied by a rising interest in group approaches. Varied forms of group work have developed and include: group therapy, group counseling, T-groups or sensitivity-training, encounter groups, and self-help/consciousness-raising groups. However, the main focus of this section is group psychotherapy.

Originally, *T-groups* were considered separately from *sensitivity-training groups*, but now the terms are used interchangeably. The purpose of T-groups is to learn, within a small-group format, problem-solving skills that may be applied to problems that arise within other types of groups (e.g., educational, social, industrial, scientific). The goal of sensitivity training is to foster personal growth through intense and sustained interaction between members, and between members and leaders; T-groups are more task-oriented and sensitivity groups are more process-oriented (Hansen, Warner, and Smith, 1980). Like T-groups and sensitivity groups, encounter groups are designed for a nonclinical population, and the goal is for adjusted individuals to become better adjusted. Unlike the former two groups, encounter groups typically employ a nonstop, marathon format of intensive group interaction over a 48- to 72-hour period. Self-help or leaderless groups (e.g., Alcoholics Anonymous, Overeaters Anonymous), are formed to promote peer support and feedback to members who share a specific problem or goal. Consciousness-raising groups are a recent offshoot of self-help groups (e.g., groups that address the changing roles of women or parenting issues of divorced fathers). Closer to group therapy in goals and procedures is group counseling. Although the distinction is difficult to maintain in practice, group counseling is considered appropriate for individuals who need assistance in coping with situational or developmental crises. Surveys of the characteristics of individuals in nontherapy groups indicate that many of the participants are more like a clinical population than a normal population with respect to symptoms and signs of distress, and that many individuals enter more than one type of group simultaneously or serially (Lieberman, 1980).

Group therapy came into prominence after World War II in response to a shortage of trained therapists. By means of a group format, the skills of a limited number of therapists could be extended to a larger number of clients and patients. The group was a cost-effective method of helping people achieve more satisfying interpersonal relationships and lead more productive lives. Unfortunately, group therapy sometimes became a dumping ground for clients or patients who were considered unsuitable for individual therapy because of limited verbal skills, weak motivation, or problems that seemed refractory to insight-based psychotherapy. However, as the use of groups expanded, practitioners realized that the modality was an effective means of treating a wide range of psychological disorders. Currently, group therapy is valued both as a supplement to and a complement of individual therapy.

In response to external pressures (e.g., clients, client-advocate groups, third-party payers), the practice of group therapy has become more pragmatic and less constrained by theoretical considerations. With this shift, many practitioners have sought to devise an optimal combination of individual and group therapy for their clients. Although some clients are unsuited to individual therapy and others to group therapy, the large majority would likely benefit from individual therapy's emphasis on intrapersonal learning and group therapy's emphasis on interpersonal learning. A client may start with individual therapy and then proceed to a series of group sessions, or they may receive both modalities concurrently in order to blend intrapersonal and interpersonal learning.

The length of group therapy varies according to the therapist's orientation, the number and diversity of goals, and the adjustment level of the members. Long-term groups (generally 20 or more sessions) can give equal attention to intrapersonal and interpersonal issues; in short-term groups (generally 10 to 20 sessions) interpersonal learning is primary and intrapersonal learning is secondary. Brief groups (less than 10 sessions) are primarily supportive in nature; that is, they assist the individual to recover a level of functioning that has been impaired by a developmental or situational crisis. In general, the shorter the term of the group, the more the members need a common purpose or goal, because there is insufficient time to attend to different objectives; in long-term groups there is time to reconcile differences among the members in their purpose for being there (Levine, 1979).

To conclude the overview, the main advantages of group therapy over individual therapy are (1) experiential learning of interpersonal skills; (2) a closer approximation of the group to the "real world"; (3) vicarious learning from other members' coping efforts; (4) the advantage for therapists of observing the client's interpersonal problems instead of having to rely on the client's self-report; and (5) peer-based corrective feedback and support for change. Three limitations are (1) group therapy cannot provide a client with the sustained attention and depth of therapeutic work that individual therapy provides; (2) the rapid exposure of one's problems to members of the group is too threatening to some clients, at least in the early stages of therapy; and (3) there is a greater likelihood of breaches of confidentiality, and the courts have been slow to grant the professional's privileged communication to the nonprofessional members of a group.

Group Theory and Procedures

There is no one theory of group psychotherapy that encompasses individual member change, group-as-a-whole change, and the interface between the two. Most group therapy today represents an extension and modification of theories of individual psychotherapy. Current group orientations include: psychoanalytic, person-centered, existential, transactional analysis, gestalt, behavioral, and cognitive theories. These theories have been presented in the preceding chapter, and the reader is referred to Corey (1980) and Hansen et al. (1980) for a discussion of their application to groups.

Although not a formal psychotherapy system, psychodrama is a highly developed group therapy strategy. Founded by Jacob Moreno in the early 1930s, psychodrama employs a stage, an audience consisting of clients and others, assigned roles for group members, and structured dramatic procedures in which clients take turns in recreating their problem events and conflictual relationships (Moreno, 1978). The goal is to achieve self-understanding, and eventually self-directed change, by reliving conflictual intrapersonal and interpersonal experiences of the past or the present. Due to its longer history as a group therapy approach (since the 1920s), psychodrama has influenced the concepts and methods of other theoretical approaches (e.g., family of origin work, use of sculpting and doubling with family members).

As in the case of the dyadic modality, many group therapists employ an eclectic model of practice, though the authors are not aware of a formal eclectic model of group psychotherapy. Basically, the eclectic group therapist incorporates concepts from various theories into a new conceptual framework, incorporates change strategies that are commonly used by different group approaches, and then employs specific techniques which have demonstrated utility for particular kinds of groups and therapeutic goals. Although the eclectic group therapist by no means uses a montage of techniques, he has a clear rationale for selecting a technique from one theory on one occasion, and a technique from another theory on another occasion (Hansen et al., 1980).

Group Outcome and Group Dynamics

Simplistically stated, the difference between group outcome and group dynamics is the distinction between the *what* and the *how* of group therapy. The term *outcome* refers to what the group members gain for themselves, and the extent to which they are able to maintain the gains following termination of the group experience. The term *group dynamics* refers to how individual members use the group to accomplish their individual goals.

Some writers subdivide group dynamics into (1) group development, or the phases which a group moves through and the salient themes of each phase, and (2) group process, or the interaction between members, and between members and the therapist. Group development and group process are linked by the tasks within each developmental phase that reflect the salient themes of each phase.

There are at least four phases of group development, and the number of sessions for each phase varies from group to group. More often than not the phases overlap, and groups differ in the ease with which they move from one phase to the next. The first phase is joining and testing the waters; the primary task is goal-setting in which members state their desired outcomes (Hansen et al., 1980). As part of that primary task, a member must develop an accepting and trusting relationship with the therapist and other members. Yalom (1975) lists five themes: advice-giving, identifying members' similarities, symptom description, search for the meaning of therapy, and dependence on the therapist for direction and healing.

The second phase is characterized by negativity, conflict, and confrontation, as members seek to protect themselves from the power of the group. The primary task is to set individual limits on self-exposure and maintain control over what happens and how it happens. Yalom (1975) identifies themes of dominance, control, and power, which are played out confrontively and conflictually between members, and between members and the therapist.

The third phase has been characterized by several writers (Yalom, 1975; Saretsky, 1977; Hansen et al., 1980) as cohesiveness. The major task is to develop insight into intrapersonal and interpersonal reactions as a basis for making constructive personality changes. Additional tasks include assuming more responsibility for what is happening in the group, and perceiving and responding more realistically to the therapist and members. Typically, there is more self-disclosure, self-acceptance, and tolerance of others, along with evidence of genuine caring and closeness. The primary theme is intimacy (Yalom, 1975) and productiveness (Hansen et al., 1980).

The fourth phase is termination. The primary task is to put new intra- and interpersonal learning into practice outside the group. A related task is resolving "unfinished business" with the therapist and/or with other members. The major themes are loss (of the group) and anticipation (of an improved life adjustment). To conclude, there is no clean separation between group dynamics and group outcome; their purposes are inextricably interwoven and their effects are synergistic.

Effectiveness of Group Therapy

Over the years the effectiveness of group therapy has been subject to acrimonious debate. Research support for the efficacy of group therapy is not as solid as it is for individual therapy. Admittedly, the problems of demonstrating effectiveness are formidable and include the following: difficulty in sorting out individual member goals from group-as-a-whole goals; number and diversity of personalities and adjustment levels within a single group; the confounding of treatment effects due to the concurrent use of another therapy modality with group therapy; lack of a clear description of what type of group is used; absence of comparable treatment groups or a control group; vague specification of criteria for improvement, and insufficient evidence of the maintenance and generalization of client improvement.

Despite the methodological difficulties, there appears to

be a growing consensus that group therapy has a salubrious effect for the majority of clients (Meltzoff and Kornreich, 1970; Meyer and Smith, 1977; Bednar and Kaul, 1978). Both therapists and clients are more likely to report some improvement rather than no improvement, or negative effects, although the improvement may not be discerned by other interested parties. Evidence for the superiority of one theory over another has not been forthcoming. However, cognitive–behavioral group therapy is proving to be a potent and cost-effective approach to social skills training (Rose, Tolman, and Tallent, 1985).

The now-classical study of Lieberman, Yalom, and Miles (1973), which compared 18 different systems in an encounter group format, found the group experience to be effective for the majority of undergraduate student participants, though there was some slippage of positive reports after six months. The study also identified approximately 10 percent of the participants who experienced a negative outcome, a figure that has held up in other outcome studies. The study also was one of the first in the field of psychotherapy research to find that successful outcome can best be predicted by the personality of the therapist, the clients, and the therapeutic relationship between the two, rather than by the theoretical orientation of the therapist. More recently, support for the relation between negative outcome and leadership styles has been reported by Dies and Teleska (1984).

For successful outcome, the therapist must make a careful assessment of a group in order to establish reachable goals and provide workable tasks (Ferber and Rantz, 1972). A continuing challenge for group therapy research and practice is to specify which type of group and leadership style is effective for which types of clients with which kinds of psychological disorders.

MARITAL–FAMILY THERAPY

Overview

In the first two decades of this century help for troubled marriages was obtained from social workers and clergy who adopted a pragmatic and often moralistic approach (Barker,

1984). Beginning in the 1930s, other professional disciplines entered the field and applied their knowledge and methods to the understanding and improvement of marital relationships. As was true for all forms of psychotherapy, the aftermath of World War II created a strong impetus for the development of marital therapy. The impetus was sustained during the fifties as a result of the high value placed on the preservation of marriage and "couple togetherness" (Barker, 1984). The terms, *marital counseling* and *marital therapy* have been used interchangeably.

The basic premise of marital therapy is that the couple is the client and the therapist treats the relationship. In shifting the focus from therapist–client to therapist–couple, marital therapy became a forerunner of treating family members (Goldenberg, 1983, chapter 12). Family therapy, which grew out of efforts to treat schizophrenics by involving their families in the treatment, was at first an adjunct to individual and marital therapy. Since 1960, family therapy has become a treatment modality in its own right, and marital therapy, with its variations of sex therapy, couples group therapy, and marriage encounter groups, may be considered a specialty within family therapy or a separate therapy modality. In this section marital therapy is considered as a part of family therapy.

With the current trend of adapting psychotherapy to the needs of clients, family therapy may include individual, group, or marital therapy in order to achieve a broad-based treatment strategy. With any family, the therapist must set reachable goals and give workable tasks (Ferber and Rantz, 1972).

At least three stages of family therapy can be delineated. In the first stage, family members are provided with a rationale for being seen together, rapport is developed, problems are identified, and goals are set. Barker (1984) subdivides goals into outcome goals (what the family expects to achieve by the end of therapy), and process goals, or specific objectives that represent successive approximations to the outcome goals. The second stage is the application of interventions to improve the functioning of each family member and the family as a whole. A major focus is to foster interactions that increase cohesiveness, common purposes, and improved communication. The third or termination stage is designed to decrease dependence on the therapist by assisting family members to transfer positive changes from the session to the home environment.

Formerly, the presence of the whole family was considered the sine qua non for doing family therapy; however, today the essential ingredient is a sustained focus on family relationships and interactions regardless of the number of members present in a session. Although family therapy is a type of group therapy, the group's composition of individuals who have a history and a future together sets it apart from other group approaches.

Family Theory and Procedures

With the exception of psychoanalytic and behavioral theories which have been adapted to a family format, current theories are based on the family as a system. This conceptual focus of *treating the family system instead of one member* is the key element of family therapy (Jones, 1980). The family as a system derives from several theoretical propositions which have been advanced by numerous writers: the locus of an individual problem or symptom is in the interactions with others; causation is reciprocal, that is, a member's problem is both a stimulus for and a response to the behavior of other members: the family system has an explicit hierarchical structure (e.g., power, control, knowledge); a change in one member creates change in the others; and the family seeks stability, or the maintenance and preservation of its structure and function, even at the expense of one member (often the one who is labeled the problem). Following is a summary of five widely used theoretical models. For a comprehensive coverage of these five theoretical models and others, the reader is referred to Jones (1980) and Nichols (1984).

The Psychoanalytic Model. Current family problems are considered to stem from parents' unresolved conflicts with their family of origin. Relationship problems in the family of origin are introjected and then projected onto the spouse and one or more children. As therapy progresses, parents transfer their unresolved conflicts with their parents to the therapist, and in so doing give the therapist a direct and immediate opportunity to help them resolve the conflicts. Although the emphasis is on past intrapersonal issues of the parents, therapists do address current interactions of family members during a session. The assumption is that as spouses perceive and react to their own parents as real people rather than fantasized figures, they will begin to perceive and react to each other and to their children as individuals rather than as fantasized figures. One strength of the psychoanalytic approach lies in showing how each parent's conflictual relationships with his or her family of origin contribute to current relationship problems with each other and with their children. One limitation is insufficient emphasis on the reciprocal interaction of family members.

The Bowen Model. Founded by Murray Bowen, the model postulates that a dysfunctional family system is a response to long-standing negative emotions which have been displaced from the parents' family of origin to the marital and parental relationships.

Two major concepts are triangulation and self-differentiation. Triangulation occurs when parents use a child's problem to avoid facing a marital problem. The therapist puts himself in the triangle in place of the child and refocuses the parents' attention on their relationship problem. Self-differentiation means that parents must complete the developmental process of growing out of the child role and into the adult role with their own parents. The therapist works with each spouse alone and with both together in order to help them achieve a clear and stable self-differentiation. One strength of the Bowen model is demonstrating how a child's problem may be created and perpetuated by the parents' fear of confronting problems in the marital relationship. One limitation is that much of the therapeutic work involves only the parents, singly or together, instead of the family as a whole.

The Structural Model. Originated by Salvador Minuchin and collaborators, the structure of the family system is considered to be the basis for maladaptive or adaptive functioning. The family structure is defined by its subsystems (e.g., marital, parental, parent–child), and by its specific boundaries; that is, rules that define how subsystems relate to each other and how members within a subsystem relate. For example, rigid boundaries or rules result in distance between family members, and weak boundaries or rules result in enmeshment of one or more family members. The goal of the structural family therapist is to change the family structure, first by accepting it, then evaluating it, and finally creating conditions for specific changes in the structure (Jones, 1980). One strength of this approach is the careful delineation of the structure of the family system as a basis for deciding when, where, and how to intervene. One limitation is an overemphasis on the total family and a relative neglect of the growth of individual family members.

The Interactional Model. This model subsumes the approaches of several well-known family therapists, notably Jay Haley, Don Jackson, Virginia Satir, Paul Watzlawick. Although there are important differences between interactional theories, they do have a common emphasis on family communication patterns and the analysis of family interactions. The family is a system which maintains and perpetuates itself through rule-based communication patterns. Problems within an individual member or between members develop because the communication rules are ambiguous, contradictory, or confusing, with the result that relationships become conflictual or disorganized. The overall goal of therapy is to clarify, modify, or add to the rules so that communication becomes direct, clear, and consistent. One strength of this approach is the view that the essence of relationships is communication, and that relationship problems are mirrored in the form and content of family members' communication. One weakness is the strong tendency to define symptoms as exclusively interpersonal, and to conceptualize all family problems in terms of reciprocal interactions.

The Behavioral Model. The family is conceptualized as a system of interlocking reciprocal actions, whereby each member responds to the actions of every other member (Jones, 1980). Family problems result from maladaptive learning in which inappropriate actions of one or more members are reinforced, perpetuated, and generalized. The task of the therapist is to teach family members how to identify and reinforce desirable actions, and how to eliminate undesirable actions. In recognition of the hierarchical component in systems (e.g., power, control), the therapist concentrates on changing the parents' behavior. Evaluation of interventions and follow-up contacts are integral components of the treatment strategy. One strength of the behavioral approach is the emphasis on specific targeted behaviors and explicit therapeutic techniques to implement changes in the targeted behaviors; one limitation is insufficient attention to the emotional aspects of the family members' relationships.

As is true for psychotherapy in general, there is a strong eclectic trend among family practitioners; that is, they search for commonalities among different theories and incorporate the best features of each system. Examples of commonalities are: (1) in varying degrees all the models have a systems orientation (an individual's symptoms express a family problem); (2) an interpersonal focus (interactions between members); and (3) an educational component (teaching families). In a survey of over 1,000 family therapists, the largest percentage, 38 percent, identified themselves as eclectic (Green and Kolevson, 1982). Grebstein (1986) notes that the development of family therapy has reached the point where eclectic models that integrate theories and techniques are being published, and he cites examples of eclectic models, including his own.

Effectiveness of Marital–Family Therapy

In comparing family therapy with no formal treatment, slightly more than 70 percent of the studies report significant gains for those in family therapy (Gurman and Kniskern, 1981), which is roughly equivalent to the improvement rate reported for individual psychotherapy by Garfield and Bergin (1978) and Smith et al. (1980). In comparison with other modalities, family therapy was found to be at least as effective, and more effective for some problems [e.g., psychosomatic problems (Gurman and Kniskern, 1978)], though the review of studies by Wells and Dezen (1978) gave a more qualified support for the superiority of family therapy. Gurman and Kniskern (1978) also noted a deterioration or negative outcome rate of 2–3 percent, which held up across different theories and appeared to be related to deficiencies in therapists' knowledge and therapeutic style.

Gurman and Kniskern (1978) also report a two-thirds improvement rate for nonbehavioral marital therapy. Goldenberg (1983) states that for couples with sexual dysfunction and no serious relationship problems, behaviorally oriented sex therapy is the treatment of choice in terms of reported improvement rates.

In reviewing studies on effectiveness, Jones (1980) concludes that Minuchin's structural approach and Patterson's behavioral approach have received the most research attention, that the structural approach has been found to be especially effective for psychosomatic disorders in a family member, and that the behavioral approach is well suited to acting-out problems of children.

In a "review of reviews," Parkinson (1983) concludes: family therapy is more effective than no therapy and is superior to other modalities for adolescent psychosomatic problems and drug addiction; deterioration rates are uniformly low; inclusion of the father is a critical factor in session attendance and in outcome; the therapist's interpersonal skills are strong contributing factors to successful outcome; and with the exception of the structural and behavioral theories, there is a lack of well-designed and competently executed research.

As in other modalities, the lack of conceptual clarity and methodological rigor makes interpretation of research findings tentative. Since no one approach is consistently superior to all others, the challenge, as others have noted, is for researchers to discover what approaches and procedures are most effective for which types of families and problems.

CRISIS–BRIEF THERAPY MODALITY

Overview

Although crisis intervention and time-limited therapy have been a part of the history of psychotherapy (e.g., treating combat-related disorders in World War II), the systematic development of theory and practice was a response to the community mental health movement of the sixties. Crisis intervention, along with inpatient, outpatient, partial hospitalization, and education–consultation services, were mandated components of comprehensive mental health centers. Crisis intervention and brief psychotherapy were consistent with the emphasis placed on prevention (e.g., intervening before problems became serious and chronic), provision of prompt, round-the-clock assistance for psychological emergencies, and offering time-limited therapy to a large segment of the community who were not in need of long-term therapy. The goal of getting people on their feet so they could deal with their problems, even if they needed to return for additional assistance later, was perceived as a more efficient and effective strategy than protracted, dependency-fostering psychotherapy.

Relatedly, the rise of the human potential movement with its emphasis on personal growth instead of psychopathology, and the advent of behavioral psychotherapy which stressed time-limited, symptom-directed treatment, created an additional impetus for psychotherapy that would be quickly and easily accessible, directive and structured in its approach, and solution focused, with clients as active participants in their own recovery. As a result, the parameters of psychotherapy changed in terms of the range of clients served, methods used, length and frequency of sessions, and goals (e.g., relief of symptomatic distress, strengthening coping skills). Since the sixties, virtually all psychotherapy systems have developed crisis intervention strategies and brief therapeutic procedures.

Crisis Intervention

Crises are usually defined as developmental (e.g., transition from one life stage to the next) or situational (e.g., divorce, death of a loved one), and precipitating factors are considered more critical than long-standing, predisposing factors. Goldenberg (1983, chapter 13) identifies several premises on which crisis intervention theory is based: optimal functioning requires a balance between psychological strengths and weaknesses, and between healthy and toxic environmental influences; disruption of the balance may lead to a crisis; during a crisis an individual is more receptive to suggestion and change than during periods of stability; a qualitatively different adjustment usually follows the resolution of a crisis; and balance is restored by changing one's environment, one's response to stress, or both.

Crisis intervention models which have developed from the pioneering work of John Bowlby, Gerald Caplan, and Erich Lindeman, are characterized by brief, intensive therapy to alleviate stress, eliminate disabling symptoms, and return clients to their previous level of functioning. Typical methods include giving relevant information, encouraging problem-solving attitudes, activating personal strengths and environmental resources, and preparing for future crises. Crisis intervention services are available in a variety of settings: outpatient clinics, hospital emergency rooms, suicide prevention centers, domestic assault and rape centers, and "free" clinics for alcohol and drug related crises. Paraprofessionals, with back-up support from professionals, deliver crisis services by means of telephone hot-lines, face-to-face contact, or mobile crisis units. Jacobson, Stricker, and Morley (1968) delineate four levels of crisis intervention: (1) environmental manipulation (e.g., making referrals, removing hazards such as sleeping pills); (2) psychological support (e.g., empathy, assistance in decision making; (3) psychoeducational procedures for coping with a particular type of crisis, such as grief; and (4) longer-term counseling for individuals whose psychological makeup renders them susceptible to crises. The third and fourth levels may involve parents, spouses, and close friends as adjunctive helpers or as coparticipants in the crisis. For additional information on crisis intervention models, the reader is referred to Aguilera and Messick (1982).

Brief Psychotherapy

Even in the absence of a crisis, brief psychotherapy (ordinarily 5–20 sessions) has acquired a solid place in the practice of most therapists, either as a specialty area or as an alternative to longer-term therapy. Budman and Gurman (1983) state that brief psychotherapy is developing on two fronts: (1) highly specific, manual-directed approaches, and (2) due to external pressures, e.g., third-party payers, practitioners are having to "think brief."

The goal of brief therapy is to improve efforts to cope with circumscribed problems of living, while strengthening the client's overall self-supporting ability (Goldenberg, 1983, chapter 13). Therapists have adapted interventions to more circumscribed goals and to a limited number of sessions. More so than long-term therapy, brief psychotherapy is (1) characterized by rapid assessment of problems; (2) contractually based in terms of session agenda and between session assignments; and (3) present-centered with the major focus on changing specific thought–feeling–action patterns. The therapist is more active and directive in the sessions, and puts more pressure on the client to initiate changes. Clients who are most likely to benefit from brief therapy present circumscribed problems of recent onset, have a history of adaptive coping, and can quickly establish a collaborative relationship with a therapist. Brief psychotherapy is also associated with irregularly spaced sessions, and session length may be more or less than the conventional 50-minute hour.

Brief psychotherapy is congruent with the reported staying power of clients (or therapists' holding power). Several studies (Lorion, 1974; Garfield, 1978) indicate that after about five to seven sessions many clients terminate for various reasons. Typical reasons are financial constraints, satisfaction with a modicum of improvement, positive changes in life circumstances, insufficient progress, or incompatibility with the therapist's personal style or orientation. To sum up, brief psychotherapy is compatible with the trend in the health care field to make treatment cost-effective. As Cummings (1977) points out, brief therapy makes it economically feasible to provide long-term therapy to the 10 percent of patients who require it. Small (1979) gives a comprehensive coverage of the various forms of brief psychotherapy.

Effectiveness of Crisis Intervention and Brief Therapy

Evaluating the effectiveness of crisis intervention has been difficult due to client's anonymity, telephone-conducted sessions, and other obstacles in designing a pre- and posttreatment study. Reviews of studies on the effectiveness of brief psychotherapy indicate that this modality is about as effective as longer-term therapy (Luborsky et al., 1975; Butcher and Koss, 1978; Small, 1979; Swenson and Hartsough, 1983). A similar finding is reported for brief marital–family therapy (Gurman and Kniskern, 1978), and brief group therapy (Budman, Demby, Feldstein, and Gold, 1984; Klein, 1985). Although differences in favor of long-term therapy appear at termination, the differences tend to disappear with time, which suggests that with brief psychotherapy clients need additional time to implement gains (Butcher and Koss, 1978).

PROFESSIONAL AND PERSONAL GROWTH

Stresses and Satisfactions

In a survey of therapists' satisfactions and stresses, Farber and Heifetz (1981) state: "Psychotherapy is a difficult, albeit fulfilling career, one that may generate personal as well as professional strains" (p. 629). Commonly mentioned satisfactions are promoting growth and change in self and clients, having an intimate involvement in clients' lives, and achieving professional status and respect. Stresses include feeling personally depleted after long hours of therapy, balancing objectivity and intimacy in the therapeutic relationship, and coping with severe psychopathological symptoms and resistant behaviors. For the most part, the therapist's experience level was not a significant variable, and institutionally based therapists reported greater stress levels than did private practitioners.

Although private practitioners are protected from the bureaucratic frustrations of institutional settings, their rapidly growing numbers are creating stiff competition, and both private and institutional therapists face continual pressure to satisfy externally imposed accountability standards.

Regardless of experience level, work setting, or type of therapy modality, therapists must cope with a variety of strains inherent in the practice of therapy. Sank and Prout (1978) identify recurring types of strains: transference–countertransference, client problems alien to the therapist's life experiences, value conflicts, and similarity between therapist and client with respect to personal problems and coping styles.

LaPerriere (1979) underscores a frequently occurring stress in family therapy: "Finally, some families present us with problems so alien, with world views so unacceptable, that we cannot find access to the common humanity we need to ply our trade because we are busy denying that we feel angry, or scared, or repelled" (p. 883).

The ratio of stresses to satisfactions is critical, and when there is a chronic imbalance of stresses over satisfactions, therapists are susceptible to burnout (Farber and Heifetz, 1982). Not only is burnout debilitating to therapists, but it also vitiates the quality of therapy rendered.

In a survey of therapists, Deutsch (1985) found over half had experienced relationship, depression, and other personal problems; over half had had therapy, with women more likely than men to avail themselves of psychotherapy and medication. In recent years the American Psychological Association (APA), through its Committee on Distressed Psychologists, has sought to provide a network of professional assistance for practitioners with psychological problems. One group, Psychologists for Helping Psychologists (PHP), is a self-help group for psychologists with chemical dependency problems (Thoreson, Nathan, Skorina, and Kilburg, 1983). In large urban areas, practitioners have organized informal self-help or peer consultation groups in which therapists receive as well as give assistance (Greenburg, Lewis, and Johnson, 1985). A problem that surfaces with regularity in self-help groups is what Gibbs (1984) labels "the therapist as imposter." The "imposter" reaction refers to nagging doubts about one's therapeutic potency. Gibbs attributes the imposter reaction to a lack of contingent reinforcement; for example, having to measure one's success rate against a spontaneous remission rate of one-third to one-half, lack of knowledge of how one's success rate compares with that of the profession as a whole, and uncertainty about which therapeutic actions contribute to a client's improvement.

On balance, the profession has made notable strides in providing opportunities for professional growth through continuing education programs, and in assisting therapists with psychological problems stemming from their work or personal life.

Training

A therapist's professional and personal growth begins during graduate training, and by and large reviews of training have recommended more emphasis on skill development, supervised practica, and personal growth; for example, provision of peer-group experiential learning about self and others, and personal therapy (Ford, 1977, 1979; Garfield, 1981; Kalafat and Neigher, 1983). In addition, systematic evaluation of the quality of training is lacking. When evaluation is conducted, too much reliance is placed on impressionistic judgments, qualitative comparison data, anecdotal reports from supervisors and supervisees, and assessment of the end-product without maintaining quality control throughout the program (Levy, 1983; Norcross and Stevenson, 1984; Stevenson and Norcross, 1985).

To ensure the development of specific skills, several writers have urged adoption of programmatic formats, or "manual-guided" therapies, as an effective and efficient method to teach students intervention skills (Ford, 1977; Kalafat and Neigher, 1983; Schacht, 1984). Two examples are Beck, Rush, Shaw, and Emery's (1979) cognitive therapy for depression, and Strupp and Binder's (1982) time-limited dynamic psychotherapy. The advantages are that a manual-guided teaching format specifies the interventions to be learned, provides instructive demonstration of how and when to apply interventions, and establishes acceptable levels of performance. The major objective of the programmatic skill-based training is to prepare trainees to conduct interventions in a clinical facility under supervision.

Despite the key position that supervision occupies in therapy training, it has not drawn as much theoretical and empirical attention as other therapy issues (Schmidt, 1979; Lambert, 1980; Schaefer, 1981). In training programs, supervision is a critical link between the didactic learning in formal coursework and the experiential learning in clinical practica. The tutorial format individualizes and personalizes the trainee's learning of therapeutic interventions, relationship-building skills, and ethical sensitivity.

Regardless of the supervision model (e.g., psychoanalytic, cognitive-behavioral, process-oriented) or the supervisory modality (e.g., one-to-one, cotherapy, group), there is a consensus that supervision should provide a professional growth experience rather than provide personal therapy, which is best arranged by the student independent of the training program. On the other hand, professional growth shades into personal growth insofar as the supervisor assists the supervisee to cope with feelings, needs, and attitudes that vitiate his ability to listen objectively, respond empathically, and intervene appropriately.

Too often, supervision is defined narrowly (case consultation) and confined to later stages of training (practicum and internship). A broader perspective is needed, one in which supervision begins with the student's entry into a program and continues through the program, and is an integral part of the making of a psychotherapist.

Although conducting personal therapy ought not to be a part of the supervisor's job, opinion is divided over whether provision for personal therapy is a necessary or even desirable component of a training program (Wampler and Strupp, 1976; Sank and Prout, 1978). It can be argued that experience in the client role increases the trainee's understanding of how his personal dynamics impact adversely on the conduct of therapy, and gives an important perspective on the therapeutic relationship that cannot be acquired solely in the therapist's role. In fact, a sizable number of practitioners do obtain therapy in their postgraduate years, and in retrospect state that it should be a part of one's training as a practitioner (Norcross and Prochaska, 1982c). In our judgment, experiential familiarity with the client role (either as an actual client or as a quasi-client in training sessions) is a decided advantage in learning how to initiate and maintain a therapeutically productive interaction, as well as knowing at what point the relationship has served its purpose.

Aside from the issue of personal therapy, there is a need for more emphasis on the development of interpersonal skills. Noteworthy is a statement by Lambert and Bergin (1983) that until technical skills can be demonstrated to be more potent than and independent of the therapist's personal qualities, training programs should give students the opportunity to develop effective interpersonal skills.

To conclude, programs should design training experiences that blend personal and professional growth, so that students learn to combine relationship-building skills that foster trust, hope, and a sense of self-efficacy, with the technical skills needed to match intervention strategies to clients' personalities, problems, and environmental resources.

TRENDS, CHALLENGES, AND NEW DIRECTIONS

Trends

One emerging trend is the convergence or integration of psychotherapeutic approaches. Faced with a glut of therapies and mounting pressures for accountability, an increasing number of practitioners are seeking efficient and effective treatment approaches that combine conceptual breadth with commonly used intervention strategies (Goldfried, 1980, 1982; Smith, 1982; Korchin and Sands, 1983). Smith comments on "a greater interest at this time in therapy systems that emphasize the integration of affect, cognition, and behavior, and that stress intervention strategies more than heavily theoretical approaches" (p. 808).

A related trend is the differential application of interventions. With a large number of interventions and specific techniques from which to choose, therapists can be selective and apply what works best with different types of clients with particular kinds of disorders. More pragmatic and less theory-conscious than in the past, therapists are learning how to tailor intervention strategies to the client's personality, problems, and stage of therapy (Beutler, 1983; Prochaska and DiClemente, 1984). A Delphi poll (experts give their opinion on an issue, and then with feedback from the first survey are polled a second time) of researchers, theoreticians, and trainers predicted that the three interventions most likely to increase in frequency of usage would be self-change methods, cognitive restructuring, and problem-solving techniques; the three least likely to increase in usage would be relaxation, contingency management, and biofeedback (Prochaska and Norcross, 1982).

Another trend can be discerned in the expanding network

of continuing professional education programs. Both experienced and newly degreed practitioners are faced with an "information explosion" and a rapidly increasing obsolescence of current knowledge. The trend toward establishment of continuing education networks integrated on a national, regional, and local level will assist practitioners to stay abreast of new developments in change technology and to translate research findings into practice.

Still another trend is the expansion of psychotherapy from the mental health sector to the general health-care delivery system and to the industry-sponsored employee assistance programs. The full range of psychotherapeutic services (individual, group, marital–family) are being utilized in the treatment of psychologically related illnesses and impaired job performance and productivity, as well as in the reduction of medical services through promotion of healthy life-styles. However, to take advantage of the funding sources for the wider utilization of psychotherapy, practitioners must be able to deliver prompt, cost-effective therapy to large numbers of people (Fox and Bent, 1984). To do so, practitioners will have to operate within large, well-organized practice groups or health maintenance organizations (HMOs), develop proficiency with brief or short-term psychotherapy, and exploit the full potential of group-based, programmatic, or manual-guided therapies.

Challenges

A pressing challenge is to correct the underutilization of psychotherapeutic services by minorities by removing the cultural, social class, age, and gender bias in the practice of psychotherapy. Dahlquist and Fay (1983) cite several areas of potential (and actual) class, cultural, age, and sex bias: language usage, expression of emotions, nonverbal communication styles, client–patient expectations of therapy (and therapist expectations), and degree of similarity between client and therapist. Even the goals of therapy, and the assumptions about normal or socially appropriate behavior, can be significantly affected by bias.

With respect to age bias, Fox and Bent (1984) point out

that by the end of this century one-sixth of the population will be 65 or older. That statistic, and the fact that only a few clinical psychology programs train students to work with the elderly, underscore the need for psychotherapy training suited to the needs of an increasing elderly population.

To minimize bias and to provide psychotherapy that is relevant for special populations, Dahlquist and Fay (1983) recommend use of a cross-cultural model that is based on general, panhuman characteristics of adaptive functioning, yet allows for client differences in gender, social class, age, and cultural background. To implement a broad-based model, therapists must develop a flexible communication style that can accommodate to clients of differing backgrounds, and choose goals and interventions that are compatible with the values, beliefs, and interpersonal styles of their clients. As Dahlquist and Fay aptly note, more psychotherapy research with special populations is needed. In addition, training programs must provide therapy experience with special populations, as well as recruit students and faculty who represent various minority groups. For an extended discussion of psychotherapy with ethnic minorities, the reader is referred to Dudley and Rawlins (1985). Hare-Mustin (1983) has written an incisive appraisal of bias in psychotherapy with women.

A second challenge, which derives from the field of health psychology, is to develop a better understanding of client noncompliance and effective ways to foster compliance. Very little research is available on the severity, assessment, causes, and treatment of noncompliance, except in follow-up studies of premature termination (Flanders and McNamara, 1984). According to Flanders and McNamara, client noncompliance, in contrast to client resistance to assimilating painful insights within sessions, is a failure to follow the therapist's suggestions and recommendations outside the sessions. They conclude that client–patient compliance may be a strong, nonspecific variable in therapy outcome. In addition, Beutler (1986) cites studies that show therapist compliance with planned therapeutic procedures to be a strong contributor to positive outcome.

A third challenge is to develop a common language to communicate about psychotherapy (Ryle, 1978; Goldfried,

1982). A theoretically neutral, agreed-upon language would serve three purposes: (1) facilitate collaboration among theoreticians, among researchers, and among practitioners, and between the three groups; (2) create a conceptual tool to explicate and refine what Wachtel (1977) identifies as a therapeutic "underground" of therapy wisdom; and (3) enable trainees to discern and appreciate the similarities and specific contributions of current therapy systems.

A fourth challenge, which overlaps with the other three, is for practitioners, researchers, and theoreticians to set aside their parochial disputes and adversarial postures in a collaborative effort to develop therapeutic approaches that are comprehensible, relevant, and cost-effective. A derivative of the challenge is to fully operationalize treatment procedures and to conceptualize, as much as possible, therapist decision-making processes (Norcross, 1986a).

New Directions

Rubenstein (1985) summarizes the predictions made at a retreat attended by APA's Division of Psychotherapy Board Members.

> (1) Psychotherapists will be part of the medical team of large corporations and provide short-term crises intervention. Only more "serious" cases will be referred to outside practitioners. The number of these private practitioners will be vastly less than today. (2) Psychotherapists will function more as "family Medicine practitioners" who are available for work with individuals and/or families throughout their life span. In this regard they will provide intervention and treatment at different developmental stages and at times of transition. In a sense they might be called "family transition educators." (3) Psychotherapists will, along with other mental health disciples (i.e., psycho-educational specialists, social workers, counselors), either directly or more indirectly contract with school districts to provide ongoing developmental as well as crisis intervention service to the entire school-age population as well as other families. (4) Psychotherapists

will become closely aligned with the legal profession in direct work with divorce mediation and resultant child custody issues. A specialization we are now only minimally involved in. (5) Psychotherapists will become major providers to and consultants for law enforcement agencies and the whole prison and judicial system. Many of us will have training in both criminal justice and psychology. (6) Psychotherapists will become involved in all sorts of public relations programs for both government and private industry. Our communication skills will be utilized to help these groups reach a wide variety of populations. We will greatly increase our attention to issues of mass communication. (7) Psychotherapists will function as media experts in both film and the video marketplace. We will be making greater and greater use of the media for prevention and treatment of large groups of people [p. 9].

Chapter 7

Normality and Abnormality: Critical Issues in Assessment

To understand, predict, and ameliorate abnormal behavior, the clinical psychologist is expected to have a firm knowledge of what constitutes normal behavior, especially the organismic and environmental variables that mediate the development and stability of normal behavior. Ironically, the clinical psychologist understands a great deal more about the absence than the presence of mental health, and is strongly inclined to define normality as a symptom-free condition. The neglect of a positive conception of normality is due in large measure to the preoccupation in training programs with learning about psychopathology, and to the lack of societal pressure to examine healthy functioning. Nevertheless, in theory if not in practice, clinical psychologists assume that accurate diagnosis of psychopathology and formulation of treatment goals presuppose an informed understanding of the range of normal psychological functioning.

NORMALITY

The terms, *normality, mental* or *psychological health, psychological maturity, adjustment, and psychological competence*, are often used interchangeably, and all lack a solid operational definition. Basically, there is considerable variation among the terms in what they denote and connote.

White (1969) points out that the meaning of a term such as *mental adjustment*, derives from the study of abnormal behavior and stresses the absence of what is negative; whereas a term such as *psychological maturity*, is preferable because it is usually based on studies of persons who have been found to cope successfully with life. However, one limitation of the term *psychological maturity* is that it has an adult reference point and is ordinarily a measure of developmental outcome rather than of developmental process.

Psychological competence is a more clinically useful term because it emphasizes the development of coping skills throughout the life span; however, it lacks the interdisciplinary usage of the other terms. A more recent term, *hygiology*, includes both the promotion of psychologically healthy behaviors and the prevention of psychopathological behavior, and thereby gives an added dimension to the traditional treatment goal of eliminating psychopathology. This section uses all of the above-mentioned terms.

Hansen and Himes (1980) delineate four conceptual models of normality, which are based partly on the earlier work of Offer and Sabskin (1974). The first is a biological model which postulates that normal behavior presupposes normal biological or genetic functioning. Simplistically stated, normal people have mostly normal genes, and abnormal behavior is the expression of abnormal genes. A more complex genetic explanation cited by the authors is one that allows for an array of genotypes, that in turn give rise to many kinds of normal behavior which may shade into abnormal functioning as a result of genetic and environmental conditions.

A second model is a sociocultural one, which includes cultural relativism (i.e., the meaning of the terms *normal* and *abnormal* is embedded in the mores and values of a particular culture), and functionalism. Behavior is evaluated in terms of the function or purpose served in relation to the total personality and societal expectations. In the sociocultural model, the primary criterion of normality is the degree of compatibility between an individual's behavior and the values and expectations of the family and the larger community.

The third model defines normality as an ideal or goal to be approximated. Hansen and Himes describe two variations: the first is a statistical ideal, which assumes that the most common or frequently occurring behavior in a particular population is normal, and uncommon or infrequent behavior deviates from normality. For example, in the normal (bell-shaped) distribution of personality test scores, the statistical ideal is the midpoint of the distribution curve, and extreme deviations in either direction denote abnormal functioning; although with a quantitative continuum there is no sharp demarcation between normal and abnormal. The other variation is a clinical ideal, in which the conception of normality is derived from a particular personality theory, and which for most theories is an optimal balance between individual needs and values, and environmental constraints (e.g., Freud's psychosexually mature person, Roger's fully functioning person, Maslow's self-actualizing person).

A clinical ideal that is both comprehensive and independent of a particular personality theory is the one advanced by Jahoda (1958). Six criteria are identified: (1) a positive attitude toward self and a stable sense of identity; (2) evidence of continued psychological growth, cognitively, emotionally, and socially; (3) integration, which includes maintaining an equilibrium of psychological forces, resistance to stress, and a unifying outlook on life; (4) autonomy and reasonable independence from social influences; (5) adequate perception of reality, which includes empathy and interpersonal sensitivity; and (6) environmental mastery, as evidenced in problem-solving efficiency and interpersonal effectiveness.

The fourth model posits a developmental basis for normality. Successful mastery of the developmental tasks of each life stage defines normality. Especially important is an individual's flexibility in adapting to the stress and strain of moving from one developmental stage to the next.

Hansen and Himes identify the following commonalities in the four models. (1) Physical health and organic factors contribute to psychological well-being. (2) The psychologically healthy person is able to establish effective and satisfying relationships with others, and has appropriate and satisfying thoughts and feelings about self. (3) Being productive is an important criterion of psychological well-being, and is age-based in terms of mastery of increasingly complex developmental tasks. (4) Psychological well-being requires a modicum of accommodation to familial, social, and cultural expectations. (5) Psychological health is a dynamic rather than a static concept; that is, it is an ongoing process that shows "normal" variations over time and in response to situational events. To round out the above, the following points might be added: that problems of living are to be expected; that each individual has a unique style of coping; and that psychological health is more than the absence of symptoms.

In addition to theoretical formulations of normality, the concept has been studied empirically in terms of correlations with specific variables. Following is a summary of findings obtained for nine variables.

Education

Educational achievement is positively related to personal adjustment, particularly self-esteem, and educational problems may either contribute to or result from poor psychological adjustment. In addition to being a significant component in educational achievement, intelligence contributes to psychological health insofar as it reflects an individual's cognitive capacity for adaptation (Hansen and Himes, 1980).

Vocation

Satisfactory progress in vocational development is also associated with psychological well-being. Super (1957) describes developmental stages in vocational adjustment, and explains how the mastery of vocational tasks in each developmental stage impacts on other areas of adjustment.

Ethnic–Racial Status

By itself, ethnic or racial status does not account for mental health or mental illness (Hansen and Himes, 1980); however, in conjunction with discrimination, poverty, and value conflicts between majority and minority cultures, racial–ethnic status does pose a threat to psychological health.

Socioeconomic Status

Earlier research that showed an inverse relationship between mental illness and socioeconomic status has come under critical scrutiny (Hansen and Himes, 1980). Although social and economic advantages are likely to enhance psychological well-being, there is no clear-cut relationship between socioeconomic status and normality, except where low socioeconomic status is associated with poverty and family disorganization.

Gender

Both biology and socialization shape the individual's psychosexual orientation, and deviations from the norm create formidable obstacles to attaining a stable and satisfactory identity. In addition, sex role dynamics have been implicated in susceptibility to various types of disorders (Sobel and Russo, 1981); for example, obesity in women, antisocial behavior in men. Furthermore, Gilbert (1981) has underscored the dangers inherent in a socialization process that fosters sex role stereotypes, which in turn limit the kinds of roles, behaviors, and personality characteristics that society endorses for each sex (e.g., women are expected to be dependent and followers, men are considered to be unsuited to the role of custodial parent).

A number of studies have addressed the concept of androgeny, whereby a person blends traits and behavior of both sexes and displays what is appropriate for each situation instead of conforming to stereotypic expectations. In a review of studies on androgyny, Gilbert (1981) concludes that androgyny is an important component of healthy psychological functioning for both men and women, and that "sex typing is not the most adjusted state—particularly for feminine women" (p. 35).

Age

The relationship between age and normality clearly reflects the notion of normality as an ongoing process of change. Within each age period, the individual must adjust to physical and psychological changes, as well as to environmental changes in the form of a new set of age norms. Erikson (1963) and Havighurst (1972) have outlined developmental stages throughout the life span. Give or take a few stages, the major ones are infancy–early childhood (0–6 years); middle childhood (6–12); adolescence (13–19); early adulthood (20–35); middle adulthood (35–60); and later adulthood. Within each stage, mastery of developmental tasks fosters psychological maturity and provides a sound basis for coping with the tasks of subsequent stages. Generally, developmental tasks are defined in terms of physical skills, cognitive skills, management of emotions, social relationships, attitudes toward self and reality, and formation of stable values (Hansen and Himes, 1980). For adult development, Levinson (1977) has described four major periods from young adulthood to old age, each with a developmental period consisting of a stable stage and transitional stage; the task common to all periods is to decide how to attain life goals and how to be true to cherished values.

Within the developmental framework, crises are not necessarily inevitable; if present, they are most likely to be the result of discrepancies between an individual's life-style and a socially expected role (LaVoie, 1980). Moreover, crises are not necessarily growth-inhibiting; the process of coping with problems and conflicts may enhance psychological health.

Social Roles

Two social roles that have commanded considerable research attention are marriage and parenthood, although the relationship to normality is complicated by other variables, such as age, education, gender, socioeconomic status, or physical health. The fact that over 90 percent of the population marry at some time during the life span, and approximately 80 percent of divorced people remarry (Barker, 1984, chapter 2), may represent conformity to strong cultural pressures. On the other hand, the statistics may also indicate that the institution of marriage contributes to psychological well-being by providing a practical way to satisfy basic psychological needs. Noteworthy is the finding that separated and divorced people are at high risk for emotional illness, and the rate of hospitalization for mental illness among the divorced is 8 to 12 times the national average (Garfield, 1982). In a review of studies on marital adjustment, L'Abate and Goodrich (1980) report that as a group married couples have a lower incidence of mental disorder than the unmarried, and that women are more susceptible than men to both marital stress and satisfaction. Moreover, among those who never marry or do not remarry, women appear to be better adjusted than men, especially in the older age population (LaVoie, 1980).

Like marriage, the relation between parenthood and normality is strongly influenced by other variables, such as socioeconomic status, rural–urban status, marital satisfaction, education, family of origin experiences, maternal employment, the parent's personal adjustment. The trend today is to examine parenthood within a developmental framework. Parental effectiveness or competence is a function of the skills, knowledge, attitudes, stress, and environmental resources associated with each developmental stage, as well as the successes and failures of the preceding stages (Kaplan, 1980). Much of the literature on psychological health and parenthood addresses the impact of parents' behavior on the child's adjustment. A neglected area is the effect of the child's behavior on the mental health of the parent, and how the child's behavior differentially affects the psychological stability of the parent.

Personality Traits

Although there is a consensus that at least several personality traits predict psychological adjustment, the importance of a particular trait varies with the developmental period. Rather than catalogue all the traits which have some association with normality, four are singled out for comment.

The first is temperament, a general trait that subsumes a number of specific traits, among which are emotionality, activity level, impulsivity, sociability, distractibility, persistence, adaptability to change, and sensory alertness. Strong evidence exists for the inheritability of traits of temperament (Buss and Plomin, 1975). Rowe (1980) concludes that as a trait, temperament appears early in a child's development, has some genetic basis, and remains stable at least through young adulthood. Thomas and Chess (1977) also conclude that temperament traits are moderately inheritable, emerge early in life, and are subject to gradual change by the environment.

High or low degrees of temperament traits (e.g., sociability, fear, activity level, aggressiveness) can facilitate or interfere with family and social relationships, magnify or attenuate environmental stressors, and reduce or exacerbate interpersonal conflicts (Rowe, 1980). Especially important in the child's psychological development is how the environment, particularly the family milieu, responds to the child's temperament.

A second trait is tolerance for ambiguity, or the degree to which an individual copes effectively with unstructured or open-ended situations, and can accept experiences that are at variance with preconceptions or conventional reality (Foxman, 1980). The trait appears to be stable through most of the life span; interindividual differences appear to be independent of gender, intelligence, education, and vocational background; and through its correlation with other adaptive traits, such as emotional resiliency, appears to be a stable component of psychological health.

A third trait is personal responsibility, or the degree to which an individual accepts and is responsible for his behaviors, and is willing to initiate self-change. The trait shows a developmental progression up to adulthood; cuts across sex, socioeconomic, ethnic–racial, and educational–vocational variables; and is a necessary, though not a sufficient, component for coping successfully with problems of living (Genthner, 1980). A longitudinal study of male children found that in comparison to children rated low on understanding, children rated high on interpersonal understanding: (1) focused more on how a conflict is perceived by all parties involved rather than how it is settled; (2) shared responsibility for conflicts and problems rather than externalizing responsibility; and (3) were more willing to work through conflicts rather than to withdraw from or reject others (Gurucharri, Phelps, and Selman, 1984).

A fourth trait is attachment, or the degree to which an individual develops and maintains close friendships. The trait has its foundation in the frequency, intensity, duration, and quality of the early parent–child bonding. With age progression comes breadth and diversity of attachments, from parents, to peers and older persons (e.g., relatives, mentors), and finally to a mate and children. Asher and Wheeler (1985) report that in comparison to socially neglected children (without friends but not disliked), rejected children (without friends and actively disliked) are more likely to continue in their rejected status and to be highly susceptible to adult maladjustment.

Most of us can say with conviction that our best moments in life are the ones we share with someone special to us. Close attachments satisfy many of our basic psychological needs, not the least of which is self-esteem, and when in distress, close friends provide us with emotional support. The loss of attachments, and the making of new ones, are inevitable and reflect sound personal and social adjustment (LaVoie, 1980). Among the elderly, the presence of a confidant is the prime characteristic that separates those living in institutions from those living in the community (Kalish and Knudtson, 1976).

SOME IMPORTANT IMPLICATIONS

As noted earlier, the clinical psychologist needs a flexible and broad conception of normality, not only as a frame of reference for understanding what abnormality is and is not, but also as a basis for appreciating the many variables that contribute to the development, maintenance, loss, and recovery of normal psychological functioning. One suggestion is that clinicians would benefit from studying the lives of psychologically competent persons, so that they develop as much sensitivity and discernment toward strengths and resources as they now have for defects and limitations. By spending some career time working with well-functioning persons, they would gain valuable experience in the practice of hygiology; that is, enhancing healthy aspects of normal individuals as well as preventing the loss of psychological health.

Especially important is the clinician's awareness of how his values and beliefs about normality influence assessment and treatment of clients. For example, clinicians must be careful not to deny their own personal responsibility by assigning all responsibility for recovery to their clients, or by making client evaluations that fail to take into account the loss of personal responsibility due to psychological disorder (Genthner, 1980). A clinician who is knowledgeable about temperament traits and their effect on a child's adjustment may alleviate behavior problems by helping parents to adjust child-rearing practices to a particular child's temperament.

Finally, with women clients, the male therapist must be careful not to let sex stereotypes interfere with promoting self-independence and self-actualization, which are part of most definitions of normality (Gilbert, 1981). For the woman client who is also a minority person, a clinician must appreciate how both sex and race discrimination are major contributors to psychological disorders, and that psychotherapy must be supplemented by educational, vocational, and social services (Olmedo and Barron, 1981).

ABNORMALITY

Like normality, many definitions of abnormality have been proposed, but not a single meaning has gained universal acceptance. Terms such as *mental illness, maladjustment, immaturity, deviance, psychopathology, psychological disorder,* are used interchangeably, and all have shortcomings. *Mental illness*, a term based on a medical model, implies an involuntary and organically based intrapsychic condition. *Immaturity* denotes a developmental lag, with a pejorative connotation. *Deviance* is often associated with legal and/or moral judgments. *Maladjustment* is a narrow-band term that refers to problems of minor or moderate severity, and sometimes is a euphemism for more serious disturbances. *Psychopathology* is a term that: (1) encompasses a wider range of abnormal behavior than maladjustment; (2) is relatively value-free compared to deviance and immaturity; and (3) more clearly denotes psychological etiology than does the term *mental illness*, but is too strong a label for the common adjustment difficulties or problems of living. *Psychological disorder* is perhaps the most desirable term, because it is not beholden to an illness model, and designates the types of clients for whom the clinical psychologist's diagnostic and therapeutic skills are best suited. In this section the terms *abnormality, mental illness, psychopathology*, and *psychological* or *mental disorder* are used interchangeably.

Because abnormal behavior is more salient than normal behavior, it is more readily identified by both laypersons and professionals. The saliency is due to the lower frequency of occurrence, but more importantly, to the presence of one or more of the following properties: suffering–distress; irrationality or incomprehensibility; unpredictability and loss of control; vividness and unconventionality; observer discomfort; violations of moral and legal standards of conduct; and interference with the goals and needs of the individual and/or society (Rosenhan and Seligman, 1984, see chapter 1). Millon (1981, chapter 1) identifies three distinguishing features of abnormal behavior: (1) adaptive inflexibility, or few coping strategies which are applied rigidly and inappropriately; (2) a vicious circle in which habitual coping methods create new problems or intensify already existing ones; and (3) tenuous emotional stability, or lack of resiliency under stress and accompanying loss of control over emotions.

In addition to the problem of which term or label is appropriate to use, the assessment of abnormality is complicated by the fact that not all of the distinguishing properties are present at any one time, or overtly displayed for that matter. Moreover, there is no sharp demarcation between normal and abnormal behavior—an individual may function normally in some areas of life (e.g., vocational–educational), and not in other areas (e.g., marital–family); and personality traits that are adaptive or at least neutral in one developmental stage may prove to be maladaptive in another developmental stage. Finally, behavior that is considered normal in one community or region of the country may be labeled as abnormal in another community or section of the country. For instance, in the late fifties one of the authors was teaching in a university in the deep south when a young black man, high-school diploma in hand, arrived on campus to register for courses. He was promptly taken into custody and committed to a state hospital on the grounds that he must be mentally ill to behave in such a fashion. Within that community and in that era, he did display some of the critical properties of abnormality identified by Rosenhan and Seligman (1984), such as producing observer discomfort, unconventionality, violation of the community's moral and legal standards, even though he was not experiencing acute distress, not evidencing irrationality and loss of control, or interfering with his goals and needs and those of society at large.

In order to have a definition of abnormality that is sufficiently inclusive to satisfy a large number of mental health professionals, the authors of the third edition of *The Diagnostic and Statistical Manual of Mental Disorders* (DSM-III) (American Psychiatric Association, 1980) have proposed the following.

> A mental disorder is conceptualized as a clinically significant behavioral or psychological syndrome or pattern that occurs in an individual and that is typically associated with either a painful symptom (distress) or impairment in one or more areas of functioning (disability). In addition, there is an inference that there is a behavioral, psychological or biological dysfunction, and that the disturbance is not only in the relationship between the individual and society. (When the disturbance is limited to a conflict between an individual and society, this may represent social deviance, which may or may not be commendable, but is not by itself a mental disorder.) [p. 6].

Like it or not, this is a critical definition for the clinical practitioner.

A CLASSIFICATION OF PSYCHOPATHOLOGY BASED ON DSM-III

Description

Nathan and Harris (1983) outline several features that differentiate DSM-III from the two previous editions (DSM-I and DSM-II). Included are (1) a separate diagnostic status for substance use disorders with an expansion of the number of subtypes; (2) a residual grouping for impulse–control disorders not classified elsewhere; (3) a reconceptualization of psychosexual disorders that is less stigmatizing and judgmental (for example, as a result of political–public policy pressures the American Psychiatric Association in 1974 decided that homosexuality was no longer a mental disorder, and only individuals who are dissatisfied with and distressed by their homosexual-arousal pattern are now included in the psychosexual disorder category; (4) a broader, more inclusive, and behavior-based description of childhood psychopathology; (5) a separate status for affective disorders, which in the previous editions had been distributed among psychoses, neuroses, and personality disorders; (6) replacement of the category of neuroses in DSM-III by affective, anxiety, somatoform, dissociative, and psychosexual disorders with greater differentiation and refinement of subcategories (e.g., anxiety disorders are divided into phobic disorders with four subtypes, anxiety states with three subtypes, and posttraumatic stress disorder with three subtypes—a change that reflects greater emphasis on a descriptive and empirical, as opposed to theoretical approach); (7) improved reliability of diagnosis by provision of empirically derived operational criteria for assignment to diagnostic categories; (8) assessment along five axes designed to increase diagnostic utility for prognosis and treatment planning. The first two axes comprise all the diagnoses, with the first axis encompassing clinical syndromes, and the second axis including personality disorders and specific developmental disorders that may accompany the clinical syndromes; a third axis designates physical disorders or conditions that may be relevant to psychological disorders; a fourth axis is used to identify sources of disorders over the previous year or anticipated problem areas; and the fifth axis indicates the highest level of adaptive functioning during the past year.

The following illustrates how a clinician might write a DSM-III diagnosis based on the five axes with diagnostic code numbers for axes I and II.

Axis I: 300.70 Hypochondriasis
Axis II: 301.60 Dependent Personality Disorder
Axis III: Rectal polyps
Axis IV: Psychosocial stressors: death of spouse Severity: 5—Severe
Axis V: Highest level of adaptive functioning past year: 4—Fair

Following is a list of the main diagnostic categories of DSM-III, with examples of the subcategories. Not included are divisions within the subcategories.

- Disorders usually first evidenced in infancy, childhood, or adolescence (e.g., mental retardation, infantile autism)
- Organic Mental Disorders (e.g., organic brain syndromes, dementia)
- Substance Use Disorders (e.g., alcohol dependence, cocaine abuse)
- Schizophrenic Disorders (e.g., disorganized type, catatonic type)
- Paranoid Disorders (e.g., paranoia, shared paranoid disorder)
- Psychologic disorders not elsewhere classified (e.g., brief reactive psychosis)
- Affective Disorders (e.g., major depression, manic episode)
- Anxiety Disorders (e.g., phobic disorders, posttraumatic stress disorders)
- Somatoform Disorders (e.g., conversion disorder, hypochondriasis)
- Dissociative Disorders (e.g., psychogenic amnesia, multiple personality)
- Psychosexual Disorders (e.g., gender identity disorder, paraphilias)
- Factitious Disorders (physical and/or psychological disorders, though voluntarily produced by the client, are then beyond the control of the client)
- Disorders of Impulse Control not elsewhere classified (e.g., explosive disorder, pyromania)
- Adjustment Disorders (e.g., depressed mood, work inhibition)
- Psychological factors affecting physical conditions (physical disorder specified on axis III)
- Personality Disorders (e.g., antisocial personality, borderline personality disorders)
- Conditions not attributable to a mental disorder that are a focus of attention or treatment (e.g., marital problem, parent–child problem)

Overall, descriptive validity (differentiating individuals in one diagnostic category from those in another category) shows only a modicum of improvement over DSM-II, and outcome validity (predicting the future course of an individual's disorder), as in the case of the two previous editions, is still questionable (Rosenhan and Seligman, 1984, chapter 9).

As Nathan and Harris (1983) and Rosenhan and Seligman (1984) point out, the increase in the number of diagnoses in DSM-III is due to its greater specificity, the highlighting of previously ambiguous or rare conditions (e.g., elaboration of the posttraumatic stress disorder in response to society's concern over the post-Vietnam syndrome), and the identification of new disorders since the publication of DSM-II (e.g., tobacco dependence).

ETIOLOGY: AN OVERVIEW OF FOUR EXPLANATORY MODELS

Biological Model

Psychopathology is viewed as an organic process that may be germ-based, genetically transmitted, anatomical–neurological, or biochemical. A frequently noted example of the germ-based explanation is the discovery of the spirochete in syphilis from which general paresis, an organic brain syndrome, develops.

Spurred by the ground-breaking research of Kallmann (1953) which posited a genetic predisposition to schizophrenia and manic-depressive disorder, considerable research has accumulated to support a genetic susceptibility to a variety of psychopathological conditions such as schizophrenia and affective disorders (cited in Rosenhan and Seligman, 1984, see chapters 13 and 17; Schwarz, 1979; Strider, 1980), and early infantile autism, hyperactivity, alcoholism, and antisocial personality (cited in Schwarz, 1979). Silver and Segal (1984) offer the following observation: "It may seem likely that over the next decade geneticists and molecular biologists will be capable of mapping parts of the human genome. Substances thus localized may serve, in turn, as markers for inherited disorders that are caused by derangements in specific areas of the genome" (p. 805). Schwarz (1979) comments: "I am beginning to suspect that all forms of psychopathology that are not clearly due to traumatic, toxic, or infectious conditions of the brain are significantly influenced in likelihood and age of onset not only by environmental factors, but also by genetic variation among individuals" (p. 879).

Explanations that stress neurological or anatomical impairment are more pertinent to organically based psychotic disorders. Rosenthal (1968) has proposed a neurologically based defect in process schizophrenia (in contrast to reactive or psychogenically based schizophrenia). However, Strider (1980) concludes that a neurological basis for process schizophrenia has yet to be empirically established.

With respect to biochemical factors (which would include nutritional deficiencies), Silver and Segal (1984) single out studies that have used PET-scans to detect hypofrontality in schizophrenia, decreased metabolism in Alzheimer's disease and various forms of dementia, and alterations of metabolic activity in affective disorders by means of the administration of drugs. Although still inconclusive, research on disordered neurotransmitter systems, abnormal metabolites, and diminished or excessive levels of one or more transmitters suggests at least a contributory role in the etiology of affective and schizophrenic disorders (Strider, 1980; cited in Rosenhan and Seligman, 1984, see chapters 13, 16).

Although biological findings are promising and at times impressive, organic causation has been limited mostly to the severe forms of adult psychopathology, which comprise only a small segment of the total range of psychological disorders. Genetic explanations, while having implications for a larger range of disorders, indicate a genetic susceptibility rather than direct, specific genetic transmission. Schwarz (1979) points out that less than half of the total variation in schizophrenia, neurosis, and character disorder is explained by genetic differences, with the rest of the variation due to environmental influences and classification error. Still to be clarified is how genetic susceptibility to psychopathology is mediated by other inherited characteristics, and how genetic susceptibility interacts differentially with familial and social influences, and developmental and situational crises. Despite advances in the study of biochemical correlates of psychopathology, the findings are tentative, and hypotheses are largely based on how disorders respond to biochemical interventions, for example, drug administrations.

As many have noted, psychology and other behavioral sciences have largely untapped contributions to make in terms of understanding and ameliorating the impact of psychopathology on the broad spectrum of an individual's behavior across the life span. At this point, for many psychological disorders and for ordinary problems of living, psychological etiology and intervention have more to offer than biological theories or interventions. For instance, the approach of health psychology, which assists individuals to cope better with medical conditions and to develop healthy lifestyles, can be utilized by clinicians to assist individuals to cope better with genetic susceptibility, neurological defects, or biochemical deficiencies. Psychology is not the whole equation, but it has been and still is on the cutting edge of progress in the assessment, rehabilitation, and prevention of psychopathology.

Sociological Model

Basically, sociological theories explain psychopathology as a response to prevailing subcultural and social influences. As Dohrenwend and Dohrenwend (1969) note, "Symptom items themselves have different meanings and hence different implications for persons in different subcultures" (p. 169). Two common hypotheses are (1) the *drift* hypothesis; that is, socially and economically deprived areas of society attract and hold individuals from all classes who have seriously disturbed personalities and marginal life adjustments, thereby accounting for the higher incidence of abnormality in deprived areas, and (2) the *breeder* hypothesis; that is, depressed and disorganized environments with high rates of unemployment, dehumanization, and hopelessness are fertile ground for the development of abnormality (Strider, 1980).

In commenting on living environments, Strole (1972) concludes that due to the greater prevalence in slum areas of parental psychopathology, economic poverty, and family disorganization, both metropolitan and rural slums are more psychopathogenic for children than are nonslum neighborhoods. Furthermore, for adults seeking a change in environment, a large urban area, under most conditions, is a more therapeutic milieu than is a small community, especially for the chronically troubled person.

Instead of an individual frame of reference, sociological and anthropological concepts are designed to explain how large units (e.g., families, social groups, ethnic–minority subcultures) contribute to the development and maintenance of psychopathology (Millon, 1981, chapter 1). For an extended discussion of the relationship of culture and psychopathology, the reader is referred to Marsella (1979) and Draguns (1980).

Psychological Model

Following is a summary of four approaches: psychodynamic–intrapsychic, phenomenological–humanistic, cognitive–behavioral, and trait–type.

The psychodynamic–intrapsychic approach, which includes classical psychoanalytic theory and neoanalytic variations, is based on (1) childhood conflicts which arise when needs cannot be satisfied due to external constraints or conscience, and produce (2) conscious or unconscious anxiety, and defense mechanisms which are designed to eliminate or decrease anxiety (Rosenhan and Seligman, 1984, chapter 4). Defense mechanisms usually involve psychological distortion of awareness and/or reality of varying degrees of severity (Strider, 1980). Defenses against anxiety undergo developmental progression compatible with maturation of sensory–motor, perceptual–cognitive, affective–motivational, and interpersonal processes. Anxieties of the earlier developmental stages become reactivated by stressful situations of adult life, and psychopathology is the outcome of escalating anxieties pressing against inadequate or weakened defenses, which results in symptoms of intrapsychic and interpersonal impairment.

The phenomenological–humanistic approach subsumes self theories, existential theory, and gestalt theory. Common to these theories is the assumption that abnormality develops when an individual's feelings, needs, values, and intentions run counter to familial and social pressures, and as a consequence, the individual experiences pervasive and protracted conflict, which eventuates in self-estrangement and self-alienation. The disturbance in self-identity interferes with developing realistic and accurate perceptions of others, which impairs interpersonal functioning. A core belief is that subordinating one's identity to real or imagined expectations results in a failure to live productively and in a satisfying manner. For further information, refer to Rosenhan and Seligman (1984, see chapter 7).

The cognitive–behavioral approach contends that the basis for development, maintenance, and generalization of maladaptive behavior is the same as for normal behavior, and abnormality refers to behaviors that an individual has learned in order to cope with stressful problems of daily living. Abnormal behavior may be acquired by (1) classical conditioning, in which abnormal responses become associated with external events; (2) operantly conditioned processes, in which abnormal behavior becomes positively or negatively reinforced; or (3) cognitive mediational processes in which maladaptive thoughts and beliefs lead to emotional distress and inappropriate actions. While the source of behavioral deficits and excesses is to be found in the methods of child rearing, once formed the deficits and excesses create environmental contingencies that strengthen and perpetuate abnormal functioning. For additional information, refer to Rosenhan and Seligman (1984, see chapters 5, 6).

The trait–type approach is more descriptive than explanatory, and is derived from classification and statistical processing of clinical observations or test data. Three commonly used methods are (1) simple, clinical description of syndromes; (2) combining of nosological classifications on the basis of clinical findings; and (3) the use of statistical methods of factor and cluster analysis of clinical data to yield clinical typologies (Strider, 1980). Examples of the trait–type approach are Cattell and Scheier's (1961) multifactorial theory, Eysenck and Rachman's (1965) three-factor theory, and Millon's (1981) system of personality classification. Millon has proposed the following classification of abnormal behavior (based on least to most modifiable behavior): (1) personality syndromes which differ in terms of trait patterns; (2) symptom disorders, which arise primarily from trait patterns and secondarily from situational stresses; and (3) behavior reactions, which are primarily responses to situational stresses rather than to trait patterns.

In addition, the four psychological approaches can be grouped under three general models: the illness model (psychodynamic), social learning (cognitive–behavioral and trait–type), and actualization model (phenomenological–humanistic). Despite some differences, central to all three models is the basic paradigm of personal distress/social impairment generated by defensive–protective reactions to conflict-centered fear–anxiety. The symptoms of the illness model are the behavioral deficits and excesses of the social learning model, and the relating and communicating failures of the actualization model.

Although differing on the issue of whether abnormality is quantitatively or qualitatively different from normality, the three models generally accept a severity continuum of psychological disorders without a sharp demarcation between normal and abnormal functioning. The three models also acknowledge a distinction between predisposing and precipitating factors, though there is less agreement on the former because the concept of predisposition is embedded in basic differences about etiology. With respect to the interaction of predisposing and precipitating variables, Zubin's (1977–1978) statement is relevant to the three models:

> One solution is to look for the common denominator running through all three models. . . . The thread . . . is the presence of a vulnerability . . . elicited by either exogenous or endogenous life events which produces sufficient stress to elicit an episode. . . . We need to find and differentiate markers of vulnerability from markers of the presence and absence of episodes. . . . The latter wax and wane with the episodes and disappear with the end of the episode, while the former persist in and out of episodes [p. 7].

Although the search for a single, all-inclusive model continues, the availability of three viable models not only provides the necessary checks and balances to correct for each model's biases, but also accommodates the differences in beliefs and values that exist among clinicians.

Developmental Model

Although the developmental approach is an example of a psychological model, it deserves a separate emphasis. Etiologically, two types of developmentally sequential interactions are considered (Cohen, 1974). The first interaction is between organismically based characteristics (sex, size, attractiveness, intelligence, psychophysiological reactivity), and socializing influences and pressures (family, school, neighborhood, peers). From this interaction, critical thought–feeling–action patterns evolve that constitute a predisposition to psychopathology. The stage is then set for the second, or developmentally later interaction between specific predispositions and precipitating events that occur at different developmental periods (e.g., the stresses of coping with normal developmental tasks as well as accidental stresses, such as loss of significant others, failures, physical traumas, and illnesses).

Implicit in the developmental conception is the notion of critical or sensitive periods of development, in which success or failure to cope successfully with the critical period influences mastery of subsequent periods (e.g., Freud's psychosexual stages of development, Erikson's psychosocial stages).

Millon (1981, chapter 3) hypothesizes three sensitive developmental phases which are based on three critical neurological growth stages, and the learning of coping behaviors is related in a determinate way to the three sensitive phases. He identifies three pathogenic conditions that lead to dysfunctional behavior styles: (1) disruptive or traumatic events that elicit coping reactions that are useful for short-term functioning, but deleterious for long-term functioning; (2) innocuous or nontraumatic events that nevertheless activate coping behavior that becomes dysfunctional through generalization to inappropriate situations or persons; and (3) insufficient learning experiences (i.e., environmental impoverishment that produces deficiencies in learning adaptive behaviors).

Schwarz (1979) proposes a model based on genetic predisposition and parental behavior. The formative stages of childhood strengthen or weaken one of three interpersonal styles: cooperation, fearful avoidance, or antagonism to others. While opportunities for changing an interpersonal style persist through childhood, the longer a child practices one of the three styles in different areas of life, the harder it will be later on to modify the style or develop an alternative one.

CURRENT AND FUTURE ISSUES

There are several areas on which the National Institute of Mental Health (NIMH) has already set or is likely to set high priorities for research attention and funding (Silver and Segal, 1984). One is the developmental area, which Silver and Segal describe as "exploring the continuities and transformations whereby individual personalities become vulnerable or invulnerable to psychopathology at various stages in the life span" (p. 808). They also comment on the new generation of research strategies and methods for longitudinal study that enable long-term patterns of personality functioning to be examined in terms of both biological factors and sociocultural influences, and that may well lead to a taxonomy of environments and life situations.

Another promising area is the family context of normality and abnormality. Silver and Segal (1984) outline three lines of research. The first is sociocultural, which studies how families, especially disadvantaged ones, cope with problems, and how support networks facilitate their coping efforts. The second is biobehavioral, which examines how family living styles interact with biological influences (e.g., temperament) to shape psychological competence in young children. A third line of investigation focuses on how specific family variables (e.g., communication style) contribute to normal or abnormal development. In reviewing family influences on psychopathology, Doane (1978) identifies the following significant differences between normal and dysfunctional families: patterns of conflict, family coalition patterns, flexibility versus rigidity, family effectiveness and efficiency, and habitual styles of communicating among family members.

An area of pressing urgency is how to correct deficiencies in treatment programs that are alternatives to hospitalization. As evidence of the need to improve treatment programs, Teplin (1984) cites research findings which indicate that deinstitutionalization has not significantly reduced the overall rate of hospitalization and rehospitalization, that the incidence and prevalence of schizophrenia is increasing due in part to the greater proportion of younger persons (18 to 30 years of age) in the population, and that increasing numbers of the mentally ill are being processed through the criminal justice system instead of the mental health system. In a similar vein, Albee (1982) takes the mental health system to task, and argues along with others for a shift of priorities from treatment to prevention. He reports that in any given year, the entire mental health delivery system (hospitals, clinics, private practitioners) sees fewer than one in five of the seriously disturbed, and only a small proportion of a much larger group who have moderate problems. He proposes a large-scale primary prevention effort that would reduce unnecessary stress, especially stress due to powerlessness, and that would enhance social competence, self-esteem, and support networks. To all who will listen, Albee sounds a clear warning: "Over and over again, surveys have found that individual psychotherapy and individual organic treatment in the form of drug therapy represent the backbone of the efforts being made in our mental health centers. As long as we plod along on that particular treadmill the situation will remain hopeless" (p. 1044).

Clearly, the relation between cumulative stress and susceptibility to childhood psychopathology is of prime importance in designing prevention programs. Magnussen (1980) cites six stress factors that have been found to be strongly associated with childhood disorders: (1) severe marital discord; (2) low social status; (3) overcrowding or large family size; (4) paternal criminality; (5) maternal psychiatric disorder; and (6) admission to the care of local authorities. When only one of these factors is present, a child is no more likely to develop serious problems than any other child. When two of the factors occur, the risk of abnormality increases fourfold, which is a persuasive argument for prevention programs to improve family functioning and environmental conditions.

To conclude, not only has our understanding of normality

relied too much on extrapolation from the study of psychopathology, but also our knowledge of psychopathology has relied too much on clinical and research findings from already existing psychological disorders. Needed is more longitudinal research on developmental variables that predispose an individual to adaptive or maladaptive functioning, along with a taxonomy of environments and life situations that facilitate or inhibit adaptive functioning. Finally, because a comprehensive understanding of normality and abnormality encompasses all of psychology, as well as the other behavioral sciences, clinical psychologists, to paraphrase from another context, do not know their own specialty if they know only that.

PERSONAL CONSIDERATIONS

To assist the reader to move toward a "personalized" meaning of normality and abnormality, the following points may be helpful. First, a key element in the terms *normality* and *abnormality* is *norm*, which can be defined as a standard or criterion. Although related to a host of variables (see pp. 186–191) and subject to gradual change over time, a norm, standard, or criterion of appropriate behavior is nevertheless essential to differentiating normal from abnormal behavior.

In clinical practice there are two norms to be considered: an external or societal norm, and an internal or personal norm. Some individuals are referred involuntarily for mental health services because their behavior, as judged by others, deviates too much from the societal norm. On the other hand, many more individuals seek mental health services voluntarily because they are not functioning in accordance with their personal standard of normality. Thus, the clinical practitioner must address both types of norms in deciding how best to assist a client to live his or her life in accordance with personal and societal standards. In this context, normality denotes success and abnormality denotes failure, as judged by personal and/or social norms, to adapt one's behavior to the changing conditions or exigencies of the psychosocial environment (Robertson, 1980).

Chapter 8

Being a Diagnostician, Part I: Clinical Assessment and Diagnosis

The father had sought the services of an independent practitioner of clinical psychology. As he described the situation: "About six years ago, just as I was finishing my college degree, my marriage fell apart. We had a few marriage counseling sessions, but it was hopeless. We had a newborn son, and the thought of giving him up almost destroyed me, but I knew I had to serve four years in the military and I knew that I had little choice but to let my ex-wife have custody of him. We didn't have much money, and I didn't even get an attorney, I just relied on what her attorney told me. Now I'm out of the military, remarried, and making a good income. I want my son back! I have filed for a modification of custody. What has happened though is that my ex-wife's attorney had her take our son to the clinic that does psychological evaluations for the courts. The psychologists and social workers there spent hours with my ex-wife and my son, interviewing them, giving them tests, observing them together, and even going to her apartment to see how they live. My attorney arranged for me and my second wife to go to the clinic too. They spent about 30 minutes talking to us, and then put my son and me into a play therapy room for 15 minutes—we were in the place less than an hour. The clinic sent a report to the court saying that my ex-wife is a far better parent than I am, and recommended that she be allowed to keep custody of my son. Somehow that just doesn't seem like we were treated equally." Indeed, that may be the case, and for a variety of reasons. The one reason, however, that should be emphasized for this chapter is that being a diagnostician requires reliable and valid methods, and data collected from a brief interview and a play session of still shorter duration would likely yield "data" of dubious reliability and validity, and would certainly seem less adequate than the data that would come from extensive interviewing and observations, comprehensive psychological testing, and a home visit.

Assessment and diagnosis form the distinguishing cornerstone for the practice of clinical psychology. In a survey of practitioners of clinical psychology, Moreland and Dahlstrom (1983) found that 91 percent of the respondents performed assessment. This same prominence has been present throughout the history of clinical psychology and, notwithstanding the increasing array of services provided by clinical psychologists, shows little or no diminution.

The reason that assessment has maintained a primary place comes from the fact that psychologists are the only clinical professionals trained to use psychological tests. While psychiatrists, clinical social workers, and other mental health professionals are prepared to conduct evaluations, they must rely on appraisal methods other than psychological tests. State licensing laws for psychologists commonly proscribe the use of psychological tests by other than a licensed psychologist. Also, the publishers of tests typically restrict the sale of certain tests, particularly those that are more clinically oriented, to psychologists.

Psychological tests have not received unquestioned acceptance. From concerned parents to Congressional subcommittees to the courts, there have been many condemnations of and inquiries about the use of psychological tests. These criticisms have centered on the client's right to privacy, discrimination because of cultural distinctions, the reliability and validity of the instruments, and the kinds of decisions that are based on test data. In some instances, a given test has been banned from use in a school system because of content (e.g., asking about values that, by public policy, are deemed to be under the exclusive aegis of the family and exempt from institutional scrutiny).

Such criticisms should not be viewed as illogical, hostile

attacks. Often there has been a just reason for questioning the use of a particular test. Too often, decisions have relied on test data when, from a validity point of view, there has been no scientific connector between the data and the criterion for the decision. For example, candidates for jobs have been screened according to tests that had minimal, if any, predictive validity for the job functions; and children have been placed in special education programs without benefit of test data directly relevant to the placement decision.

There are many reasons underlying abuse of test data. Sometimes the reason may well have been rooted in a conscious wish to discriminate, but more often the reasons have been due to a faulty understanding of testing and an ill-formulated wish to appear "professional" in the decision-making process—unfortunately, the outcome in such cases is anything but professional.

Even the well-meaning professional may share in the guilt of abusing test data. Since the profession creates a "publish or perish" dictum, particularly if the clinical psychologist is employed by a college or university, there is a never-ending quest to generate research for publication in professional journals. In order to attain the degree of originality that is necessary to win a journal editor's acceptance of a research manuscript, there seems to be a tendency to create tests; many times these are poorly developed. In providing an annotated bibliography of compendia of behavioral measurements, Reichalt (1983) asserts that tests are developed so rapidly that they frequently have not been adequately researched, noting that "approximately 70% of instruments are only used by their developer" (p. 341), yet they end up as part of published research.

These slipshod test development practices and the conscious or unconscious abuses have not gone unfettered. Both statutory and case law have imposed strong restraints on testing practices, particularly for the qualities a test must have and the decisions that can be made therefrom (Miner and Miner, 1978; Stick, 1984).

Today there are numerous federal legislative acts and state statutes that specify standards for testing, most notably Public Law 94-142, the Education for All Handicapped Children Act, that ensures, among other things, that there will be a correct and proper evaluation for any child designated as being handicapped (Martin, 1979).

Case law has also had an impact, such as the California case of *Larry P. v. Riles* which revealed that intelligence tests had been applied in such a manner that a disproportionately large number of black children had been classified as mentally retarded. The court enjoined the San Francisco school district "from placing black students in classes for the educable mentally retarded on the basis of criteria which rely primarily on the results of I.Q. tests as they are currently administered, if the consequence of use of such criteria is racial imbalance in the composition of such classes" (p. 1315). Note that some wags have chosen to interpret this legal decision incorrectly as a ban on intelligence testing. First, the decision applies, at the most, to California, but second, the decision (quite correctly) bans discriminatory use of intelligence tests, not the tests per se. However, as revealed by Stick's (1984) review, there are cases from other jurisdictions, including those from federal courts (which could potentially have a more far-reaching influence than a state court's decision), that create similar legal mandates for testing practices.

From the point of view of the clinical psychologist, the statutory and case legal decisions are joined in importance by disciplinary dictates. The collective minds for the American Educational Research Association (AERA), the American Psychological Association (APA), and the National Council on Measurements Used in Education (NCMUE) produced a jointly sponsored report on standards for tests, which is, of relevance to clinical psychologists, consonant with the *Standards for Educational and Psychological Tests and Manuals* (APA, 1966, 1974).

Moreover, the APA's (1981b) "Ethical Principles of Psychologists" is anything but silent on standards for testing. Principle 2: Competence, states (in part): "Psychologists recognize the boundaries of their competence and the limitations of their techniques. They only provide services and only use techniques for which they are qualified by training and experience" (p. 634). Principle 8: Assessment Techniques, states (in part):

> In the development, publication, and utilization of psychological assessment techniques, psychologists make every effort to promote the welfare and best interests of the client. They guard against the misuse of assessment results. They respect the client's right to know the results, the interpretations made, and the bases for their conclusions and recommendations. Psychologists make every effort to maintain the security of tests and other assessment techniques within limits of legal mandates. They strive to ensure the appropriate use of assessment techniques by others [p. 637].

In keeping with the legal principle of informed consent (whereby a patient has a right to know the positive and negative qualities of an intervention and to accept or reject it accordingly), the preceding ethical principle also states: "In reporting assessment results, psychologists indicate any reservations that exist regarding validity or reliability because of the circumstances of the assessment or the inappropriateness of the norms for the person tested" (p. 637).

All of this is well and good; to be sure, it is probable that such authoritative statements are honored by the large majority of clinical psychologists, at least in essence. If a clinical psychologist does not honor them, he or she could be subjected to disciplinary sanctions by ethics committees, state licensing boards, and courts (since ethical principles are part of the standard of care for the profession, and a breach of them could lend credence to a malpractice action against the practitioner). On the other hand, the likelihood that a clinical psychologist does, in fact, "indicate any reservations that exist regarding validity or reliability" to each and every client seems rather slight. In the end, the only "policeman at the elbow" (to rely on an old legal guide) has to be the internalized values, ethics, and standards of the individual practitioner. Of course, this underscores the importance of high quality training before entry into clinical psychology.

As a final caveat, the APA (1981d) has also promulgated "Specialty Guidelines for the Delivery of Services by Clinical Psychologists" (see chapters 3 and 4). While this document embraces the breadth of clinical psychology practices, here again there is a mandate for standards in testing and other assessment practices. To function, be it independently or under the employment of an organization, in a manner that does not live up to these guidelines would be to court a negative reaction from one's peers and, indeed, from makers of public policy.

FUNDAMENTAL CONCEPTS

There are two vantage points for viewing a person. There can be an appraisal of (1) intrapersonal distinctions; or (2) interpersonal comparisons. The principles of individuality are referred to as being "idiographic," whereas seeking laws that apply to all persons and/or making comparisons of the individual to groups of people is termed *nomothetic.*

Clinical psychologists use both idiographic and nomothetic approaches. When a set of psychological needs are gleaned from personality tests, it is an idiographic profile of the client. When test scores are presented as percentiles, they offer a nomothetic comparison of how the client performed in relation to a normative group performance. The idiographic and nomothetic concepts will receive further clarification throughout this chapter.

Terminology is a common troublemaker in professional literature; for example, there have been attempts to distinguish between the terms *measurement, evaluation, appraisal,* and *assessment.*

The first term, *measurement,* does seem distinctive. Hamersma (1972) states: "Measurement basically is the use of numbers, or numerals, and the way in which the numbers are assigned to data" (p. 6).

Measurement is commonly sequenced into four scaling levels. Level one is the nominal scale, where data are simply classified or named. Level two is the ordinal scale, where data are ranked or ordered according to some priority system. Level three is the interval scale, which relies on units that are presumably equal distances apart. Level four is the ratio scale, where the data have a zero value and progress upward with equality. Table 8.1 clarifies the levels of measurement.

The following are examples of the different levels of mea-

Table 8.1 Levels (Scales) of Measurement[a]

Level (Scale)	Procedures Involved	Restrictions	Appropriate or Permissible Statistics	Examples
I. Nominal	Classify or name data by using numerals	Only counting procedures; no arithmetic	1. Number of cases (Chi-square) 2. Mode 3. Contingency correlation 4. Nonparametric tests—Fisher exact probability test, Cochran Q test, X^2 for two or *k* independent samples	Numbers on football or baseball jerseys, coding in research
II. Ordinal	Ranking or ordering	Only ranking allowed; no arithmetic involved	1. Median 2. Percentiles 3. Nonparametric tests— Kolmogorov-Smirnov, one-sample runs test, Wilcoxon matched-pairs signed ranks, Mann-Whitney U, Wald-Wolfowitz, Moses test of extreme reactions, Friedman two-way analysis of variance, Kruskal-Wallis, Kendall rank correlation coefficient, Kendall partial rank correlation, Kendall coefficient of concordance, Spearman rank correlation coefficient	Ranking for graduate school selection, quality of cloth, etc.
III. Interval	Establishing equal-of units or differences	Addition and Subtraction allowed	1. Mean 2. Standard deviation 3. Rank-order correlation 4. Product-moment correlation 5. Nonparametric tests—Walsh test, Randomization test for matched pairs, Randomization test for two independent samples	Temperature, calendar dates, measurement of energy
IV. Ratio	Equality of units and a true "zero" point	No restrictions: addition, subtraction, multiplication, and division are all possible	1. All previously mentioned statistics are permissible including nonparametric statistics 2. Coefficient of variation 3. Logarithmic transformations 4. Nonparametric tests—all possible	Weight, height, volume, money, etc.

[a]From Hamersma (1972), with permission.

surement in a clinical psychology context. If a clinical psychologist divides a group of subjects according to "normal" versus "abnormal" (with an established data-based definition for the dichotomy), it is a nominal measurement. If a clinical psychologist observes a classroom and ranks the students for being well behaved (in sequence to being poorly behaved), for example, it is ordinal scaling. If a clinical psychologist considers intelligence quotients for a group of subjects, it is interval scaling: "Intelligence quotients (IQs) usually are considered examples of interval scale scores" (Kleinmuntz, 1982, p. 5). If a clinical psychologist does research on the incomes of clients, the money constitutes ratio scaling. Clearly, each of the levels of measurement is used in clinical psychology, but, "In personality assessment, most numerical findings are expressed in ordinal or approximate interval scales" (Kleinmuntz, 1982, p. 5).

The distinction between the terms *evaluation, appraisal*, and *assessment* is not as clear as for the term *measurement*. For example, the word *evaluation* has often been given a rather broad definition. It has also been connected to program evaluation, such as estimating how well a mental health facility fulfills its objectives.

The word *appraisal* has tended to be defined in qualitative terms, such as quantifying skills for a selection process or developing a mental status report. *Assessment* has become the preferred term for clinical psychology.

There is no shortage of definitions for the term *assessment*. To start with a brief definition, Maloney and Ward (1976) state: "A simple definition for an extremely complex process is that *psychological assessment is a process of solving problems (answering questions)* in which psychological tests are often used as *one* of the methods of collecting data" (p. 5). Kleinmuntz (1982) indicates: "Most psychologists would probably agree on the following definition: Assessment includes all systematic (or standardized) and objective procedures (or devices) for obtaining observations and scores reflecting samples of psychological behavior" (p. 6). Focusing on personality, Sundberg (1977) offers: "For our purposes personality assessment may be defined as *the set of processes used by a person or persons for developing impressions and images, making decisions and checking hypotheses about another person's pattern of characteristics which determine his or her behavior in interaction with the environment*" (pp. 21–22).

It is important to realize that clinical assessment is more than psychological testing. Maloney and Ward (1976) make the distinction:

> Psychometric testing refers to the systematic study of individual differences among people along specified traits or dimensions. The essence of the psychometric test is that the description of people is done in objective, standardized, quantifiable ways. Psychological assessment, on the other hand, is generally a process of solving problems. The basic differences in the purposes, goals, and methodologies of these two operations can be illuminated by considering the following propositions: (1) psychometric testing is primarily measurement oriented, while psychological assessment is primarily problem oriented; (2) psychometric testing is primarily concerned with describing and studying *groups* of people, while psychological assessment focuses on a description and an analysis of a particular *individual* in a problem situation; (3) psychometric testing demands little if any clinical expertise other than that of a psychometrist, while the role of the clinician or expert is crucial and integral to the process of psychological assessment [p. 38].

Kleinmuntz (1982) points out that psychological assessment encompasses virtually all types of psychological tests, as well as procedures for "systematically recording behavior observations and scoring and quantifying data gleaned from personal documents, case histories, interviewing, and behavioral analysis" (pp. 6–7). Woody (1980a) emphasizes four critical points: "First, clinical assessment is not restricted to objective, standardized, quantifiable procedures. For example, many of the data might come from interviews or observations. Second, clinical assessment is individually focused. . . . Third, clinical assessment is problem oriented. Fourth, the diagnostician, that is, the assessor, has the responsibility of applying and maintaining astute clinical acumen" (p. xxxi). Assessment does not, however, include unsystematic and/or informal techniques, unless they can, in some way, attain legitimacy by being processed through the clinical acumen of the psychologist. Assessment must be predicated on scientifically derived notions, concepts, strategies, and methods.

The previously mentioned "Specialty Guidelines for the Delivery of Services by Clinical Psychologists" (APA, 1981d) provides a final authoritative definition for assessment:

> Assessment directed toward diagnosing the nature and causes, and predicting the effects, of subjective distress; of personal, social, and work dysfunction; and of the psychological and emotional factors involved in, and consequent to, physical disease and disability. Procedures may include, but are not limited to, interviewing, and administering and interpreting tests of intellectual abilities, attitudes, emotions, motivations, personality characteristics, psychoneurological status, and other aspects of human experience and behavior relevant to the disturbance [p. 642].

In the context of clinical psychological services, assessment is joined with therapeutic interventions, consultation, program development, supervision, and evaluation of services.

CLINICAL JUDGMENT AND RELIABILITY

The scientist–practitioner model maintained by clinical psychology encounters considerable friction from the human factor inherent to assessment: the human condition sometimes rubs science the wrong way! While for the most part the experimental psychologist can be assured of scientific results by restricting data collection to tabulations of observable behavior or quantifiable performance, the clinical psychologist commonly filters data through his or her subjective ability to recognize, analyze, and interpret (i.e., clinical acumen or expertise). Thorne (1961) states: "The same laws and principles discovered by basic science psychology in relation to psychophysical judgments, perceptual discriminations, etc., also appear to apply to clinical judgments, which are not qualitatively different but simply represent quantitative complications due to the greater complexity of clinical factors requiring judgment" (p. 1).

Clinical psychologists offering assessment services must constantly make judgments, often without clear criteria for the objective under consideration. In other words, the clinical psychologist makes an individualized judgment, yet must fulfill professional standards—which means safeguarding against idiosyncratic preferences or biases.

Clinical judgments can only be made by a professional—a seemingly comparable decision by a layperson is merely a personal opinion. Through such public policy avenues as laws, society has ordained people with certain qualifications to be "professionals." The cloak of professionalism carries both benefits (e.g., status, income) and liabilities (e.g., duties, accountability for malpractice), and clinical judgment is a core ingredient to the success or failure of the professional quest. Thus, Thorne (1961) adds: "*clinical judgment* properly refers simply to the correctness of the *problem-solving thinking of a special class of persons*, namely clinically trained persons with special levels of training, experience and competence" (p. 7).

The highly personal nature of clinical judgment, even with the best-trained clinical psychologist, is always open to variability or error. It would be nice if a clinical psychologist could achieve 100 percent consistency (reliability) or accuracy (validity) with his or her judgments or in comparison with other clinical psychologists, but such does not occur—it is one of fallibilities of the assessment process.

Why is inconsistency or inaccuracy allowed in the judgments of clinical psychologists? The answer is that society has recognized that (1) someone must make clinical judgments to accommodate social order and development; (2) the person should be qualified in some manner; and (3) the profession of clinical psychology produces candidates best suited to meet the needs of society.

While research reveals difficulties with clinical judgment, it is a pragmatic creation of and for society. As Thorne (1961) states: "Even in view of the admitted invalidity or relative inefficiency of many clinical decisions, society must depend upon clinical decisions because of the practical and economic limitations of life situations" (p. 23).

Professionalism mandates that there be a constant search for scientific support and validation, with a "complete" status probably never being attainable. Further, the practitioner should only assert that he or she is doing the best that can be done (1) at this particular point in the societal–professional evolution, and (2) offered under the existing conditions, in the particular contextual framework, and to the specific client being served.

Reliability refers to the consistency of a measurement or judgment. The lack of reliability is a plague to many procedures in clinical psychology. For example, the development of a psychological test requires proof that the instrument will measure the same thing in the same way twice. The test must have "content reliability," meaning that the test items measure the same factor or construct. There are various statistical formulas for estimating content reliability; these include analysis of the scores after the same test has been administered on two (or more) occasions (called test–retest or temporal reliability), and a division of the test into parts (called the split-half or odd–even reliability).

Given the subjectivity of judgments, clinical psychology has special concern about scorer reliability. Here there are two forms: intrajudge reliability and interjudge reliability.

Early research by the senior author (RHW) exemplifies these two types of reliability. In doing his Ph.D. dissertation on the use of electroencephalography (EEG), the measurement of electrical brain wave activity, and mental abilities tests, he was struck by how the EEGer could rapidly review page after page of tracings and come up with judgments about factors that supposedly delineated the presence or absence of brain dysfunction. A search of the journals revealed little evidence to assure that the EEGer would, in fact, evaluate the same EEG protocol exactly the same way twice (i.e., that there would be intrajudge reliability). The EEGer was open minded to examining his functioning, and agreed that it was just assumed that a professional well trained in the use of EEG would be able to make exactly the same judgment twice. He cooperated with a study (Woody, 1966) that presented him with

15 EEGs from behavioral problem boys and 15 EEGs from well-behaved boys (all personal cues regarding the EEG subjects were eliminated) and he judged a series of factors that were commonly relied upon for diagnostic purposes. Eight months later, he rejudged the same EEGs (without knowledge of how he had judged a particular EEG the first time). Without going into all of the findings, suffice it to say that there were indications of problems with intrajudge reliability. As one specific finding, the EEGer was asked to classify each overall record as being in one of five well-defined categories (normal, borderline, mildly abnormal, abnormal, and markedly abnormal). The statistical analysis revealed that the initial rating and the rerating were not significantly related—there was poor intrajudge reliability, even though this was a well-trained, highly experienced EEGer operating under standard conditions.

As might be expected, this poor intrajudge reliability raised the question of interjudge reliability; that is, would two or more EEGers agree with each other? Again, a search of the journals failed to yield any answer, and a trip to one of the most prestigious neuropsychiatric institutes to interview the director of EEG (an M.D. and neurologist) met with the answer: "There's really no need to study an issue like that, we physicians know what we're doing, of course we agree with our own judgments and with those of our colleagues—the results of your first study must have been due to the EEGer being poorly trained."

To investigate the matter further, a second study (Woody, 1968b) was conducted, wherein three EEGers (with strong credentials) were hired to judge EEG protocols. The second research design was much the same as in the first (intrajudge) study, but this time the focus was on how well the three EEGers would agree with each other (i.e., interjudge reliability). Again, there were problems, this time in the realm of interjudge reliability. For example, the three EEGers were asked to simply assign each EEG protocol to either a "normal" or an "abnormal" classification (they had agreed on detailed definitions and criteria for these two classifications). Using only a normal–abnormal dichotomy, the three judges had complete agreement on only 53 percent of the cases; two-judge combinations had complete agreement on 60 to 86.7 percent of the cases. Since EEG plays such a critical role in neurological diagnosis and treatment, these findings certainly raised doubts about the reliability of clinical judgments in this area.

To be sure, clinical use of EEG has progressed since these studies were conducted. There is, however, still reason to question the reliability of judgments for EEG protocols and, indeed, any kind of clinical data (albeit that the application of computer analysis of EEG and other clinical data should assure reliability).

The message should be clear: even well-trained, highly experienced professionals may get involved in judgmental tasks that defy adequate intrajudge and/or interjudge reliability. But as was pointed out earlier, society can authorize professional practices that are less than perfect, and notwithstanding questionable reliability for clinical assessment procedures, there is public policy endorsement for the clinical judgments. As Thorne (1961) views the public policy endorsement: "The clinicians have the responsibility to go on making decisions in any situation where their predictions are even 1 or 2% better than common sense or pure chance choices" (p. 23).

VALIDITY

There is an old assessment saw that says: "You can have reliability without having validity, but you can't have validity without having reliability." This means that it is possible for, say, two clinical psychologists to agree with each other on some diagnostic notion (there would be interjudge reliability), yet their agreed-upon notion could be false (there would not be validity). But conversely, a judgment based on a diagnostic notion that is true (i.e., one that reflects a particular matter) must be consistently appraised (there must be reliability or else the validity does not obtain).

All clinical assessment procedures must be valid; that is, they must measure what they purport to measure. This is the backbone of the various authoritative statements on psychological testing and ethical practices cited earlier in this chapter.

There are several types of validity. Let us examine types that have the most relevance to clinical psychology (in the next few paragraphs on validity, the example of psychological tests will be used, but the principle applies to other diagnostic strategies as well).

Face validity refers to the fact that the test "appears" to be true. For example, the test items on a depression test look or seem as if they are the kinds of questions that should be asked about depression. Obviously this offers limited proof of validity: "face validity is *not* a genuine type of validity at all but albeit an enviable ingredient of a test" (Hamersma, 1972, p. 66).

Content validity comes from logic supporting the test. There is usually a "textbook justification" for the material. Again, there is limited proof of validity, but at least there is some academic screening. There is, however, no statistical analysis applied in either face validity or content validity.

Moving to statistical analysis, factorial validity refers to a factor analysis supporting that a test is a relatively pure measure of a given matter. Empirical validity suggests the relationship between, say, a test and a standard of observable performance. Criterion validity reveals the correlation between the score from one test and another measure (such as correlating IQ with grade point average), and moves toward, but does not fully attain, predictive power.

Construct validity is akin to criterion validity (Hamersma, 1972). For construct validity, the clinical psychologist accumulates research findings, formulates hypotheses, and tests that there is, in fact, a relationship between a test score and a behavior that it purports to measure. As Lyman (1963) describes it: "With construct validity, we predict the results which logically should be obtained if the test is valid. The prediction is stated concretely enough and precisely enough so that it can be tested statistically. In this way, we actually are checking the validity of both the test and its underlying theory" (p. 30). Construct validity seems to be the standard for psychological tests in this day and age, defined by the APA (1966) as: "The test user wishes to infer the degree to which the individual possesses some hypothetical trait or quality (construct) presumed to be reflected in test performance" (p. 12).

Federal guidelines seem to accept the content, construct, and criterion-related forms of validity, depending upon the circumstances. There is, however, a preference in federal law for criterion-related studies: "Criterion-related studies show the relationship between test performance and subsequent job performance" (Miner and Miner, 1978, p. 51).

Standardization is crucial to the validity of a psychological test, and it is here that the test departs in principle from certain other diagnostic strategies. Taking an example from personality testing, while the Minnesota Multiphasic Personality Inventory (MMPI) (see chapter 9), yields scores based on large samples of criterion-referenced groups of human subjects (thus, it has been standardized via normative sampling), the Thematic Apperception Test (TAT), which will also be described later, offers no standardized scores and relies on the subjective interpretation of the clinical psychologist. To a degree, these other diagnostic strategies, such as the TAT, have been standardized, in that there is a set way to: (1) administer the test; (2) collect and formulate the data; and (3) produce clinical interpretations. But for the most part they do not have the benefit of numerical–empirical references to large samples of human subjects. As will be presented subsequently, this does not, in any manner, mean that these nonstandardized or nonnormative diagnostic strategies do not merit inclusion in clinical psychology. Rather, it only means that they are different in nature from psychological tests, and that the data obtained by them must be viewed and treated for what they are—nonstandardized data.

When a test is developed, the statistical analysis leads to norms; that is, there is a statistical summary of how the human subjects performed on the test. Consequently, certain statistics are computed (such as the mean, the standard deviation, and other estimates of central tendency) that provide objective signposts for the clinical psychologist's interpretation. The common bell-shaped curve that reflects the normal distribution of test scores is presented in Figure 8.1. The standards of the APA (1974) have specific requirements for how normative data are established. In addition to the normative data that initially establish a test, norms should be updated, and care should be taken to avoid using the test with a client

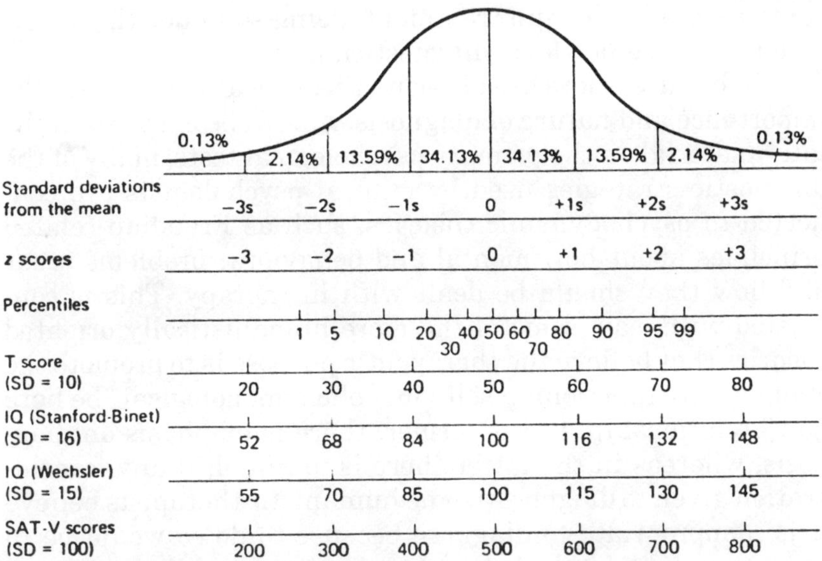

Figure 8.1 Relationships among derived scores. Adapted from "Methods of expressing test scores," Test Service Bull. No. 48. New York: The Psychological Corporation, January 1955, p.2.

or for a diagnostic issue that would not be compatible with the standardization or normative data.

DIAGNOSIS

Historically, being a diagnostician carried special prestige. To this day, many mental health treatment programs require (1) a senior-level professional to evaluate the case, perhaps by chairing an interdisciplinary case conference (wherein, for example, diagnostic ideas from a psychiatrist, a clinical psychologist, a clinical social worker, and others are pooled to formulate a comprehensive diagnostic picture); (2) the formulation of an individualized treatment plan, with the senior-level professional assuring that the approach is appropriate for and in the best interests of the particular client/patient; and (3) the assignment of the case to a therapist, one who has the skills specifically needed and who is often (but not always) a junior-level professional. Indeed, some mental health programs use paraprofessionals (persons who have only limited training in human services and who are not professionals per se) to provide follow-up treatment, doing so under the supervision of the senior-level diagnostician.

To be sure, there are differing theoretical views about the importance and nature of diagnosis. As will be clarified in the later material on the primary psychological tests, many of the diagnostic strategies used by clinical psychologists are connected to psychodynamic theories, such as Freudian-related principles about how mental and behavioral problems occur and how they should be dealt with in therapy. This is contrasted with, say, some of the more humanistically oriented theories that believe the therapeutic purpose is to promote the client's fully functioning self via a phenomenological "be here now" relationship. In the former, there is emphasis on diagnosis, whereas in the latter there is minimal, if any, consideration given to diagnosis (some humanistic therapists believe it is inappropriate to diagnose because to do so would be to tamper with and impede the client's existential flow).

While all sorts of theories and, consequently, views about diagnosis abound in clinical psychology, the prevailing stance is that psychological assessment is the foundation on which treatment ideas are built. Thus, being a diagnostician is an inextricable part of being a clinical psychologist.

Diagnostic awareness of mental conditions was present in the Stone Age and has continued through the centuries and in virtually every society and culture (Menninger, 1944). In describing the history of "mental healing," Bromberg (1975) identifies a 7,000-year-old framework that was "influenced indirectly, and sometimes directly, by political philosophies, religions and neo-religions, mythologies and folklore, science and theories of ego function, as well as economic and cultural realignments" (p. 1). Hippocrates classified mental disorders into mania, melancholia, and phrenitis. Plato studied a variety of mental cases, including those of individuals who committed criminal acts. Aristotle questioned whether mental disorders were caused by psychological factors (e.g., frustration and conflict) and tended to view them as being a reflection of underlying organic difficulties (Coleman, 1956). Through the Middle Ages, demonology, mass madness, and witchcraft prefaced a more modern awareness of mental illness.

In 1400, Bethlem Royal Hospital (Bedlam) was established (the citizenry could come and view the patients for a penny a look), and other countries followed suit. Hospitals were opened in Mexico in 1566, France in 1641, Russia in 1764, Austria in 1784.

In the United States, Benjamin Franklin guided the development of the Pennsylvania Hospital, Philadelphia (opened in 1756 with a few cells or wards for the mentally ill). In 1773, Williamsburg, Virginia was the site of the first United States hospital exclusively for mental patients (Coleman, 1956). As indicated earlier, diagnostic awareness is nothing new.

In clinical psychology, the term *nosology* refers to the naming and classification of human diseases or conditions. Throughout the evolution of mental health services, there has been a press to have a system for classifying the mental disorder or condition.

One of the first ancestors of modern-day psychiatric nosology was Emil Kraepelin (1856–1926), a German psychiatrist who conceptualized symptoms into clusters or syndromes, using the labels manic-depressive illness and dementia praecox. Eugene Bleuler, another German psychiatrist, later changed the name of the dementia praecox syndrome to schizophrenia. The Kraepelin–Bleuler efforts were the onset of a series of nosological systems embraced by diagnosis.

In dissecting the meaning of diagnosis, it should be underscored that it is more than nosology: "a diagnostic point of view fosters a way of approaching clinical issues and conceptualizing them" (Shevrin and Shectman, 1973, p. 467). Nosology provides terms or labels that are connected to carefully thought out diagnostic syndromes, categories, or classifications. Diagnosis does involve use of these terms or labels, but that is usually more for purposes of communication than for promoting diagnostic formulations. For example, Miller, Bergstrom, Cross, and Grube (1981) indicate that use of the American Psychiatric Association's *Diagnostic and Statistical Manual of Mental Disorders* (DSM) system seems to be a response to requirements of agencies (e.g., to have a means for keeping track of cases via a set classification system) and insurance companies (i.e., to assure, in part, that the therapy for which health insurance reimbursement is sought was predicated on a relevant diagnosis).

Diagnosis is usually viewed as being concerned about psychopathology. After all, seldom is a diagnosis formulated for anyone not seeking treatment. Diagnosis should, however, carry an awareness of health or hygiology as well. There should be an accommodation of normality along with recognizing abnormality.

Persons seeking the services of a clinical psychologist, even those needing psychotherapy, are not to be viewed as categorically "abnormal" or "mentally disturbed." An important attainment for our society is that there is no reason to be ashamed of needing therapy. Indeed, the term *mental illness* is secondary to the term *mental health*. Moreover, about 25% of the "normal" population suffers from a significant degree of emotional disturbance (Goldstein, Baker, and Jamison, 1980). Since there is a substantial amount of mental disturbance among "normals," comparisons of the test results from clients/patients with those of everyday folks do not always reveal abnormal distinctions; nonetheless, psychological testing of normal characteristics can aid in the understanding of the clinical issues (Comrey and Schiebel, 1983).

Diagnosis is a multifaceted process. Woody (1969) sets forth three requirements: "the present functioning or characteristics should be evaluated and described; possible causative factors or etiology should be posited; and a prognosis should be made and a treatment approach recommended" (p. 77). Determining the recommended treatment approach necessitates, in effect, making a probability statement about how the patient will respond to the various treatment alternatives (recognizing that the availability of resources will enter into the considerations; e.g., it may be that the patient would respond better to intensive psychotherapy, but the financial picture leads to only occasional supportive counseling being available). Beller (1962) posits six requirements for diagnosis: "observation, description, a delineation of causation or etiology, classification, prediction or prognosis, and control-modification or treatment plan" (p. 109). Arbuckle (1965) comments: "Diagnosis may be considered as the analysis of one's difficulties and the causes that have produced them. More clinically, it may be thought of as the determination of the nature, origin, precipitation, and maintenance of ineffective abnormal modes of behavior. More simply, it may be considered as the development by the counselor of a deeper and more accurate understanding and appreciation of the client" (p. 220). This latter definition of diagnosis is of interest because Arbuckle has generally been aligned with the humanistic approach to therapy, which (as discussed earlier) tends to value diagnosis a bit differently than the psychodynamic approach.

Diagnosis is dependent upon the qualities of the relationship between the diagnostician and the client: "In the diagnosis of mental disorders the diagnostician, through the *medium of a personal relationship, elicits and observes* a range of *psychological functioning* which he considers *relevant on some theoretical grounds* for understanding the disorder so that he can make a *recommendation* which stands a good chance of being *acted on as a basis for dealing with the disorder*" (Shevrin and Shectman, 1973, p. 451). Shectman (1973) goes further: "*Diagnosis can work when it is based not on labels but on establishing relationships which permit the observation of psychological functioning and in turn leads to an appreciation of a patient's internal experience and understanding of it and the drawing of proper conclusions*" (p. 524).

Diagnosis is not a permanent framework, be it for the client or for the profession. For the client, it is assumed that a diagnosis can and should change—therapeutic interventions are intended to alter emotions and behaviors and, therefore, the diagnosis should change accordingly.

For the profession, diagnosis is simply a product of professionalizations. Part of the public policy mandate for the mental health professions embraces diagnosis—just as public policy changes, so do the tenets of diagnosis. For example, the criteria for various DSM categories have been changed throughout the three editions to accommodate public attitudes (e.g., those regarding alcoholism, homosexuality, and so on). Rosenhan (1975) states: "Unlike most medical diagnoses, which can be validated in numerous ways, psychiatric diagnoses are maintained by consensus alone" (p. 464).

The foremost present-day nosological system is that of DSM-III (American Psychiatric Association, 1980). The basic purpose is to provide definitions of and criteria for psychiatric nomenclature, as would facilitate differential diagnosis (i.e., selecting a particular diagnosis for a given patient from the array of potential diagnoses). At this writing, the DSM-III-R, a revision, is due to be released in the near future.

Fulfilling the basic purpose is not an easy matter. Stagner (1948) states: "Much of science consists of a search for adequate definitions. This is necessary not merely because man is generally happier when he has a neat system for classifying ideas; increasing precision of definitions frequently results in focusing research more sharply and revealing important truths which had previously been ignored" (p. 1). When consideration is given to the numerous dimensions of diagnosis (e.g., description of present functioning, an etiological statement, and a prediction- or prognosis-oriented treatment plan, to use a three-dimensional model), it is obvious that the "search for adequate definitions" seems destined to encounter barriers. Since psychiatric nomenclature or nosology is applied with a multitude of professional inputs (e.g., the context of treatment, the type of patient, the disciplinary identity of the professional, and the theoretical orientation of the professional), there is equal surety that there will be controversy about the adequacy of any nosological system.

It should be noted that although the DSM system has suffered countless attacks on its adequacy it has weathered many a storm of controversy. Nathan and Harris (1983) have analyzed the structure for each of the three editions. They indicate that the first edition (American Psychiatric Association, 1952), known as the DSM-I, had 104 diagnoses, using the major categories of acute brain disorders (13 diagnoses); chronic brain disorders (25 diagnoses); mental deficiency (6 diagnoses); psychotic disorders (17 diagnoses); psychophysiologic autonomic and visceral disorders (10 diagnoses); psychoneurotic disorders (7 diagnoses); personality disorders (18 diagnoses), and transient situational personality disorders (8 diagnoses). They say that the second edition (American Psychiatric Association, 1968), DSM-II, had 146 diagnoses, using the major categories of mental retardation (6 diagnoses); organic brain syndrome (40 diagnoses); psychoses not attributed to physical conditions listed previously (24 diagnoses); neuroses (11 diagnoses); personality disorders and certain other nonpsychotic mental disorders (33 diagnoses); psychophysiologic disorders (10 diagnoses); special symptoms (10 diagnoses); transient situational disturbances (5 diagnoses); and behavior disorders of childhood and adolescence (7 diagnoses).

The reason for citing each major category and the number of possible diagnoses for each one is to point out the changes in terms and diagnoses over the 16-year period. Does the absence of a first-edition category from the second edition mean that the mental disorder has been cured and eliminated? Does a new second-edition category, one that was not included in the first edition, mean that a new mental disorder has developed and been recognized for the first time in history? Does the fact that the number of diagnoses within a category has changed from the DSM-I to the DSM-II (such as neurotic conditions increasing from 7 to 11 diagnoses) mean that the categorical mental disorder is decreasing or increasing in our society? The answer to each of these questions is no. The changes reflect Rosenhan's (1975) previously cited view: "psychiatric diagnoses are maintained by consensus alone" (p. 464).

Due to shifts in public attitudes, professional politics, and research advances (such as for understanding the efficacy of treatment alternatives), the DSM system has been and will continue to be altered. Frank (1975) asserts: "Yet despite the many revisions . . . , we have never seemed to find a truly satisfactory system of classification of psychopathology" (p. 5). The forthcoming DSM-III-R is reported to contain new classifications and criteria and proposed categories requiring further study.

The birth of the DSM-III (American Psychiatric Association, 1980) was intended to offer many improvements. Instead of a single diagnosis, it uses a multiaxial system to help treatment planning and outcome prediction (note: DSM-II was subjected to much criticism for offering little to treatment planning or case management). Thus, the DSM-III diagnosis addresses: Axis I, clinical syndromes and conditions not attributable to a mental disorder and that are the focus of attention or treatment; Axis II, personality disorders and specific developmental disorders; Axis III, physical disorders and conditions; Axis IV, severity of psychosocial stressors; and Axis V, highest level of adaptive functioning during the past year. The DSM-III-R reportedly revises, reorganizes, and refines the multiaxial system, including a new scale for measuring the overall level of psychopathology and functioning.

Nathan and Harris (1983) point out that DSM-III involves 216 diagnoses. The major categories and the number of diagnoses for each are as follow:

Organic Mental Disorders (58 diagnoses)
Substance Use Disorders (19 diagnoses)
Schizophrenic Disorders (5 diagnoses)
Paranoid Disorders (4 diagnoses)
Psychotic Disorders Not Elsewhere Classified (4 diagnoses)
Affective Disorders (9 diagnoses)
Anxiety Disorders (10 diagnoses)
Somatoform Disorders (5 diagnoses)
Dissociative Disorders (5 diagnoses)
Psychosexual Disorders (22 diagnoses)
Factitious Disorders (3 diagnoses)
Disorders of Impulse Control (6 diagnoses)
Adjustment Disorders (8 diagnoses)
Psychological Factors Affecting Physical Condition (1 diagnosis)
Personality Disorders (12 diagnoses)

DSM-III also has "V codes" for conditions without manifest psychiatric disorder that receive professional attention or treatment. These include: malingering, borderline intellectual functioning, adult antisocial behavior, childhood or adolescent antisocial behavior, academic problem, occupational problem, uncomplicated bereavement, noncompliance with medical treatment, phase of life problem or other life circumstance problem, marital problem, parent–child problem, other specified family circumstances, and other interpersonal problems. (Further discussion of DSM-III may be found in Chapter 7.)

In summarizing the differentiating features of DSM-III from the previous editions, Nathan and Harris (1983) identify:

(1) a marked modification of major diagnostic groupings to highlight, for the first time, the Substance Use, Gender

> Identity, and Psychosexual Disorders, the Disorders of Impulse Control, and the component syndromes of what were the Neurotic Disorders in DSM-II; (2) a dramatic expansion in the Childhood and Substance Use Disorders; (3) development of multiaxial diagnosis, designed to heighten the diagnostic utility; (4) provision for diagnosis from operational criteria—designed to increase reliability; (5) extensive field testing of the instrument prior to its publication; and (6) expansion of the textual material in the *Manual* to include discussion of issues of differential diagnosis, etiology, treatment, prognosis, and management [p. 341].

Interfacing these six differentiations pinpointed by Nathan and Harris (1983) with the previously mentioned reasons for changes in the DSM system (i.e., shifts in public attitudes, professional politics, and research–academic advances), it is possible to detect varying motives inherent to DSM-III. For example, there has been concern that DSM-III was structured, at least in part, to exclude nonmedical professionals. Schacht and Nathan (1977) suggest that DSM-III may be a promotion of psychiatry's control over the other mental health professions, as opposed to being an honorable attempt to meet the mental health needs of our society. Nathan and Harris (1983) acknowledge a psychiatric denial of this alleged motive but conclude "suspicion persists among some psychologists" (p. 309). This sort of controversy has minimal, if any, public policy benefits: "The message seems to be that the classification of emotional and behavioral disorders will receive a great deal of professional attention in the foreseeable future, but regrettably that attention may be motivated by professional self-interest (such as political and legal power to increase economic rewards to practitioners) rather than by the desire to develop a classification system that could be used for the benefit of patients" (Woody, 1980a, p. xxxvi).

While there is controversy about and criticisms of the DSM system, it is still the approach to classification and diagnosis that is most relied upon by clinical psychologists. This was confirmed by a survey of practicing psychologists conducted by Miller, Bergstrom, Cross, and Grube (1981); they conclude: "Despite the criticisms made of the DSM system

. . . the overwhelming majority of practicing psychologists continue to use it" (p. 389).

Whatever the approach to classification, including the DSM system, a realistic view must be maintained; the clinical psychologist should keep the diagnostic system subservient to the diagnostic processes. Furthermore, diagnosis should use classification in a technical–adjunctive manner, rather than classification dictating or controlling the diagnosis.

Chapter 9

Being a Diagnostician, Part II: Assessment Methods and Psychological Tests in Clinical Psychology

Mike's performance in sales and public relations had been outstanding. At the middle level of management, he had been trustworthy and tireless in his efforts for the company. The Chief Executive Officer (CEO) concluded that Mike should be rewarded with a promotion, but being prudent, she decided to give him the title "Acting Director" of a large department before finalizing the appointment. To the amazement and chagrin of all, Mike floundered hopelessly in the new role. The CEO telephoned the clinical psychologist, saying: "I just can't understand it, Mike has always done so well. He deals with clients and co-workers with qualities that I would like to possess. He has been aggressive and committed to our organization. He has seemed bright and up-to-date in his ideas. He seemed like a natural for the job of Director, but he acts totally differently. It's as if he isn't intelligent enough to handle it." When Mike came to see the clinical psychologist, he was understandably upset, but spoke logically about wanting to find out what was happening. He acknowledged that he just could not grasp the data that he had to work with all day. As it turned out, the data were all fed to him by computer. In fact, the entire department was heavily reliant upon computerized systems, and this was the first time that Mike had encountered computerization. After taking his case history, the clinical psychologist had no clear-cut clues to go on. One of the first psychological tests to be administered was the Wechsler Adult

Intelligence Scale-Revised. While Mike's overall intelligence was well above average, the pattern of the 11 subtests made the clinical psychologist suspicious of a possible neurological problem. Use of neuropsychological tests seemed to confirm the hypothesis. Retracing Mike's history resulted in his recalling, "Oh, yes, I was in an automobile accident about eight years ago. I had a pretty nasty bump on the head, but I got over it okay. I'm sorry I forgot to mention it when you asked me about injuries." The psychological assessment supported the presence of neurological damage, and Mike was referred to a neurologist for further evaluation. The psychological and neurological data were consonant—Mike had apparently suffered a closed-head injury that was restricting his ability to learn new concepts and to deal with computerized data. The CEO was helpful. She knew Mike was a valuable asset to the company, and recognized that he was in the wrong job. After talking with Mike, she tactfully channeled him to another high level position—one that capitalized on his ability to communicate well with people. In a follow-up session with the clinical psychologist, Mike seemed pleased at what he called "the brain detective work" and was happy with his success in his most recent assignment.

While the preceding chapter discussed an academically oriented framework for psychological assessment and diagnosis, this chapter is devoted to describing the assessment methods, techniques, and instruments that are employed in clinical psychology. The focus will be on the ways in which clinical data are collected, analyzed, interpreted, communicated, and transformed into clinical psychology services.

As a preface, clinical assessment has borne the brunt of much criticism because of its subjectivity. Meehl (1954) authored a much-heralded monograph titled *Clinical Versus Statistical Prediction* in which he examined the theory and method inherent to psychometric (i.e., statistical) and nonpsychometric (i.e., clinical) data sources. His views, which many behavioral scientists found to be convincing, supported the supposition that psychological test results could best be interpreted by a set of rules or an actuarial method. He asserted that interpretations dependent upon the subjective or clinical acumen of the diagnostician would be vulnerable to greater error.

Rather than review three decades of scholarly debate (which, on occasion, defensive emotions have rendered "pseudoscholarly") or make a futile excursion into an idiosyncratic opinion, suffice it to say that there is, indeed, reason to be skeptical of a clinician's subjectively derived judgments—recall the electroencephalography (EEG) reliability studies presented in the previous chapter (Woody, 1966, 1968b). Consequently, there is a mandate to objectify clinical interpretations as much as possible.

This mandate may lead to computer analyses, as is the case with personality tests. There is a trend toward computer-generated psychological reports. The motive for this trend may be economic (computer analyses are cheaper) as much as or more than being an assurance of reliability and validity.

Short of a computer analysis, the diagnostician must adhere to clear-cut criteria for judgments. For example, there should, whenever possible, be a set of criteria that are checked off to ascertain the most appropriate clinical judgment.

In an era when there is a computer on every desk, it is tempting to side with the actuarial approach. Unfortunately, this would be an affront to the public policy that has allowed the development of clinical psychology as a profession. That is, while science may be at the point where a machine can replace a human, society has not reached the stage where it will universally accept such a replacement.

Clinical psychology is one of the *human services*. The full meaning of the term is that humans are served by humans. Science and technology should be used to the optimum level, but to date this does not mean at the exclusion of the diagnostician's clinical judgment.

It is important to recognize that there is no single strategy or instrument that is adequate for any one diagnostic task. Every assessment method and every psychological test has weaknesses. For example, there will be limits to reliability and validity, and this might be evident in the wrongful use of a test. That is, there is often research to suggest that a test developed and standardized for one purpose can probably be used for another purpose (such as estimating intelligence from a single-factor perceptual test). But under most circumstances, all but the wary could be led astray if they used the test in such a way.

Clinical assessment is best performed by relying on *multiple* sources for collecting data. This would include having more than one method to assess the same quality, such as having two measures of depression to cross-validate a judgment about the presence or absence of the mood.

Not only should there be multiple sources, there should be *different* types of data-collection sources. When a computer analysis of a personality test is made, it will be reliable and as valid as the interpretations that are programmed into it. On the negative side, a computer analysis is restricted by its program—it cannot accommodate the client's idiosyncratic features. Of course a clinical psychologist can be restricted to his or her "mental program" (i.e., the fixed ideas that dominate diagnostic thinking and concept formation). The solution is to cultivate a diagnostic set that will allow the clinical psychologist to maintain reliable and valid indices, yet integrate any idiosyncratic feature of the client that deserves consideration.

Data-collection sources could include, for example, using data from standardized personality tests to formulate tentative ideas or diagnostic hypotheses that are then checked out or "tested" against the information obtained from a clinical interview and/or a life history questionnaire (a second type of data-collection source). Thus, if a personality test score reflected social introversion, yet anecdotal information from a clinical interview or from a life history questionnaire reflected social extraversion, there would be reason to inquire further as to which data source, if any, was reliable and valid on the introversion versus extraversion question.

If there is any universally accepted notion in diagnostics, it is that clinical assessments should make use of multiple psychological tests, not just a single test, no matter how powerful it may be. A battery of tests is preferred for differential diagnosis (Schafer, 1950), because it can eliminate the deficiencies of a single test. Rapaport, Gill, and Schafer (1968) point out: "The advantages of such a battery of tests are that indicators that for some reason are absent from one or several of the tests are likely to be present in others; that indicators in the different tests are likely to support and supplement each other; and that the presence of indicators in some of the tests may call attention to more subtle indicators in others which might otherwise be overlooked" (p. 48).

There is no one set of tests for an "ideal" psychological assessment battery. What constitutes the best battery will depend on numerous considerations, such as the client's needs, what resources will allow, and the diagnostician's competencies. It seems logical that a test battery should be selected for the particular case, with an allowance for improvisation (additions to or deletions from) as new considerations emerge (Lezak, 1983).

From analysis of assessment practices (Lubin, Larsen, and Matarazzo, 1984; Piotrowski and Keller, 1984) and professional experience, it would seem that the seven main dimensions of a clinical assessment should be

1. Personal History
2. Behavioral Observations
3. Intelligence
4. Academic Achievement
5. Perception
6. Neuropsychology
7. Personality

In selecting assessment methods and psychological tests to be used as examples of the seven dimensions, there has been reliance on Woody's (1980b, 1980c) encyclopedic review of clinical assessment. Moreover, Lubin et al. (1984) provide the patterns of use for specific psychological tests from 1935 to 1982, and the most used psychological tests will serve as examples for dimensions of clinical assessment.

PERSONAL HISTORY

Clinical assessment is predicated upon the client's personal history. While some humanistically oriented psychologists might allege that knowledge of the client's personal history could preordain a diagnostic impression (i.e., knowledge of certain past events could be overvalued), most clinical psychologists believe that every assessment strategy should be tailored to the particular client and that this can best be established by considering the psychosocial history. As Kleinmuntz (1982) states: "The fundamental assumption underlying the collection of case history data is that a person's present personality is part of a continuous process of development" (p. 187). Or as Sundberg (1977) indicates: "Each assessor is to some extent a historian, analyzing the meaning of the person's background for the purposes of today's decisions" (p. 85).

The personal history can be obtained in several ways. For present purposes consideration will be given to (1) record analysis; (2) use of a life history questionnaire; and (3) clinical interviewing.

Record analysis involves obtaining all relevant written materials on the client that predate the clinical psychologist's intervention. Relevance would, of course, be defined by the needs and characteristics of the particular client, but usually it requires obtaining educational, psychological, and medical records. Since such records will not be released without the client's approval, it is typically necessary for the client to sign a written release of confidential or privileged communication and to transmit it to the previous service facility or professional.

Upon receipt of these records, the clinical psychologist analyzes the documents for the purposes of (1) an understanding of the influences (positive and negative) in the client's psychological makeup; (2) identifying any special considerations; (3) evaluating the findings of other assessment data sources; (4) weighing the efficacy of past interventions (i.e., how successful or unsuccessful they have been); and (5) formulating a psychodiagnostic preface for the client that will allow subsequent assessment strategies and other interventions to be optimally beneficial and efficient.

Since the client's records may contain assessment data quite similar in nature to what the clinical psychologist will collect, the selection of strategies or psychological tests for the present evaluation can be based, in part, on omissions in the psychosocial data. Eventually, there can be a comparison of the earlier data with the contemporary data. Thus, the records can create a psychosocial profile that will assist in instant assessment and that can serve as a baseline for interpreting the present findings.

Records vary considerably in quality. It is often impossible to know the reliability or validity of a comment in a record. Thus, any record analysis is limited to tentative impressions, but they can then be cross-checked by other data sources.

To acquire an up-to-date factual picture, a life history questionnaire may be used. This is usually composed of a set of questions developed by the individual clinical psychologist that covers what is regarded as being essential information.

Generally the questions cover factual matters: the client's name, address, telephone number, employer, social security number, health insurance carrier, spouse's name, names and ages of children, other persons in the household, and so on. Also, it is likely that there will be questions about educational, employment, marital, and health histories. From this point on, the questions will be tailored according to three considerations: (1) the theory espoused by the clinical psychologist (e.g., a clinical psychologist who is a behaviorist would pose questions that would reveal reinforcement contingencies, whereas one who is psychodynamically oriented would pose questions that would reveal emotional conflicts and ego defense mechanisms); (2) the context in which the client is being seen (e.g., a sexual dysfunction clinic would make use of questions about health, marital, and sexual behavior, whereas a vocational counseling center would make use of questions about work, education, training, aptitudes, and interests); and (3) the special needs of the client (e.g., there could be alternative questionnaires, with one being for clients seeking individual therapy and another being used for those coming for family therapy).

The life history questionnaire is usually a document that is either mailed to the client prior to the first appointment or that is completed in the waiting room upon his or her first arrival. A secretary or psychological assistant may oversee the answers. For example, if the client has limited ability to read or write, the questions may be asked and the client's answers written down by the secretary or psychological assistant. In these instances, the life history questionnaire has become, in a sense, a structured interview.

To return to the issue of reliability and validity for the

life history questionnaire (and this also has relevance to clinical interviewing), it should be underscored that any inferences based on these data sources should be regarded as tentative. Studies reveal that there are numerous errors in personal history information given by clients and their family members; often the incorrect information is given in the belief that it is true, but sometimes the error is a result of psychological reasons (e.g., conscious or unconscious dissembling, paranoid exaggeration, and so on) (Kleinmuntz, 1982).

Clinical interviewing is a continuation of the acquisition of life history data, but it is also more. The first contact between the clinical psychologist and the client may, in fact, be the most significant influence on the entire therapeutic formulation, for it is at this time that both parties create a lasting impression of each other. While there will surely be changes in these mutual perceptions as the relationship evolves, the first impression is of crucial importance. Consequently, the clinical psychologist is careful to use the first session to, among other things, foster "facilitative conditions," those qualities in the relationship that will maximize rapport and communication between the two of them, as well as promote psychological growth for the client:

> Facilitative dimensions in communication are those behaviors whereby a message is sent from one person (or speaker) to another person (or listener). Successful communication is facilitated by speakers through *owning of feeling* (identifying and disclosing their reactions to themselves and others), *commitment to change* (resolving to work at maintaining and improving communication), *differentiation of stimuli* (identifying and discriminating between various sources of affect and anxiety and the corresponding reactions they stimulate), and *internalization* (immediate awareness of their actions and feelings, with appropriate recognition of the effects and impact of their behaviors). Listeners facilitate communication through *empathic understanding* (responding clearly and directly to the speaker so as to demonstrate hearing and understanding of what the speaker is saying), *concreteness* (responding so as to aid speakers in identifying and

> discussing their most relevant concerns), *genuineness* (demonstrating spontaneous and congruent reactions in a constructive manner), *respect* (the communication of regard and caring for the speaker's worth as a person), *confrontation* (constructively confronting the speaker with inconsistencies or conflicts which the listener experiences in the interaction), and *immediacy* (the expression of an awareness of dynamics between speaker and listener at any point in the relationship) [Schauble, 1980, pp. 1035–1036].

These facilitative conditions, therefore, accomplish both the collection of data for clinical assessment purposes *and* therapeutic growth for the client from the first contact with the clinical psychologist.

The first clinical interview is commonly referred to as *the intake*. The term connotes that the client is being taken into the clinical fold. From that initial point on, there is a professional responsibility to the client.

The structure of the clinical interview can vary greatly; essentially for the three reasons stated earlier as the bases for the contents of the life history questionnaire (namely the theoretical orientation of the clinical psychologist, the context of the services, and the needs of the client).

A standardized or structured interview follows the same format (i.e., the same general questions are used) with every client. While this may yield a lot of information (of which some could be quantified by the interviewer), it is rather rigid, may foster a interrogation-type of communication, and does not accommodate individual differences between clients.

The unstructured interview "goes with the flow." While certain general topics will likely be covered with every client, the specific questions and their sequence will be different with each client.

Is either the standardized or unstructured interview superior to the other? Kleinmuntz (1982) believes that: "In summary, the advantages and disadvantages of each form of interview . . . are about equal" (p. 180).

As might be inferred, there are different categories of information that may be obtained by clinical interviewing.

For general clinical purposes, these would include (but not necessarily be limited to): identifying data; reason for coming; present situation; family constellation; early recollections; birth and development; health; education and training; work record; recreation and interests; sexual development; marital and family data; self-description; choices and turning points in life; views of the future; and any further material (Sundberg, 1977).

Covering these categories adequately can require varying lengths of time, though Sundberg (1977) points out that "with a talkative adult it could easily take two or three hours" (p. 98). This would be to simply give superficial facts—exploration of the issues, which would mean a clear-cut entry into therapy, would likely take much longer. Further, even the "intake" is not limited to a single session, there can be as many interview sessions as are needed for diagnostic purposes, and diagnosis and treatment blend together in clinical interviewing.

The father of clinical interviewing is Harry Stack Sullivan, a psychiatrist, psychoanalyst, and founder of the Washington School of Psychiatry. The crux of Sullivan's (1954) approach is that the psychiatric interview contains the essential characteristics and movements of prolonged therapy. As Houck and Hansen (1972) put it: "The diagnostic interview as seen by Sullivan is in essence a therapeutic interview" (p. 125).

Sullivan emphasizes the relationship between the interviewer and the client. Consequently, his approach can be considered to presage the facilitative conditions (Schauble, 1980) which were discussed earlier, and can be aligned with the unstructured form:

> It is the interpersonal events and the pattern of their course which generate the data of the interview; that is, the interviewer experiences the ways in which the interpersonal events follow each other, what seeming relationships they have to one another, what striking inconsistencies occur, and so on. Thus the data of the interview may come, not so much from the answers to questions, but from the timing and stress of what was said, the slight misunderstandings here and there, the

> occasions when the interviewee got off the subject, perhaps volunteering very important facts which had not been asked for, and so on [Sullivan, 1954, p. 54].

The foregoing does not mean that the interview is not purposeful. On the contrary: "In other words, the interviewer is quite clearly aware of the type of significant data that he may reasonably expect in different phases of the interview; he takes steps to secure these data; he validates, or marks for subsequent validation, anything which seems needlessly indefinite or improbable; and he notes most carefully any occasion when material reasonably to be expected *has not* come forth" (Sullivan, 1954, p. 55).

Sullivan conceptualizes the interview into four stages. Stage I is the formal inception, wherein there is an exchange of preliminary information, such as would be needed for defining the situation and problems (but no interpretations are given). Stage II is the reconnaissance, a survey of factors that contribute (positively or negatively) to the client's psychosocial condition (with a focus on problems); tentative formulations about therapy are made. Stage III is the detailed inquiry, where an interpersonal data analysis is made; impressions are validated. Stage IV is the termination stage, and "the therapist makes a clear, explicit statement of the possibility for therapy and the procedure to be used, including the purposes of the particular procedures and the possibility for progress in therapy" (Houck and Hansen, 1972, p. 129); the statement should be supportive, with an avoidance of negativism.

Sullivan's approach lends itself nicely to the definitions of diagnosis discussed in the preceding chapter. It certainly can provide data that will be useful in clinical assessment, for example, through complementing the results of psychological testing, and it ushers in a therapeutic framework at an early, critical point in the client's contact with professionals.

The Sullivanian interview, with the necessary termination statement, has contributed to the popularity of the "case conference" in interdisciplinary settings (of course, there are other reasons for the case conference as well). In the case conference, intake data collected by, for example, a clinical social worker will be presented to an interdisciplinary mental health team. The team will pool diagnostic and treatment ideas. Usually a senior clinician, such as a clinical psychologist or psychiatrist, coordinates or supervises the decision making.

There is also a time-honored allegiance to a mental status examination. For practical purposes, this may be viewed as a model for a medically oriented diagnosis of a client's psychiatric condition. Kleinmuntz (1982) identifies six dimensions for the mental status interview or examination: (1) general appearance, attitude, and behavior; (2) discourse (manner of speaking); (3) mood and affective fluctuations; (4) sensorium and intellect (orientation to place, person, and time; memory; mental abilities); (5) mental content and specific preoccupations (thoughts, obsessions, delusions, hallucinations); and (6) insight (e.g., regarding the need for treatment). The mental status interview or examination is supposed to provide a clear-cut statement, according to the six dimensions, of the client's psychiatric status, that would support a DSM-type diagnostic classification.

BEHAVIORAL OBSERVATIONS

As a clinical assessment method, behavioral observations require that there be a scientifically based plan for the monitoring, recording, analysis, and interpretation of a client's behavior. This plan may be informal to some extent, but to qualify as an assessment method there must be a certain degree of academic formality.

In many ways, the data gleaned from behavioral observations will be comparable to that gained through clinical interviewing. The data are anecdotal or episodic and reveal only what the client is willing and/or able to communicate to the clinical psychologist. Making use of these data is dependent upon an inference that the sampling is a reliable and valid reflection of the client's true psychosocial state. The reliability and validity problems that plague data from clinical interviewing also plague data from behavioral observations.

When doing behavioral observations, the clinical psychologist is an "observer." In order to have access to the most usable behavioral sample, the observer may have to participate in the activity. Thus the question arises as to whether the observer's presence or participation leads to different client behavior than if the observer were able to sample the client's behavior unobtrusively (i.e., without the client's knowing that a behavioral observation was being made. This is sometimes true and sometimes not. The observer's presence may be partially accountable for the behavior, but it will be difficult or impossible to estimate how much influence observer participation produced.

Observation can be either direct or indirect. Direct observation requires having firsthand access to the client's behavior, whereas indirect observation relies on secondhand accounts, such as questionnaires (perhaps completed by the client, i.e., self-reports, or by some other person, say a family member or teacher, who is familiar with the client's behavior).

The observational framework can be either naturalistic or controlled. Naturalistic observation is conducted in the client's usual life sphere, such as in the home, on the job, in the classroom, and so on, whereas controlled observation relies on experiences that are contrived by the professional to trigger a kind of behavior that is of clinical interest, such as how the client behaves in a problem-solving group, an interaction with family members, a stress-provoking situation, and so on.

Before beginning a behavioral observation, the clinical psychologist must decide on a scientifically based plan for monitoring, recording, analyzing, and interpreting the client behavior that will be accessed. The initial step is to define the "target behavior"; i.e., the behavior that is of clinical interest and that motivated the clinical psychologist to implement behavioral observation in the first place.

In defining a target behavior there must be enough specificity to be able to distinguish when the behavior does or does not occur; and, of course, for interjudge reliability, it would have to be specific enough to allow multiple observers to identify the behavioral occurrence. Specificity means fulfilling the criteria of objectivity, clarity, and completeness:

> To be *objective*, the definition should refer to observable characteristics of behavior or environmental events. Def-

> initions should not refer to inner states of the individual such as aggressiveness or emotional disturbance. To be *clear*, the definition should be so unambiguous that it could be read, repeated, and paraphrased by observers. Reading the definition should provide a sufficient basis for beginning actual observations. To be *complete*, the boundary conditions of the definition must be delineated so that the responses to be included and excluded are enumerated [Kazdin, 1980, p. 71].

As is evident in this statement, the definition should counteract reliability problems, such as by avoiding emotional states that could be defined differently and promoting clear-cut behaviors.

The recording phase means noting the occurrence or amount of the discrete behavioral response. Frequency counts can be made: This requires recording the number of times that the behavior was demonstrated in a prescribed timeframe. This method of "incident sampling" is concerned with occurrence and not with the time of the selected behavior. Here there is an implied assumption that the quality of the behavior is the same, regardless of when it occurs (i.e., a behavior is a behavior), and that the timeframe will yield a sampling of the behavior that is representative of the universal occurrence of the behavior. Discrete categorizations can be made. This requires, among other options, rating the quality of a behavior (e.g., degree of application to a specified task), the alignment with a criterion (e.g., appropriate or inappropriate for the stimulus), or distinguishing one behavior from another (e.g., having a list of behaviors, and noting which do and which do not occur). The recording can also note how many of a pool of subjects behave in a certain way to a specified stimulus or reinforcing context. Interval recording uses units of time to track behavior (e.g., a time sampling). Relatedly, the amount of time that is devoted to a behavior can be a useful measure.

Selecting a behavioral sampling strategy depends, to a large extent, on the type of behavior being studied. The goal or purpose of the strategy has to be matched with the goal or purpose of the clinical assessment.

A noteworthy behavioral recording strategy, known as

Interaction Process Analysis, has been developed by Bales (1950). Without going into the methodological details, suffice it to say that a trained observer watches the interactions between people. The focus could be on how an individual client interacts with others (e.g., the client with family members), or the focus could be on how a group of clients (e.g., a psychotherapy group) interacts. The observer may be in the room with the people in question, or may observe their behavior through a one-way window. Using any one of a variety of sampling techniques (e.g., incident sampling, time sampling, etc.), as discussed previously, the examiner records interactions according to a 12-category system. Figure 9.1 clarifies the 12 categories, and points out that consideration is also given to the task area (social–emotional positive, neutral, and negative), the problematic nature of each of the 12 categories (problems of communication, evaluation, control, decision, tension reduction, or reintegration), and the thrust of each of the 12 categories (positive reactions, attempted answers, questions, or negative reactions). All of the attendant reliability and validity difficulties that are present with other behavioral sampling strategies are also present with Bales's interaction process analysis.

As for the rationale for recordation, Olmsted (1959) says: "The recording procedure of interaction process analysis rests on the assumption that the observer can judge the dominant function or meaning of an act and that in the long run the true tendencies of individual and group behavior will be portrayed with acceptable accuracy even though in any given instance the subsidiary function of the act will be lost" (p. 124).

The recorded classification of interactions leads to an interaction profile analysis: "A profile is a straightforward summary of how much an individual, or all individuals, in a group gives and receives in the various categories; it can be portrayed numerically or graphically. Inspection of group profiles can show differences between types of groups . . . " (Olmsted, 1959, p. 125). The analysis also reveals channels of communication, phase movement (where the person or the group is at a given phase of the life of the group; e.g., early in a session versus late in the session), and role relationships.

Area	Category	Item	Problem
Social–Emotional Area: Positive	A	1. Shows solidarity, raises other's status, gives help, reward	f
		2. Shows tension release, jokes, laughs, shows satisfaction	e
		3. Agrees, shows passive acceptance, understands, concurs, complies	d
Task Area: Neutral	B	4. Gives suggestion, direction, implying autonomy for other	c
		5. Gives opinion, evaluation, analysis, expresses feeling, wish	b
		6. Gives orientaiton, information, repeats, clarifies, confirms	a
	C	7. Asks for orientation, information, repetition, conformation	a
		8. Asks for opinion, evaluation, analysis, expression of feeling	b
		9. Asks for suggestion, direction, possible ways of action	c
Social–Emotional Area: Negative	D	10. Disagrees, shows passive rejection, formality, withholds help	d
		11. Shows tension, asks for help, withdraws out of field	e
		12. Shows antagonism, deflates other's status, defends or asserts self	f

Figure 9.1 Bales' system of observational categories.

Key:
- a Problems of communication
- b Problems of evaluation
- c Problems of control
- d Problems of decision
- e Problems of tension reduction
- f Problems of reintegration

- A Positive reactions
- B Attempted answers
- C Questions
- D Negative reactions

From Bales, R. F., *Interaction Process Analysis.* Reading, MA: Addision-Wesley Publishing Co., 1950, p. 9.

Bales's interaction process analysis is singled out for discussion here because: (1) it exemplifies a useful behavioral analysis strategy; (2) it has proven to be one of the more worthwhile approaches for behavioral analysis in clinical psychology; and (3) it can be applied, with a fairly limited orientation, by even the novice at behavioral observation (it is a good strategy for the student of clinical psychology to try out).

The foregoing comments underscore the need for objectification for the monitoring and recording phases. For the analysis phase, however, subjectivity reenters the clinical picture. In discussing the use of behavioral observation for the analysis of children's behavior, Palmer (1983) states:

> The analysis of such observations is often more "unstructured" than the sample. In clinical practice (as distinct from research studies), the observed behavior is seldom scored or rated in metric fashion. The fairly reliable rating scales constructed in development research studies have not been adopted in clinical use. The careful assessor who makes detailed notes may be able to detect patterns of repeated reactions or sequences of reactions in the child's behavior, however. If enough observations in a variety of situations are made, an observer may be able to demarcate recurrent themes in the child's behavior. If the assessor falls back on some intuitive global impression, the conclusions are also likely to be global and nonspecific [p. 99].

In other words, behavioral observation has numerous strategies available to it for objectifying and quantifying the data, yet the analysis is likely to be highly subjective.

As with analysis, the interpretation of behavioral observations is usually without an actuarial guideline. Consequently, the clinical acumen of the observer will determine the reliability and validity of the interpretive ideas. Presumably, the clinical psychologist will base the interpretation of behavioral observations on a scientific rationale; that is, interpretations will draw upon familiarity with the research on the correlates of a behavior. As with so many aspects of clinical assessment, however, there is, unfortunately, no quality assurance for the interpretation of behavioral observations.

The theory supported by the clinical psychologist will, of course, influence how the data from behavioral observations are transformed into services to the client. If the clinical psychologist is committed to behaviorism, the data will provide the basis for establishing reinforcement contingencies to accommodate behavioral modification. But if the clinical psychologist is committed to a psychodynamic approach, the data will be formulated into a profile of emotional dimensions.

INTELLIGENCE

The evaluation of intelligence or mental abilities was the threshold at which psychologists crossed into the realm of clinical services. Prior to the development of intelligence tests, there had been a few attempts to apply the methods of the psychological laboratory to human behavior, but true clinical psychology obtained its greatest initial impetus from intelligence testing.

There are as many definitions of "intelligence" as there are professionals dealing with the topic. From his review of the history and theories of intelligence, A. J. Edwards (1971) recommends dealing with it as a construct, and the nature of intelligence gains definition by the observable behaviors (which are prescribed by the given intelligence test that is used for measurement).

Intelligence testing began with the hallmark efforts of Alfred Binet. From 1892, when he joined the psychological laboratory at the Sorbonne in Paris until his death in 1911, Binet and his colleagues pursued the study of individual differences, particularly as measured by intelligence scales. Binet considered intelligence to encompass 10 mental functions: memory, imagery, imagination, attention, comprehension, suggestibility, aesthetic appreciation, moral sentiments, muscular force or willpower, and motor skill (A. J. Edwards, 1971).

While the mental functions delineated by Binet have been refined, renamed, and supplemented, for example by Spearman's (1904) concept of "general intelligence," the gist of these functions has continued, but now specific functions seem more defined by the test contents than by theory per se.

Binet's turn-of-the-century intelligence materials were translated for American use by Lewis M. Terman of Stanford University. In 1916, the Binet–Simon Scale was made available to American psychologists. With the 1937 Revision of the Binet–Simon Scales, the intelligence testing boom occurred: "Probably never again will a single test be as widely used as the 1937 Revision of the Binet–Simon Scales" (A. J. Edwards, 1972, p. 4).

In 1960, another version of the Stanford–Binet Intelligence Scale became available; and the norms were updated in 1972. At this writing, the Stanford–Binet IV has now become available. While this test is still in use, it has come to be viewed as being heavily weighted for verbal mental abilities, and thus is not as useful as other intelligence tests (such as the Wechsler series) for certain types of clients, especially those with limited verbal mental abilities. Yet Lubin et al. (1984) found that the Stanford–Binet is still ranked sixteenth for frequency of use among all available psychological tests.

The Stanford–Binet provides mental age measures from age 2 through superior adult (with the latter divided into three levels). The test items are structured to provide an estimate of the client's age-equivalent performance, which yields a mental age. By comparing the client's mental age to his or her chronological age, an intelligence quotient can be computed. Wilhelm Stern (1914) developed the concept of the intelligence quotient for comparing children's Binet performances. The formula for computing an intelligence quotient is: intelligence quotient = the mental age divided by the chronological age, multiplied by 100. While the computation can be made individually (using months to express the numerator and the denominator), the *Manual* (Terman and Merrill, 1960) provides tables upon which the intelligence quotient can easily be located.

At present, the most popular intelligence tests are in the Wechsler series. Without going into the history, the Wechsler series has evolved to three instruments: the Wechsler Preschool and Primary Scale of Intelligence (WPPSI) (Wechsler, 1967) is used with children between 4 and 6½ years of age; the Wechsler Intelligence Scale for Children-Revised (WISC-R) (Wechsler, 1974) is used with children between 5 years and

15 years and 11 months of age; and the Wechsler Adult Intelligence Scale-Revised (WAIS-R) (Wechsler, 1981) is used with persons 16 years of age or older.

The Wechsler tests are very similar in structure and contents (except as relevant to age). Each is based on a point-scale concept (meaning one or more points are earned by successfully answering a question or responding to a task). Items of a like nature are grouped together to form a mental ability subtest. Essentially the same set of mental abilities are estimated by the coterie of subtests. Finally, each Wechsler test yields subtest scaled scores and three intelligence quotients (a verbal scale IQ, a performance scale IQ, and a full scale IQ).

For the purposes herein, the focus will be on the WAIS-R, but as indicated in the preceding paragraph, it is similar to and thus exemplary of the two Wechsler tests for children. Intelligence quotients are classified according to Table 9.1, and Table 9.2 shows the standard deviation and percentile rank for intelligence quotients at five-point intervals.

The WAIS-R has 11 subtests. The respective name, nature, and objective for each of the subtests are as follows (Ogdon, 1982):

INFORMATION: factual questions that reveal academic achievement, and richness of environment;
DIGIT SPAN: requires repeating series of numbers (forward and backward) as a measure of immediate attention, memory, and recall (anxiety and distractibility may enter into the performance);
VOCABULARY: defining words, which is dependent upon learning ability and early educational environment (the best single measure of intelligence);
ARITHMETIC: solving arithmetic problems (without paper and pencil), requiring concentration, mental alertness, and academic achievement;
COMPREHENSION: deriving solutions to everyday problem-solving situations, as dependent upon logical reasoning and judgment;
SIMILARITIES: recognizing and expressing relationships

Table 9.1
Intelligence Classifications

IQ	Classification	Percent Included: Theoretical Normal Curve	Percent Included: Actual Sample[b]
130 and above	Very Superior	2.2	2.6
120–129	Superior	6.7	6.9
110–119	High Average[c]	16.1	16.6
90–109	Average	50.0	49.1
80–89	Low Average[c]	16.1	16.1
70–79	Borderline	6.7	6.4
69 and below	Mentally Retarded[c]	2.2	2.3

[a]Reproduced by permission from the WECHSLER ADULT INTELLIGENCE SCALE-REVISED. Copyright © 1981 by The Psychological Corporation. All rights reserved. Source adapted from WAIS-R Manual, New York, The Psychological Corporation, p. 28.
[b]The percents shown are for Full-Scale IQ, and are based on the total standardization sample (N = 1,880). The percents obtained for Verbal IQ and Performance IQ are essentially the same.
[c]The terms High Average, Low Average, and Mentally Retarded correspond to the terms Bright Normal, Dull Normal, and Mental Defective, respectively, used in the 1955 WAIS Manual.

TABLE 9.2
Relation of IQs to Deviations
from the Mean and Percentile Ranks[a]

Verbal, Performance, or Full Scale IQ	Number of SDs from the Mean	Percentile Rank	Verbal, Performance, or Full Scale IQ	Number of SDs from the Mean	Percentile Rank
145	+3	99.9	100	0 (Mean)	50
140	+2⅔	99.6	95	−⅓	37
135	+2⅓	99	90	−⅔	25
130	+2	98	85	−1	16
125	+1⅔	95	80	−1⅓	9
120	+1⅓	91	75	−1⅔	5
115	+1	84	70	−2	2
110	+⅔	75	65	−2⅓	1
105	+⅓	63	60	−2⅔	0.4
			55	−3	0.1

[a]Reproduced by permission from the WECHSLER ADULT INTELLIGENCE SCALE-REVISED. Copyright © 1981 by The Psychological Corporation. All Rights reserved. Source adapted from WAIS-R Manual, New York, The Psychological Corporation, p. 27.

between verbal stimuli, necessitating verbal concept formation and logical reasoning (an estimate of true verbal learning potential);
PICTURE COMPLETION: identifying a missing part from a picture of an object, which is a non-linguistic measure of general intelligence and involves concentration, reasoning, and attention to details;
PICTURE ARRANGEMENT: ordering pictures to make a sensible story, revealing an ability to plan, perceive cause-and-effect relationships, and social intelligence;
BLOCK DESIGN: reproducing pictorial designs with colored blocks, demanding visual–motor coordination, perceptual analysis, synthesis, and abstract reasoning;
OBJECT ASSEMBLY: fitting puzzle pieces together, bringing out visual perception and organization, sensory–motor feedback, and concentration; and
DIGIT SYMBOL: translating a symbol–number code into new learning, requiring visual–motor activity and coordination, concentration, and psychomotor speed.

Note that the first six subtests comprise the verbal scale, and the last five subtests comprise the performance scale. For each subtest, the items or tasks: (1) start easy and become more difficult; (2) earn varying amounts of points; and (3) may or may not be timed.

Interpretation of the WAIS-R or the other Wechsler tests is not restricted to the level of intelligence per se. This is, of course, a primary concern, and the contents of Tables 9.1 and 9.2 provide the framework for considering the client's level of intelligence.

An interpretation is also made of the level of each mental ability. The subtest scores are analyzed individually and comparatively. For example, subsequent assessment and intervention strategies could be tailored accordingly if scores on subtests that suggest general and/or social learning potential (e.g., Similarities, Vocabulary, Picture Completion, Picture Arangement) are significantly higher than scores on subtests that suggest verbally oriented academic achievement (e.g., Information, Arithmetic, Vocabulary). In such a case, a diagnostic hypothesis might be that the client has been an underachiever, subjected to a culturally impoverished environment, and/or thwarted in fulfilling his or her intellectual potential by some psychosocial factor (e.g., poor motivation, anxiety, low achievement need).

Consideration is also given to the scatter of the subtests. This is similar to a comparative analysis of two or more subtests, but requires considering, among other things, the extent of the variance of the subtests and the particular pattern of highs and lows created by the subtest scores. While there are many reference sources upon which a clinical psychologist can rely for guidance in this sort of profile analysis (and there is a growing number of computer programs for profile analysis), there are conflicting research-based opinions about the meaning of particular profiles. Thus, the clinical acumen of the diagnostician remains crucial. As a rule of thumb, the clinical notion is that everyone should have differences in mental abilities (i.e., stronger in one area and weaker in another), but a great deal of subtest scatter or variance can trigger a concern for barriers (cultural, mental disorder, organic) to intellectual development.

A comparison is also made of the level of verbal intelligence and performance intelligence. Again there are varying research-based opinions about what a difference in levels means. As one view, Ogdon (1982) suggests that having a verbal IQ significantly above the performance IQ is characteristic of most mental disorders (including neuroses, psychoses, and organic conditions), whereas a performance IQ significantly above the verbal IQ is found primarily amongst persons with "acting out" tendencies (including adolescent delinquents, sociopaths, persons wih poor academic achievement).

The Wechsler series has gained support for differential diagnosis. That is, while the adult Wechsler is the most popular test for intellectual assessment, research has been amassed to support that it can distinguish emotional conditions and neurological dysfunctioning (Woody, 1967, 1968a; Sattler, 1974; A. J. Edwards, 1975; Walsh, 1978; Ogdon, 1982; Lezak, 1983).

The WAIS-R is, as its name reflects, a revision. Its predecessor, the WAIS (Wechsler, 1955), had essentially the same structure, but was criticized for being outdated. There have been comparisons of the results obtained by the WAIS and the WAIS-R. The research studies indicate that the WAIS-R leads to significantly lower scores than those obtained by the WAIS (Rabourn, 1983; Smith, 1983). In fact, Lippold and Claiborn (1983) assert: "The difference found between IQ means is large enough to alter clinical decisions based on IQ scores" (p. 315); and they caution that the two tests should not be considered as producing equivalent scores.

The 11 subtests for the WAIS and/or the WAIS-R typically require from one to two hours to administer (and possibly more, depending upon the response style of the client). In the name of efficiency, efforts have been made to develop a short form. That is, researchers have investigated using only a few subtests to gain the same clinical picture as would come from all 11 of the subtests. Silverstein (1982) posits that Vocabulary and Block Design can be used for a two-subtest short form, or that Arithmetic, Vocabulary, Block Design, and Picture Arrangement can be used for a four-subtest short form.

However, as seems to be true with short forms for other tests (such as for the MMPI), even the most honorable attempts to shorten the instrument lead to sacrifices in reliability and validity. For example, Ryan, Larsen, and Prifitera (1983) found high correlations between the IQs from Silverstein's short forms and WAIS-R full-scale IQs, but concluded: "short forms should be used with caution where precise IQ measurements are required" (p. 460). Roth, Hughes, Monkowski, and Crosson (1984) applied Silverstein's short forms to patients suspected of having brain impairment, and found that they overestimated full-scale IQ (FSIQ). Roth et al. concluded: "short forms do not appear adequate for estimating the FSIQ of patients suspected of brain impairment" (p. 723).

The WAIS-R is typically viewed as the foundation upon which the psychological assessment is built. It is the most used intelligence test and the second most used psychological test (Lubin et al., 1984).

ACHIEVEMENT TESTS

Psychological assessment usually involves some estimate of educational or academic achievement. As mentioned previously, several subtests on each of the Wechsler instruments have a connection to educational achievement (e.g., the Information subtest). When the contents of the tests are linked to the generally accepted ideas about how intelligence is defined, it is not surprising that intelligence and achievement test scores have significant correlations (Henderson, Butler, and Goffeney, 1969).

Academic achievement may also reflect the diagnosis of the client. Sattler (1974) states: "Children placed in learning disability classes usually (a) have normal or above normal intellectual capacity, as indicated by an IQ above 90; (b) display academic deficiencies in one or more of reading, arithmetic, spelling, and handwriting; and (c) have difficulties, other than those noted in (b), associated with syndromes of learning disabilities, such as hyperactivity, deficits in expressive language, or attentional difficulties" (p. 332). Woody (1968a) compared the mental abilities and achievement scores of well-behaved and behavioral problem boys (matched groups), and found that the well-behaved boys scored significantly higher than the behavioral problem boys in both reading and arithmetic achievement (the two groups were also significantly different on 7 of 11 Wechsler subtests). Virtually any emotional or neurological condition could impact upon academic achievement, and thus, while it does not make a differential diagnosis per se, it should be evaluated.

There are many achievement tests available to clinical psychologists, but none can be considered as being in a most favored position. Depending on the nature and purpose of the clinical assessment, it is likely that measures of reading (word recognition and/or comprehension), arithmetic, and spelling would be useful.

It is important to recognize that academic achievement is not the end goal. Our society is highly oriented toward achievement, and the achievement motive is powerful in one's personality structure—but there is more to life. Noted intelligence theorist George D. Stoddard (1943) commented: "Knowledge indiscriminately gathered in for its own sake has no place in our concept of intelligence-at-work, nor is it . . . to be highly regarded as a preparation for life" (p. 432). Also, Albert Einstein (1936) stated: "The development of general ability for independent thinking and judgment should always be placed foremost, not the acquisition of special knowledge" (p. 47). In other words, achievement is necessary for the welfare of both the individual and society, but the proper perspective places it in a more diversified psychological framework. In clinical assessment, therefore, it is but one of many factors that will enter into the appraisal of the person.

PERCEPTUAL FUNCTIONING

Perceptual functioning is a dimension of intelligence, and has implications as well for personality and achievement. While a brief definition could emphasize thinking, imagination, and perception forming a continuum of perceptual functioning, perceptual functioning does not accommodate a succinct definition (Lezak, 1983).

While perception is part of a client's response to virtually any test (and the Wechsler instruments include subtests that purposely rely on perceptual functioning), the most used specialized test of perceptual functioning is the Bender-Gestalt test, which ranks as the third most used of all psychological tests (Lubin et al., 1984). Its creator, Lauretta Bender (1938), sets forth the rationale:

> The gestalt function may be defined as that function of the integrated organism whereby it responds to a given constellation of stimuli as a whole; the response itself being a constellation, or pattern, or gestalt. All integrative processes within the nervous system occur in constellations, or patterns, or gestalten. Integration occurs not by summation or subtraction or association but by differentiation, or by increasing or decreasing the internal complexity of the pattern in its setting. It appears that an integrated organism never responds in any other way. The whole setting of the stimulus and the whole integrative state of the organism determine the pattern of the response [pp. 3–4].

In order to attain a measure of perceptual functioning, the Bender-Gestalt test consists of nine designs, and the client is asked to draw them.

The manner in which the designs are reproduced allows for clinical impressions. There are numerous factors that are considered by the clinical psychologist, including modifications in size (e.g., expanding or reducing the drawings from the size depicted on the standardized cards); the arrangement of the designs (e.g., rigid, methodical, confused, collisions, logical); unusual modes of reproduction (e.g., angulation changes, circles or dots modified, closure difficulties, overlapping, perseveration, reversals, sloping deviations, and so on) (Ogdon, 1982). For a few interpretive examples, angulation changes, perseveration, reversals, rotations, and destruction of a design's configuration might be suggestive of organicity, whereas closure difficulty, circles or dots modified, overlapping, sketching, and expansion or reduction in size might be suggestive of emotional disturbances (Ogdon, 1982).

The origination of the Bender–Gestalt test was predicated on neurological functioning, and it is still used in conjunction with neuropsychological assessment. Rightly or wrongly, it has been extended to nonneurological issues as well. Hutt and Briskin (1960) capture the reasoning: "Mature, healthy perception, according to the Gestalt school, consists of the integration of a triad of factors: (1) the innate tendency of organisms to organize perceptual data as it is affected by (2) temporal factors and (3) maturational level. It tends to follow that any other factors, emotional, toxic, organic or traumatic, that affect these perceptual processes would also be reflected in some way in the patient's response (verbal or written) to his perceptual experience" (p. 9). Consequently, Hutt and Briskin offer guidelines for using the Bender-Gestalt test for other than neurological matters (see also Hutt, 1980). Piotrowski and Keller (1984) found that the Bender-Gestalt test was the fifth most endorsed projective personality test used in the training of clinical psychology candidates.

Despite its professional popularity, there has been much criticism of the Bender-Gestalt test. Too often, no systematic scoring system is used (even though there are several scoring systems available whose developers have made reasonable efforts to establish reliability, validity, and interpretive guidelines). Too often, a clinical judgment is based on the Bender-Gestalt test results in isolation, as opposed to being part of a comprehensive psychological test battery.

After critiquing the studies of the use of the Bender-Gestalt test as a singular measure of neurological functioning, Bigler and Ehrfurth (1981) conclude the following about the instrument (which they refer to as the BVMG, meaning the Bender Visual Motor Gestalt): "Because of its simplicity, short administrative time, and initial studies of its success, the BVMG rapidly became the revered test for establishing organicity" (p. 562) and that "continued misinterpretation of much of the data on the BVMG has taken place" (p. 563); and there is a "high rate of false negatives yielded by the BVMG and other single tests of organicity . . ." (p. 567), and consequently, "The use of Bender-Gestalt as the only measure to assess organic status should not continue" (p. 568).

In point of fact, experience supports that it is not necessarily the use of the single test per se that leads to false positives (i.e., judging a client to possess a clinical condition, such as organicity, when, in fact, he or she does not possess the clinical condition). Rather, it is the clinical psychologist's failure to apply a standardized system for administration, scoring, analysis, and interpretation, whether the instrument be for perceptual functioning or personality, and so on.

NEUROPSYCHOLOGY

Only a few short years ago, a work of this sort would not have included material on neuropsychology. While certain tests, such as the various Wechsler intelligence scales and those that tap into perception, were interpreted for neurological implications, the prevailing view was that the clinical psychologist should studiously avoid direct commentary on neurological functioning—to do otherwise would be to risk an inappropriate excursion into the realm of medicine, namely the practice of neurology.

Care must still be maintained to avoid going beyond the practice of psychology, but it is now generally accepted (including by medical practitioners) that clinical neuropsychology is an appropriate service for clinical psychologists to render. It is recognized that clinical neuropsychology can make a substantial contribution to the practice of medicine in general, and in particular to the practice of neurology; in other words, the neuropsychologist and the physician (such as a neurologist) engage in teamwork.

Clinical neuropsychology is devoted to the psychological assessment of brain-related behavior. Luria (1970) sets forth the fundamental premise of clinical neuropsychology: "First by pinpointing the brain lesion responsible for specific behavior disorders we hope to develop a means of early diagnosis and precise location of brain injuries. . . . Second, neuropsychological investigation should provide us with a factor analysis that will lead to better understanding of the components of complex psychological functions for which the operations of the different parts of the brain are responsible" (p. 66). The assessment challenge becomes: "(1) the presence or absence of neurologically based cerebral impairment, and (2) the lateralization and localization of the lesion" (Walsh, 1978, p. 285).

The clinical neuropsychologist can offer far more than diagnostic test information. While assessment is likely to be ever present, Lezak (1983) points out that there are three basic purposes of neuropsychology: "diagnosis, patient care—including questions about treatment and planning, and research" (p. 8). To exemplify the connection between clinical neuropsychology and treatment, consider the following from Walsh (1978):

> Neuropsychological assessment also provides an important method of evaluating various forms of treatment such as neurosurgical procedures and drug therapy. The neurosurgical procedures include resections for tumour and epilepsy, the insertion of shunts in cases of so-called normal pressure hydrocephalus, and the special procedures loosely referred to as psychosurgery. Assessment is also valuable in checking progress after vascular surgery such as endarterectomy for stenosis of the vessesls [sic] supplying the cerebrum [p. 285].

As is evident in this quote, the clinical psychologist will be required to have training that may or may not be part of the traditional curriculum.

The concept of treatment extends into therapy and rehabilitation, and here again the clinical neuropsychologist can play a critical role:

> Rehabilitation of closed head trauma patients is best accomplished when the interdisciplinary team approach is used to provide for the wide variety of behaviors and disabilities exhibited by this population. When possible, team members should routinely include representatives from psychiatry, neurology, speech–language pathology, psychology, physical therapy, occupational therapy, nursing, social service, vocational rehabilitation, therapeutic recreation, medical and other consultants as indicated, and family members or significant persons in the patient's life [Adamovich, Henderson, and Auerbach, 1985, p. 4].

It seems well accepted by the health care professions that the patient with neurological difficulties will usually require rehabilitation services of some form, that the multidisciplinary model of service delivery is the most logical, and that clinical neuropsychology is capable of making a critical contribution to the rehabilitation program, whether it be through assessment, consultation, research, or therapy–counseling (Ylvisaker, 1985).

This is not the place for a detailed discussion of brain-related behavior or the conditions associated with neurological damage or dysfunctioning, but the key dimensions can be recognized. Lezak (1983) states: "Behavior may be conceptualized in terms of three functional systems: (1) *intellect*, which is the information-handling aspect of behavior; (2) *emotionality*, which concerns feelings and motivation; and (3) *control*, which has to do with how behavior is expressed" (p. 18). All three of these systems are within the professional purview of clinical neuropsychology.

Scholarly debate continues as to whether or not psychological tests can reliably and validly measure brain functioning. To counter the critics, neuropsychologists have moved toward statistical documentation of the "hit rates"; that is, how well neuropsychological test results predict a particular brain condition. For example, Golden, Hammeke, and Purisch (1980) cite cross-validation studies (e.g., comparing the test data of brain injured patients with normal-control subjects) for the Luria-Nebraska Neuropsychological Battery (LNNB), and they compared the data from the LNNB with "such medical and laboratory data as the CAT scan, EEG, angiogram, pneumoencephalogram, skull x-rays, neurological history, and/or surgery, according to the patient's condition" (p. 4). While there have been many studies on the reliability and validity of the LNNB and each study has yielded unique results, the general posture taken because of the research is: "hit rates ranging from 62 to 80% for the brain-injured group and from 72 to 98% for the control group" (p. 8).

Some neuropsychologists believe that the best approach is to select numerous single-factor tests to create a battery of instruments designed especially for a particular patient (Lezak, 1983). Other neuropsychologists maintain that reliability and validity are enhanced by having a specific battery of tests designed for brain-related behavior and using the same battery with all relevant patients, thereby allowing the clinical neuropsychologist to build up a common frame of reference for diagnosis, treatment, and rehabilitation.

While there are numerous standardized neurological test batteries (Lezak, 1983), the two foremost batteries are the Halstead-Reitan Battery (Halstead, 1947; Reitan and Davison, 1974) and the previously mentioned LNNB. Without going into all of the subtests within each of the batteries, suffice it to say that each battery consists of a collection of tests that is believed to measure the important facets of brain functioning. The names of the LNNB scales are the most revealing of the scope of measurement: motor, rhythm, tactile, visual, receptive speech, expressive speech, writing, reading, arithmetic, memory, intellectual processes, pathognomonic (items highly indicative of brain damage), left hemisphere, and right hemisphere (the latter two scales are constructed to estimate lateralization of damage).

Neuropsychological tests go beyond assessment of a brain injured person, such as being useful for evaluating the development of children (Townes, Trupin, Martin, and Goldstein, 1980); health conditions, such as asthma (Dunleavy and Baade, 1980); the effects of aging (Bak and Greene, 1980); propensities toward violence (Bryant, Scott, Golden, and Tori,

1984); and a host of other human qualities that are essential to clinical assessment.

Neuropsychology requires that the clinical psychologist have an advanced academic understanding of physiological processes and specialized skills. Since clinical neuropsychology is relatively new, training opportunities in this area are still emerging. Golden and Kuperman (1980a) found that at least 30% of APA-approved clinical psychology training programs offer enough training in neuropsychology to accommodate specialization. Golden and Kuperman (1980b) provide a list of neuropsychology internships. They conclude: "However, most students do not get adequate training to enable them to claim a specialty in neuropsychology" (p. 917). While the latter may still be true, it should be noted that their survey was conducted in 1978, and it is probable that far more training opportunities have been created since that time.

It seems likely that today's clinical psychology students will be expected to have a greater preparation in neuropsychology than did earlier generations. Indeed, the American Board of Professional Psychology (ABPP) is now conducting examinations for the status of Diplomate in Clinical Neuropsychology.

PERSONALITY

As with the term *intelligence* and so many other psychological terms, *personality* has been defined in all sorts of ways. The theoretical orientation of the clinical psychologist (such as psychoanalytic, behavioral, or humanistic) will have a major influence on the definition endorsed, but even within those major rubrics, there are many variations on an orientational theme. Hall and Lindzey (1957) say: "It is our conviction that *no substantive definition of personality can be applied with any generality*" (p. 9); and they add: "Thus, we submit that *personality is defined by the particular empirical concepts which are a part of the theory of personality employed by the observer*" (p. 9).

While the foregoing seems accurate from an academic perspective, it is necessary to establish a practical framework. For present purposes, Maddi (1980) offers a succinct definition:

"*Personality is a stable set of characteristics and tendencies that determine those commonalities and differences in the psychological behavior (thoughts, feelings, and actions) of people that have continuity in time and that may not be easily understood as the sole result of the social and biological pressures of the moment*" (p. 10). Placing personality into clinical assessment, Beck (1981) states:

> The task before a psychology of personality is to delineate the forces, the constancies (hypothetical constructs, to be sure), that are the sources of the observables. A corollary from the hypotheses of the constancies is that they enable us to predict the behavior of others. This inheres in the sheer fact that they are constants. In our transactions with one another we are, in fact, always predicting. We are pretty sure regarding what a person is likely to do, sure that what he does today he will do tomorrow, and on another morrow. These are the judgments of everyday life and its wisdoms [p. 24].

Notice how Beck's tracking of personality into clinical assessment is consonant with the definition of diagnosis set forth in the preceding chapter, especially as is relevant to transforming the appraisal of the past (etiology) and present functioning into a prognostication or prediction.

There are (literally) thousands of personality tests. Recall the comments in the preceding chapter about how many "tests" fail to reach acceptable standards. Partly because of the nebulous nature of and diverse theories for personality, the problem is seemingly more pronounced for the clinical assessment of personality than for certain other areas, such as achievement, aptitudes, and vocational interests.

For simplicity, personality assessment tests can be dichotomized as being objective or projective (Graham, 1977; Piotrowski and Keller, 1984). In this context, "objective" does not convey anything about reliability and validity, because both objective and projective instruments lay claim to those qualities.

An objective personality test: (1) has specific stimulus items (such as questions about the client); (2) requires the client to give a discrete response (such as true or false, or a rating, say on a 1 to 5 scale, or to choose which of X number of descriptors is preferred most and which is preferred least)—that is, the objectivity comes, in part, from the form of the response; (3) obtains a codification (usually in writing) of the client's responses (such as a self-report); (4) yields numerical measurements; and (5) has a standardization (such as norms to assist in the interpretation).

A projective personality test relies on the psychoanalytic principle of projection. For now, the term *projection* refers to "a method of studying personality by confronting the subject with a situation to which he will respond according to what the situation means to him and how he feels when so responding" (Frank, 1948, p. 46). This might, for instance, involve having the client look at a picture, and let his or her imagination produce a story. The story will then be analyzed by the clinical psychologist as a product of the client's personality structure.

The selection of personality assessment tests for illustrative purposes will rely on the survey by Lubin et al. (1984), which found that the top three personality tests (in order of frequency of usage) were: (1) the MMPI; (2) the Rorschach Inkblots Method; and (3) the TAT.

The Minnesota Multiphasic Personality Inventory (MMPI)

The MMPI (Hathaway and McKinley, 1967), is an objective instrument. It is comprised of 566 true or false items, with the client responding to each item to reflect how it does or does not apply to him. From a larger pool of statements and a series of standardization studies on both normals and clinical patients, selected items were used to form subtests or scales by criterion keying (meaning that a given clinical scale, say Scale 2 = Depression, was formed by the responses of patients with a particular diagnosis, such as a psychiatric diagnosis of depression).

Just as the Wechsler subtests create a mental abilities profile, the MMPI scales form a personality profile. The patterning of the scales (i.e., the profile) is the basis for interpretation, not just the high or low level of a score for an individual scale.

A unique feature of the MMPI is that there are four validity scales that are devoted to detecting unusual or deviant approaches to responding. The "Cannot Say" scale is the total number of omitted items (or those that were marked both true and false), and a high number of these responses could raise doubts about whether the profile can accommodate a meaningful interpretation. The "L" or "Lie" scale can reveal whether the client is trying to answer in a manner that will be overly favorable for him or her (i.e., faking good), whereas the "F" scale can be used to identify the client who does not answer with a normal test-taking attitude (as might invalidate the scale, such as by claiming to be more troubled than is actually true, i.e., faking bad). Finally, the "K" scale reveals defensiveness, such as denial of symptoms.

While an elevation on any one of these validity scales has potential clinical relevance, the patterning (particularly of the L, F, and K) can yield more refined information about the client's test-taking attitude. Extensive research has been conducted on the validity scales to allow the diagnostician scientifically based guidelines for interpretation.

Before reviewing the clinical scales, the means for interpreting the MMPI should be noted. There are essentially three approaches.

Clinical Judgment. If the clinical psychologist has extensive experience with the MMPI and with clinical assessment, he can make the interpretation based on clinical acumen. However, as discussed in the preceding chapter, this can lead to problems in reliability of judgments, and the criteria for a given diagnosis, even if reliably applied, could have dubious validity.

Computer Analysis. If the clinical psychologist has very little experience with MMPI or with clinical assessment, he can transmit the client's responses for a computerized interpretation. These services are available from a variety of sources. This option affords the expertise of an eminent MMPI specialist, whose interpretations were used in the computer programming. The advantage is that the interpretive processes will have 100% reliability and proven validity. The disadvantage is that the idiosyncratic nature of the client's case history cannot be incorporated into the computer's interpretation.

Reference to Cookbooks. The most common approach is for the clinical psychologist to rely upon a "cookbook." There are numerous references, such as those offered by Gilberstadt and Duker (1965), Lachar (1974), and Graham (1977).

Minnesota Multiphasic Personality Inventory "cookbooks" are the offspring of the movement to use actuarial methods in clinical assessment (Meehl, 1954, 1956). This type of reference provides clinical summaries for combinations of elevated clinical scales. The clinical psychologist simply: (1) notes the configuration of the validity scales (and the cookbook will have summaries for alternative validity scale patterns); (2) determines the clinical scales that are elevated (usually any T-score above 70, i.e., two standard deviations above the mean or about at the 97.7 percentile, is considered to be significant clinically); and (3) looks up combinations of two and/or three elevated scales in one of the authoritative references or "cookbooks." Each of these sources provides a clinical description for each of the clinical scales individually; but it is clear that a more refined clinical picture can be obtained by combining scales into two- or three-scale patterns.

At first blush, the use of a cookbook might seem unprofessional, but such is not the case. There are so many possible two- or three-scale combinations that the clinical psychologist would be taxed if he had to memorize all the nuances. Moreover, the clinical summaries in the cookbooks are based on amalgamations of research, thereby affording optimal reliability and validity.

There are 10 basic MMPI clinical scales (number 1 through 0). The scales and brief symptomatic definitions, derived from Graham (1977), are as follows:

- Scale 1 (Hypochondriasis): "preoccupation with the body and concomitant fears of illness and disease" (p. 34).
- Scale 2 (Depression): "The primary characteristics of symptomatic depression are poor morale, lack of hope in the future, and a general dissatisfaction with one's own life situation" (p. 36).

- Scale 3 (Hysteria): "involuntary psychogenic loss or disorder of function" (p. 38).
- Scale 4 (Psychopathic Deviate): "such delinquent acts as lying, stealing, sexual promiscuity, excessive drinking, and the like" (p. 41).
- Scale 5 (Masculinity–Femininity): gender-based preferences relevant to "interests in work, hobbies and pastimes, worries, fears, and sensitivities, social activities, religious preferences, and family relationships" (p. 45).
- Scale 6 (Paranoia): "ideas of reference, feelings of persecution, grandiose self-concepts, suspiciousness, excessive sensitivity, and rigid opinions and attitudes" (p. 48).
- Scale 7 (Psychasthenia): "thinking characterized by excessive doubts, compulsions, obsessions, and unreasonable fears" (p. 52).
- Scale 8 (Schizophrenia): "disturbances of thinking, mood, and behavior. Misinterpretation of reality, delusions, and hallucinations" (p. 55).
- Scale 9 (Hypomania): "elevated mood, accelerated speech and motor activity, irritability, flights of ideas, and brief periods of depression" (p. 57).
- Scale 0 (Social Introversion): "tendencies to withdraw from social contacts and responsibilities" (p. 60).

There are also numerous supplementary scales. Dahlstrom, Welsh, and Dahlstrom (1972, 1975) offer over 450 ancillary scales, from typical clinical matters (e.g., Dominance) to specialized matters (e.g., Success in Baseball). While a certain amount of research has gone into the supplemental scales, only a few have received widespread acceptance. Most recently, the standard profile sheet has been revised to include four clinical scales in addition to the 10 previously cited clinical scales; they include: Anxiety, Repression, Ego Strength, and the MacAndrew Addiction.

To illustrate how combining MMPI scales works, consider a client with elevated scores (more than two standard deviations above the mean) on the Depression and Psychopathic Deviate Scales, that is, a 2-4 code. In a refinement beyond the symptomatic definitions for the individual scales given previously, Graham's (1977) description of the 2-4 code is

> When persons with the 24/42 code come to the attention of professionals, it usually is after they have been in trouble with the law or with their families. 24/42 individuals are impulsive and unable to delay gratification of their impulses. They have little respect for social standards and often find themselves in direct conflict with societal values. Their acting out behavior is likely to involve excessive use of alcohol, and their histories include alcoholic benders, arrests, job loss, and family discord associated with drinking [p. 68].

This is just a partial description, but it captures the essence of a "cookbook" interpretation.

Some of the reference sources provide elements of diagnosis, such as prognosis. For the 2-4 code, Lachar (1974) states: "The depression abates when escape from stress is effective or manipulations promise to be effective. While the insight these persons show may be good and their verbal protestations of resolve to do better may seem genuine, long-range prognosis for behavior change is poor. Recurrence of acting out and subsequent exaggerated guilt are common" (p. 74). He adds: "The modal diagnosis was Personality Trait Disturbance" (p. 75).

Just as efforts have been made to find short forms for the Wechsler tests, clinical psychologists have devised various short forms for the MMPI. Basically, the same advantages and disadvantages for short forms of the Wechsler tests apply to short forms of the MMPI. Butcher, Kendall, and Hoffman (1980) conclude that it is unwarranted to believe that MMPI short forms are "accurate substitutes for the standard form MMPI in predicting objective measures of psychopathology" (p. 278). Similarly, Helmes and McLaughlin (1983) compared three MMPI short forms, and decided: "the rate of correct classification by all three major short forms is insufficient for clinical use" (p. 787). From a survey of practicing clinical psychologists, Moreland and Dahlstrom (1983) found that 91 percent of the respondents did assessment, and 67 percent used the MMPI; there was limited acceptance accorded to short forms, but a positive reception for computerized interpretations and supplementary scales.

Of concern is whether the MMPI meets legal and ethical

standards; for example, whether it "overpathologizes" for black clients (Butcher, Braswell, and Raney, 1983). Pritchard and Rosenblatt (1980) found no evidence that the MMPI is racially biased. Giving consideration to socioeconomic level, presenting complaints, diagnoses, and demographic information, Butcher, Braswell, and Raney (1983) did a cross-cultural comparison of American Indian, black, and white inpatients using the MMPI, and they concluded that any differences were due to symptomatic distinctions; that is, the MMPI did not overpathologize for black patients, and "minority status alone does not account for the obtained differences between black and white psychiatric patients" (p. 593).

There has also been concern about the possibility of the MMPI items and standardization being outdated (much of the research was done in the 1940s). This concern is not supported when the MMPI is interpreted by those with proper clinical acumen. Nonetheless, it has been reported that research is underway to obtain contemporary normative data and investigate possible new items.

The MMPI is a self-report, that is, the client is asked to read questions and answer them honestly. Here is the problem: Some clients may wish to answer openly and honestly, but their personality leads them to denial or defensiveness or some other quality that produces other than a penetrating revelation of the true characteristics. Hamersma (1972) states: "Self-report inventories are highly susceptible to faking, malingering, and response sets . . ." (p. 102).

There are several types of response bias. Clients may give the socially desirable response (i.e., they say what they think the clinical psychologist wants to hear). Some clients, such as those being evaluated in a child custody dispute and those who want the clinical psychologist to believe that they are the better parent for meeting the best interests of the child, may give only (or predominantly) responses that will make them look good. Conversely, some clients, such as those being evaluated for rehabilitation benefits, may give only (or predominantly) responses that will make them appear to need services or financial support. There may also be an unrealistic commitment to respond in a certain manner (i.e., positively or negatively); this response set ignores the contents of the item.

The validity scales of the MMPI are helpful for detecting these detriments to clinical assessment, and in fact the MMPI is one of the few self-report inventories that offers any measurement of these biasing factors. A. L. Edwards (1964), the creator of a popular self-report inventory known as the Edwards Personal Preference Schedule (1954), asserts that a client's responses to an objective personality test, such as the MMPI, should be viewed as only revealing what the client is willing to endorse as acceptable, as opposed to being viewed as a realistic portrayal of the personality. Since penetrating the response bias is a goal of projective personality tests, this leads to the use of the Rorschach Inkblots Method and the TAT.

The Projection Hypothesis

Early on, projection was regarded as an ego-defense mechanism associated with paranoid and other disorders (Freud, 1911). While the term still has that meaning, its use has been expanded to describe an influence on sense perceptions (Freud, 1919); that is, how the person perceives the outer world may be influenced by the projection of personality features.

The projection principle underlies so-called projective techniques. As Symonds (1946) describes it: "In projective techniques there is the implication that as a person expresses himself in any kind of constructive or interpretive activity he is acting out inner fantasy. If he is telling a story it is believed that he projects into the characters in the story his own impulses, feelings, and thoughts" (p. 515). Or, as Frank (1948) puts it: "*The essential feature of a projective technique is that it evokes from the subject what is in various ways expressive of his private world and personality process*" (p. 47).

Lindzey (1961) states: "*A projective technique is an instrument that is considered especially sensitive to covert or unconscious aspects of behavior, it permits or encourages a wide variety of subject responses, is highly multidimensional, and it evokes unusually rich or profuse response data with a minimum of subject awareness concerning the purpose of the test*" (p. 45).

Of importance to the interpretation of projective techniques, the clinical psychologist usually avoids nomothetic ideas, while focusing on idiographic ideas. As Rabin (1968) says: "the task of the examiner–interpreter is complex, for his analysis is holistic–ideographic, and he attributes to the responses that he obtains a multidimensionality necessary for such analysis" (p. 12).

The Rorschach Inkblots Method

The Rorschach Inkblots Method is derived from studies of perception. It involves a series of 10 inkblots (selected from thousands of trial inkblots). The client is told that people see different things in the inkblots, and is asked to tell the clinical psychologist what he sees in them.

The Rorschach Inkblots Method was developed by the Swiss psychiatrist Hermann Rorschach. He was born on November 8, 1884, and he died of appendicular peritonitis at the age of 38. Perhaps (in part) because his father was a professor of drawing, Rorschach had a long-term professional interest in the drawings of patients. Pichot (1984) provides a detailed account of Rorschach's life, focusing on how the present-day inkblots came into being. In describing the method, Klopfer and Davidson (1962) state: "A basic assumption underlying the Rorschach techniques is that there is a relationship between perception and personality. The way in which an individual organizes or 'structures' the ink blots in forming his perceptions reflects fundamental aspects of his psychological functioning. Ink blots are suitable as stimuli because they are relatively ambiguous or 'unstructured,' i.e., they do not elicit particular learned responses, but permit a variety of possible responses" (p. 14). Thus, there are no "correct answers" as such.

As will be discussed shortly, there are certain factors within a client's responses to the Rorschach that lead to an impression of the client's perceptual connection to reality, but the primary interest is in the "distortions" that are unique to the client. Beck (1981) clarifies: "A person's perception, his cognitive functioning, is in instances erratic because he distorts the object. He sees it not as it is, meaning not in accordance with the experienced reality of a normative segment of the population. That is, he sees it not as it is, but as he, the patient, is. Here we enter on the problem of the whole personality as a psychological determinant" (p. 31). Obviously the projective hypothesis is applicable: "His perceptions are selected and organized in terms of his 'projective' needs, experiences, and habitual patterns of response as well as by the physical properties of the blots themselves" (Klopfer and Davidson, 1962, p. 14).

The responses given by the client are scored according to different categories or factors. The original Rorschach approach supported that the responses to inkblots could reveal basic personality tendencies only if the responses were analyzed systematically. This meant having categories that would accommodate precise identification and measurement; that is, "Accordingly, when abstracting from the complex test performance certain components for analysis, he concentrated primarily on formal categories and only secondarily on content categories" (Rickers-Ovsiankina, 1977, p. 4).

There are several alternative systems for scoring and interpreting the Rorschach, such as those by Beck (Beck, Beck, Levitt, and Molish, 1961) and Exner (1974). As might be expected, advocates for each system claim superiority. For present purposes it would be ill-advised to enter into a debate on the merits of the alternative systems. Rather, the Klopfer system will be used as an example. In it, there are five major scoring categories:

1. LOCATION: Where on the card was the concept seen?
2. DETERMINANT: How was the concept seen? What qualities of blot determined it?
3. CONTENT: What was the subject matter of the concept seen?
4. POPULARITY–ORIGINALITY, P-O: How commonly is the concept seen by other subjects? . . . Many responses are neither popular nor original. . . .
5. FORM LEVEL: How accurately is the concept seen? How closely does the concept fit the blot area used? Also, what is the degree of elaboration of the concept? [Klopfer and Davidson, 1962, pp. 48–49].

The use of a scoring system, whichever one may be chosen, is intended to facilitate reliability and validity.

There is more to the analysis of a Rorschach protocol than simply totaling up the scores for a set of categories. As Phillips and Smith (1953) describe it: "Formal scoring represents only a part of the categorization of Rorschach data. The Rorschach test situation elicits far more than the scored perceptual reactions. Such things as the style with which material is developed, elaborations of percepts, and direct responses to the examiner have been shown to be related to significant extra-Rorschach behavior and these reactions too must be categorized" (p. 257). One of the foremost focal points has been the content of and/or the symbolic imagery associated with the responses: "the essential nature of the personality is reflected equally in the content, the quality, and the scoring category of a subject's response" (Miale, 1977, p. 452). This is, however, an area of great controversy, particularly because of dubious reliability and validity. Mindess (1955) asserted: "In the Rorschach literature generally, a visible confusion surrounds the problem of content analysis" (p. 248).

It would be beneficial if there were irrefutable correlations between Rorschach scores and behavior and/or mental processes, but such is not the case. There has, however, been extensive research (on some systems more than others) that provides guidelines for interpretation that overcomes the problems of reliability and validity that plague most, if not all, clinical assessment strategies. In his summary of guidelines, Ogdon (1982) indicates that a protocol that has a greater than average number of responses involving movement (e.g., a *flying* bat, or two *dancing* women) might support the following: "Introversive, thoughtful, or inhibitory characteristics in normal individuals"; "Above average intelligence and academic achievement at all ages and with many clinical as well as normal populations"; "High creativity, inventiveness or creative potential, especially in linguistic and artistic activities"; "Good ego functioning: the Reality Principle dominates with good planning ability, impulse control and the ability to tolerate frustration, positive and consistent self-orientation, minimal feelings of vulnerability or fragility, and good prognosis in therapy" (p. 23); and other hypotheses as well. Conversely, Ogdon posits that a protocol that has a subnormal number of responses with movement might support the following: "Ego weakness as found in many neurotic conditions associated with a lack of normal flexibility and resistance to change"; "Anxiety, tension or hysteria"; "Low intelligence, low mental age, and possible mental retardation" (p. 24); and other hypotheses as well.

With the number of quite divergent hypotheses that are possible from the same single Rorschach score, it is readily apparent that the interpretation is dependent upon the expertise of the clinical psychologist. That is, while the scoring system can help establish a respectable intrajudge and/or interjudge reliability, the research to date does not assure interpretive validity, even when multiple scores are used: "Direct behavioral parallels may not always exist . . ." (Klopfer and Davidson, 1962, p. 15).

A potential solution may be in the offing. Efforts are underway to create computerized interpretations for the Rorschach Inkblots Method, much like what has been done for the MMPI. It is premature, however, to give one's blessing to this approach.

The Thematic Apperception Test (TAT)

The TAT lacks the traditional properties of a psychometric test. Based on the projective hypothesis, the TAT was created by Henry A. Murray (Morgan and Murray, 1935), and was predicated on his translation of psychoanalytically oriented principles into a theory of "personology." This theory is directed at understanding the total functioning of the individual, which necessitates appraisal of the human organism and its placement in an environmental context. Murray focused on the normal personality, as opposed to the disordered one.

The TAT consists of pictures depicting, for the most part, people and scenes. While there are several possible administrative alternatives, the general approach is to ask the client to: "Tell what has led up to the event shown in the picture, describe what is happening at the moment, what the characters are feeling and thinking; and then give the outcome. Speak your thoughts as they come to your mind" (Murray, 1943, p. 3). The contents of the stories are analyzed.

As with the Rorschach, there are several alternative systems for analyzing and interpreting the client's TAT responses. Only a few of the systems provide for quantifying the responses.

To place analysis and interpretation in a nutshell, Murray (1938) supported "analyzing each successive event in a story into (a) the force or forces emanating from the hero, and (b) the force or forces emanating from the environment" (p. 6). Murray's content analysis dissects the responses for needs (provoked by internal and/or external sources); presses (environmental determinants that facilitate or impede goal-related efforts); thema (the need–press interaction); need integrate (the integration between the need and the environmental object's image-thought); unity–thema (dominant needs formed into an interrelated compound); and regnant processes (mutually dependent processes that constitute dominant configurations in the brain). Intellectual functioning, imaginative processes, family dynamics, inner adjustment, emotional reactivity, sexual adjustment, and patterning of overt behavior are just a few of the dimensions that can be obtained from an analysis of the form and content of the client's TAT protocol (Henry, 1956).

It should be noted that there have been numerous thematic apperception strategies; that is, telling stories about pictures. For example, two of the more popular ones are the Children's Apperception Test (CAT) and the Senior Apperception Technique (SAT) (Bellak, 1975); both of these strategies are similar to the TAT in rationale, structure, administration, analysis, and interpretation, but are tailored, respectively, to children and to older adults.

The Reliability and Validity of Projective Techniques

As mentioned, the TAT is not (and has not aspired to be) a psychometric test. This is also basically true for the Rorschach, albeit some scoring systems have confused matters by seeking quantifiable data and developing indices for differential diagnosis (note the complex, quantifiable Rorschach system offered by Exner, 1974). Further, all projective techniques are highly dependent on the clinical expertise of the diagnostician.

As a result, there has been much criticism of the reliability and validity of projective techniques: "Little that is encouraging can be said about projective techniques, the literature on which continues to reflect a lack of interest in the generally accepted standards of empirical validation" (Lanyon, 1984, p. 692).

It must be remembered that the interpretation of projective data is for meaning, not for a probability statement (Schwartz and Lazar, 1979). Conventional reliability methods do not find relevance with the TAT (Harrison, 1965).

There are many reasons, beyond the nature of the TAT, why this is true: (1) The pictures were not chosen to be paired or to accommodate a split-half analysis; (2) the expectation that a client receiving a clinical intervention will not remain in a fixed psychological state; (3) the lack of benefit from gaining an identical second performance on the TAT; and (4) intervening influences that are likely to occur over a course of clinical evaluation or treatment (Karon, 1981).

Harrison's (1965) survey of research led him to conclude that intrajudge and interjudge reliabilities are sufficiently positive. Validity also has support (Harrison, 1965; Bellak, 1975), but the importance of the clinical psychologist's expertise is highlighted by the summary statement: "The 'test' is still a test of the tester" (Harrison, 1965, p. 597).

It is necessary to be practical about projective techniques. By its revered training model, clinical psychology involves both science and practice; and by public policy, practice is endowed with a duty to rely on "art"—within bounds.

The clinical psychologist should recognize that certain assessment strategies, such as (perhaps) projective techniques, do not always attain unimpeachable scientific status. Yet, as was discussed in the preceding chapter, the role that society has assigned to clinical psychologists necessitates the use of certain procedures that are known to be fallible. The important safeguard is, of course, that the clinical psychologist must recognize the strengths and weaknesses of all interventions, be they diagnostic or therapeutic, and must make accommodations accordingly.

PERSONAL CONSIDERATIONS

There are several considerations that are accentuated by being a diagnostician. These include: employability, confidence and competence, creativity, and clinical acumen.

Diagnosis, in general, is understood and endorsed by professionals and laypersons alike. The clinical assessment strategies and their purposes are usually discrete and clear-cut. For example, the evaluation of mental abilities is accomplished by an intelligence test, and the level of intellectual functioning, or the IQ, reflects the person's learning and development patterns—even elementary school children are aware of intelligence testing and its purpose.

As a result of the foregoing, being a diagnostician means that the clinical psychologist has distinctly marketable skills. There is usually a good possibility that an employer, such as a mental health clinic, will recognize the need for employees for assessment services.

Clinical assessment is a primary service within clinical psychology, and often such functions as the administration of psychological tests or the intake interviewing (e.g., history taking) of clients will be assigned to someone who welcomes a role that is somewhat circumspect. It is rather common for this role, especially if it is technical in nature (e.g., administering psychological tests), to be fulfilled by a fairly junior-level professional, and the job title might be psychometrist or psychometrician instead of psychologist. This does not mean that diagnosis in the complete sense does not require advanced skills. Diagnosis does, in fact, necessitate refined clinical expertise—yet certain functions can be performed well without the sagacity of the senior clinical psychologist.

Confidence is essential to being an effective diagnostician. Obviously this quality cannot be obtained simply by completing university courses in clinical assessment; rather, it is dependent, to a marked degree, on the personality composite of the clinical psychologist.

Why is confidence essential? Because the diagnostician routinely makes judgments that have a far-reaching impact on the lives of many people. For example, when a child's intelligence is assessed to be lower than average, it impacts on the child and his or her entire family, and may shape their lives for years to come. Also, in many jurisdictions, the expert opinions of the Ph.D.-clinical psychologist and the M.D.-psychiatrist are accorded equal authority for a wide variety of legal decisions, such as in the involuntary commitment of a person to a mental hospital or for supporting or contradicting a defendant's use of the insanity defense to avoid guilt or responsibility for a crime.

Connected to confidence is competence: In order to function effectively as a diagnostician, there must be a realistic sense of competence; that is, knowledge of one's professional abilities and limitations. This has ethical implications; for example, it is unethical to offer any psychological service without adequate competence. There are also legal implications (e.g., avoiding allegations of malpractice by only offering services that are compatible with one's established competence). Much of the decision making about confidence and competence comes from the clinical psychologist's self-regulation on a day-to-day basis (see chapter 4).

Being a diagnostician can be boring! If one works all day, every day in assessment, it is likely that the same tests will be used repeatedly, reports following the same format will be produced, and the same phrases will be relied upon. These days it is possible for reports to be generated by computer—that is how repetitive and structured the contents can become. On the other hand, assessment can be a highly creative process. If the services become perfunctory, it is a movement toward being nonprofessional.

There are other pitfalls: One school superintendent insisted that the psychologists "provide IQ numbers, that's what it takes to get reimbursement from the state"; and since he had heard that culturally disadvantaged children tended to score lower on the Binet than on the Wechsler, he urged the use of the Binet "until we have the special education classrooms full."

Regrettably, it is not uncommon for an employer, particularly one who is not a mental health professional, to have objectives (e.g., gaining state financial reimbursement for handicapped children) that do not honor the objectives of psychodiagnosis (e.g., substituting a minimal testing for a comprehensive clinical assessment). In instances of conflicting objectives, the clinical psychologist may be channeled toward an inappropriate role, such as one in which he merely records IQs. Not only is this potentially unprofessional (e.g., it could be unethical to make diagnostic decisions without adequate assessment data), it certainly constricts the clinical psychologist's identity.

Creativity is the hallmark of high quality diagnostics. From a comprehensive base of assessment data, the clinical psychologist creates idiographic and nomothetic analyzes and interpretations that justify the sacrosanct role afforded to clinical psychology by public policy, and honors the best interests of the client. On a personal level, it is creativity that furthers the rewards of being a diagnostician.

Clinical acumen is not easily gained. Confidence, competence, and creativity join with academic knowledge, professional experience, and the clinical psychologist's personality to bring about the sagacity that distinguishes being a diagnostician from other psychological roles and from the opinions of laypersons. Clinical acumen is never fully realized, rather, the quest for it is constant throughout the career of the clinical psychologist.

Chapter 10

Afterword: The Future of Clinical Psychology

Clinical psychology moved into the 1980s in the wake of the "New Federalism," which envisioned a shift of fiscal responsibility for mental health care from the federal government to the states. The combination of reduction of federal funds for the traditional jobs of teaching, research, and practice, tightening of restrictions by many third-party payers, and growing competition for private and public dollars by a rapidly expanding number of service providers created a sharp impetus within the profession to develop alternative roles, work settings, and sources of income.

OBSTACLES TO GROWTH

Fox, Barclay, and Rogers (1982) identify several obstacles that professional psychology must overcome. One is the lack of a generic definition of professional psychology that would encompass all of the applied areas. They comment that the terms *clinical psychology* and *professional psychology* are used interchangeably to the chagrin of many, and that health psychology fails as a generic definition because it excludes industrial and school speciality areas. They also point out that APA accredits speciality areas, even though states (with very few exceptions) license generically; this creates confusion in the minds of the public and other professions. The lack of a generic definition of the profession may be due to a long-standing, implicit assumption that the generic definition of a psychologist is that of a scientist whose specialization may be professional practice.

Another obstacle identified by Fox et al. is that the public will not have a clear expectation of the scope and competency of professional education as long as training takes place outside psychology departments (e.g., schools of medicine, education, or business) or outside a university (e.g., free-standing schools).

A potential, though not current, obstacle to further growth is the possibility that clinical psychology will become so professionalized, so institutionalized, so preoccupied with proprietary concerns, that it will lose the flexibility and readiness to respond swiftly to changing priorities. This could result in psychologists' ceasing to be on the cutting edge of new developments. It would be well for all to heed Strickland's (1983b) assertion that, "all of us are already nested in our traditional areas and specialties, are constrained by law, and are concerned about economic security" (p. 54).

PROPOSALS FOR GROWTH

Levy (1984) describes internal and external forces that will continue to shape clinical psychology's future. Examples of internal forces are: (1) community psychology, which shifts the focus from the treatment orientation of a practitioner and client dyad to the prevention of illness and improvement of the quality of life within a community; (2) the rapidly developing areas of neuropsychology, health psychology, and rehabilitation psychology (which are outgrowing their status as subspecialities of clinical psychology); and (3) the increased delivery of mental health services within an education format by nonclinical psychologists (e.g., stress reduction programs, parent effectiveness training, remediation of social-skill deficits). As examples of external forces, Levy cites: (1) the secularization of mental health care by the lay person's claims to a larger role in deciding what services are delivered, by whom, and how they are evaluated; (2) the need for nontraditional approaches to what the 1980 Mental Health Systems Act describes as "the unserved, underserved and inappropriately served populations"; and (3) the changing priorities for federal funding that place a high value on prevention and the general health care field.

A number of psychologists have proposed generic definitions of professional psychology. Fox et al. (1982) suggest that professional psychology's purpose is to enhance the effectiveness of human functioning. Levy (1984) describes a human services psychology that promotes well-being through the treatment and prevention of psychological and physical disorders, has an interdisciplinary reach, and utilizes a systems-based biopsychosocial model of human functioning. Fox et al. urge the establishment of schools of psychology within university settings, or within nonprofit structures managed by public boards with standards comparable to those of university graduate education. They also support developing psychological practicum and internship centers to provide hands-on training by, with, and for psychologists, with a degree credential that clearly differentiates the preparation of practitioner psychologists from that of nonpractitioner psychologists. Levy (1984) argues for APA accreditation of broad-based human services training programs that subsume specialty and subspeciality areas, and whose graduates will have professional and occupational titles for which their specific training qualifies them.

CURRENT TRENDS

Six distinct trends should lead clinical psychology into the future. They are: mass communication media; computerization; therapeutic integration; systematic conceptualizations; the practitioner training model; and shifts in professional roles.

Trend 1: Mass Communication Media

In 1981, the Association for Media Psychology was founded to study the use of media for the advancement of the profession. Bouhoutas (1983) outlines four purposes: (1) to demonstrate the relevance of psychology for funding; (2) to improve the image of psychology; (3) to increase demand for services; and (4) to provide primary preventions to the general public. The American Psychological Association (APA) has already taken decisive action on the first and second purposes with its formation of committees to coordinate and disseminate information to the public. Bouhoutas foresees even greater use of the media by and on behalf of psychologists.

From the technological side, the synthesis of cable TV and computers offers considerable potential benefits for the profession. According to Turkat (1983), interactive videocomputer cable systems will impact dramatically on the application of psychological interventions. Clinical psychologists will be able to provide consultation and therapeutic services to the public through the interactive videocomputer cable systems. Noting that psychotherapy over the videoscreen already occurs in some rural areas and within some institutions, Turkat predicts that the next stage will be regional videocomputer facilities for clinical psychologists, and ultimately a national network available for psychological services.

Trend 2: Computerization

Computers are also paving the way for developments in assessment and diagnosis. Computerized testing with microcomputers is already altering the way clinical psychologists administer, score, and interpret tests. Test scores are available within minutes instead of days or weeks. Psychologists are relieved of the time-consuming features of traditional assessment and can redirect their energies into other areas. Also, many clients prefer the anonymity of the computer-based test administration.

A host of problems are coming in the wake of the trend; for example, confidentiality, reliability, and validity of test interpretation, supervision, copyright infringement, and ethical standards (APA, 1984c). Two APA committees have been charged with the responsibility to develop standards and guidelines for computerized assessment and diagnosis. Johnson and Culbert (1984) predict that computerized assessment will become more portable, and that assessment in remote areas will be facilitated by compact systems and systems networks that allow for the sharing of equipment and normative data bases.

Trend 3: Therapeutic Integration

With respect to psychotherapeutic approaches, the current trend is toward integration of and rapprochement between competing theories. The proliferation of therapy schools will be curbed as clinical psychology develops its knowledge base and begins to identify which clients respond to which particular treatments, therapists' proficiencies and personalities, and living environments (Beutler, 1983). The concept of compliance, which was developed in the context of health psychology, is beginning to surface in discussions of treatment of psychosocial disorders. Preliminary research indicates that compliance may be a strong, nonspecific treatment effect by itself, and that therapists of all persuasions are well advised to attend to the causes of patient and client noncompliance and to develop methods to treat noncompliance (Flanders and McNamara, 1984).

Trend 4: Systematic Conceptualizations

Some authors foresee greater use of systems concepts in the application of assessment and intervention. O'Connor and Lubin (1984, chapter 1) conceptualize: (1) health as a relationship between a person and the systems which make up the person's living environment; and (2) health as a relationship that maximizes the functioning of both the person and the relevant systems. Assessment and intervention must be planned to include not only the individual, but also the individual's family, the individual's social network, and the community organizations and institutions. O'Connor and Lubin describe psychotherapy as the mechanism by which the individual client/patient and the relevant systems correct the unhealthy pattern of existing relationships. Community interventions and preventative mental health require corrective measures applied to family systems and to the interaction between family systems and multiple sociocultural contexts (Woody and Springer, 1985).

Schwartz (1982) conceptualizes client participation as a biopsychosocial system. Assessment and treatment must be applied to each of the three levels with due consideration for the interaction between levels, between treatment disciplines, and between treatments at each level of the biopsychosocial system. The role of clinical psychology belongs in the middle (it is to be hoped not the excluded middle) level of the system. To move from the high-powered dialogue of systems concepts to in vivo implementation requires the assistance of sophisticated technology, such as the videocomputer.

Trend 5: The Practitioner Training Model

The trend toward practitioner-oriented training will surely continue but is likely to be in a more conservative direction. Some free-standing schools will merge with a tightening of standards and upgrading of quality; others will affiliate with university campuses or extension centers. More psychology departments will offer the Psy.D. option. Some university-based schools of psychology will become administrative units within colleges of health and human services. Another possibility, admittedly a more radical one, would be for professional psychology to decentralize in university divisions of law, medicine, education, and business.

Training models will be shaped to some degree by what action is taken on the larger issue of generic versus specialty status of professional psychology. The various forms of professional accreditation only recognize the specialties of clinical, school, counseling, and industrial psychology, even though statutory accreditation in most states is generic.

The APA's regulatory guidance (which provides a code of ethics, peer review procedures, accreditation of training programs, and the general and specific guidelines for service providers) largely addresses concerns unique to the specialty areas within the profession. Faced with pressure from many of the newer and professionally oriented divisions to declare as specialities, APA for several years has sought a consensus for regulating the formation of new specialties and for periodically reviewing the continuing status of specialities (APA *News*, 1982).

Waiting in the wings are two options that purport to bring a measure of order and consistency to the profession's multiple identities that often overlap or conflict. One option is to develop a definition of professional psychology that has generic standards and training requirements that apply to the whole spectrum of professional practice. Then criteria would be drawn up to differentiate specialities from subspecialties. The other option is to define clinical psychology as a generic discipline that would include school, counseling, and other areas that meet the criteria of a human service specialty. Many recently formed APA divisions could become sections of established divisions, as has happened in the division of clinical psychology with sections for women, continuing professional development, pediatric psychology, experimental behavioral science, and clinical child psychology. This shift from division to section status would serve to allay APA's fear that professional interests are dominating the organization's divisional structure.

Trend 6: Shifts in Professional Roles

Fox and Bent (1984) anticipate several changes in the modus operandi of practitioners. Noting the shift from mental health institutions to general health, industrial, or corporate settings, Fox and Bent predict that practitioners will more often than not ply their trade in some form of organized group, and the group practice of the future is likely to include cooperative linkages with other practice groups within a national network. They believe that the market for future services will be less illness oriented and more oriented toward maintaining and enhancing human effectiveness in individuals, groups, and organizations.

Already there are nationally based leasing corporations that provide fringe benefit packages to some types of workers who are leased out to small firms on a time-limited basis. It may come to pass that similar leasing corporations will lease individual practitioners, or even practitioner groups, on a time-limited, contractual basis to physical and mental health care facilities that are unable or unwilling to provide full-time employment with all the fringe accoutrements. Like so many others, Fox and Bent also underscore the need to establish large psychological centers for service, research, and training that will give public visibility and professional stature comparable to that of medical centers. The position adopted by Fox and Bent is that, in the final analysis, professional psychology will be judged by the degree to which it rests solidly on a respected, productive, and growing basic psychological science. In their words: "the two groups [science and profession] have much to gain by working together and this seems to be happening" (p. 287).

Finally, perhaps, psychological practice and psychological science are prepared to build an enduring coalition based on shared goals and common needs; to wit, they are ready to cooperate because each can supply something important to the other.

Nearly 100 years have passed since Lightner Witmer performed his midwifery role in the birth of clinical psychology, which a half-century later matured into the "Holy Trinity of postwar clinical psychology" (Korchin, 1976, p. 45) with the unique blend of teaching, research, and practice. In a few short years clinical psychology will be celebrating its first centennial; and indeed, there will be much to celebrate, while at the same time clinical psychologists must consider the rapidly approaching 21st century. One might hope that graduate students in the next century would study these first hundred years, not only to know their roots, but also because "the past is prologue."

References

Adamovich, B. B., Henderson, J. A., & Auerbach, S. (1985), *Cognitive Rehabilitation of Closed Head Injured Patients: A Dynamic Approach*. San Diego: College-Hill Press.

Adler, A. (1929), *Problems of Neurosis: A Book of Case-Histories*. New York: Harper Torchbooks, 1964.

Aguilera, D. C., & Messick, J. M. (1982), *Crisis Intervention: Theory and Methodology*, 4th ed. St. Louis, MO: Mosby.

Albee, G. (1966–67), Give us a place to stand and we will move the earth. *Clin. Psycholog.* 20:1–4.

——— (1970), The uncertain future of clinical psychology. *Amer. Psycholog.*, 25:1071–1080.

——— (1977), The uncertain future of the MA clinical psychologist. *Prof. Psychol.: Res. & Pract.*, 8:122–124.

——— (1982), Preventing psychopathology and promoting human potential. *Amer. Psycholog.*, 37:1043–1050.

American Psychiatric Association (1952), *Diagnostic and Statistical Manual of Mental Disorders*. Washington, DC: American Psychiatric Association.

American Psychiatric Association (1968), *Diagnostic and Statistical Manual of Mental Disorders*, 2nd ed. Washington, DC: American Psychiatric Association.

American Psychiatric Association (1980), *Diagnostic and Statistical Manual of Mental Disorders*, 3rd ed. Washington, DC: American Psychiatric Association.

American Psychological Association (1966), *Standards for Educational and Psychological Tests*. Washington, DC: American Psychological Association.

American Psychological Association (1974), *Standards for Educational and Psychological Tests*. Washington, DC: American Psychological Association.

American Psychological Association (1975), Graduate study in psychology 1976–77. Washington, DC: American Psychological Association.

American Psychological Association (1976), *Policy on Training Psychologists Wishing to Change Their Specialty*. Washington, DC: American Psychological Association.

American Psychological Association (1977), *Standards for Providers of Psychological Services*, rev. ed. Washington, DC: American Psychological Association.

American Psychological Association (1980), *APA/CHAMPUS Outpatient Psychological Providers Manual.* Washington, DC: American Psychological Association.

American Psychological Association, Committee on Professional Standards (1981a), Casebook for providers of psychological services. *Amer. Psycholog.*, 36:682–685.

American Psychological Association, Committee on Scientific and Professional Ethics and Conduct (1981b), Ethical principles of psychologists. *Amer. Psycholog.*, 36:633–638.

American Psychological Association, Committee on Professional Standards (1981c), Specialty guidelines for the delivery of services. *Amer. Psycholog.*, 36:639–685.

American Psychological Association, Committee on Professional Standards (1981d), Specialty guidelines for the delivery of services by clinical psychologists. *Amer. Psycholog.*, 36:640–651.

American Psychological Association (1983a), *Accreditation Handbook.* Washington, DC: American Psychological Association.

American Psychological Association (1983b), Door slowly opens for psychologists asking retraining. *APA Monitor*, 14(7):6–7.

American Psychological Association (1984a), APA-approved sponsors of continuing education in psychology. *Amer. Psycholog.*, 39:679–686.

American Psychological Association (1984b), Council to debate altering peer review. *APA Monitor*, 15(1):1, 26.

American Psychological Association (1984c), The growing use and abuse of computer testing. *APA Monitor*, 15(1):7, 26.

American Psychological Association, Board of Professional Affairs (Subcommittee on Specialization) (1984d), *Specialization in Psychology: Principles.* Washington, DC: American Psychological Association.

American Psychological Association (1985a), APA efforts outlined in report to NIMH advisory council. *APA Monitor*, 16(2):6–7.

American Psychological Association (1985b), *Directory.* Washington, DC: American Psychological Association.

American Psychological Association (1985c), Education, training to hold steady as student loans cut. *APA Monitor*, 16(3):13.

American Psychological Association (1986a), *Graduate Study in Psychology and Associated Fields*, annual ed. Washington, DC: American Psychological Association.

American Psychological Association (1986b), A grand slam helps in '86. *APA Monitor*, 17(2):6–7.

American Psychological Association NEWS (1982), APA considers new recognition for psychology. *Clin. Psycholog.*, 35(4):11–12.

Anderson, J., Parenté, F., & Gordon, C. (1981), A forecast of the future of the mental health profession. *Amer. Psycholog.*, 36:848–855.

Annis, L. V., Tucker, G. H., & Baker, D. A. (1978), What happens to Ph.D. program applicants who have master's degrees? *Amer. Psycholog.*, 33:703–705.

Arbuckle, D. S. (1965), *Counseling: Philosophy, Theory, and Practice.* Boston: Allyn & Bacon.

Ardila, R. (1982), International psychology. *Amer. Psycholog.*, 37:323–329.

Arlow, J. A. (1984), Psychoanalysis. In: *Current Psychotherapies*, ed. R. J. Corsini. Itasca, IL: F. E. Peacock, pp. 14–55.

Asher, S. R., & Wheeler, V. A. (1985), Children's loneliness: A comparison of rejected and neglected peer status. *J. Consult. Clin. Psychol.*, 53:500–505.

Association of Psychology Internship Centers (1986–87), *Directory of Internship Programs in Professional Psychology*, 15th ed. Association of Psychology Internship Centers.

Bak, J. S. & Greene, R. L. (1980), Changes in neuropsychological functioning in an aging population. *J. Consult. Clin. Psychol.*, 48:395–399.

Balch, P., & Harper, R. (1976), Prevention, psychologists, and economics: A reply to Wolf. *Prof. Psychol.: Res. & Pract.*, 7:650–653.

Bales, R. F. (1950), *Interaction Process Analysis*. Reading, MA: Addison-Wesley Publishing Co.

Barker, R. L. (1984), *Treating Couples in Crisis*. New York: Free Press.

Barron, J. (1977–78), An early working draft for special standards in clinical psychology. *Clin. Psycholog.*, 31(2):9–17, 30.

——— Fabrikant, B., & Krasner, J. D. (1971), *Psychotherapy: A Psychological Perspective*. New York: Selected Academic Readings/Simon & Schuster.

Beck, A. T. (1976), *Cognitive Therapy and Emotional Disorders*. New York: International Universities Press.

——— Rush, A. J., Shaw, B. F., Emergy, G. (1979), *Cognitive Therapy of Depression: A Treatment Manual*. New York: Guilford Press.

Beck, S. J. (1981), Reality, Rorschach, and perceptual theory. In: *Assessment with Projective Techniques: A Concise Introduction*, ed. I. Rabin. New York: Springer Publishing, pp. 23–46.

——— Beck, A. G., Levitt, E. E., & Molish, H. B. (1961), *Rorschach's Test: I. Basic Processes*, 3rd ed. New York: Grune & Stratton.

Bednar, R. L., & Kaul, T. J. (1978), Experiential group research: Current perspectives. In: *Handbook of Psychotherapy and Behavior Change: An Empirical Analysis*, 2nd ed., ed. S. L. Garfield & A. E. Bergin. New York: John Wiley.

Belar, C. E., & Orgel, S. A. (1980), Survival guide for intern applicants. *Prof. Psychol.: Res. & Pract.*, 11:672–675.

Bellak, A., & Hersen, M. (1980), *Introduction to Clinical Psychology*. New York: Oxford University Press.

Bellak, L. (1975), *The Thematic Apperception Test, The Children's Apperception Test, and the Senior Apperception Technique*, 3rd ed. New York: Grune & Stratton.

Beller, E. K. (1962), *Clinical Process: The Assessment of Data in Childhood Personality Disorders*. New York: Free Press.

Bender, L. (1983), *A Visual Motor Gestalt Test and its Clinical Use*. New York: American Orthopsychiatric Association.

Benjamin, L. S. (1984), "No shortcuts." *Clin. Psycholog.*, 37(1):24.

Bent, R. J. (1982), The quality assurance process as a management method for psychology training programs. *Prof. Psychol.: Res. & Pract.*, 13:98–104.

Bergin, A. E. (1971), The evaluation of therapeutic outcomes. In: *Handbook of Psychotherapy and Behavior Change*, ed. A. E. Bergin & S. L. Garfield. New York: John Wiley, pp. 217–270.

——— Lambert, M. J. (1978), The evaluation of therapeutic outcomes. In: *Handbook of Psychotherapy and Behavior Change: An Empirical Analysis*, 2nd ed. ed. S. L. Garfield & A. E. Bergin. New York: John Wiley, pp. 139–190.

Berman, P. J. (1979), Graduate student selection at the George Washington University. *Clin. Psycholog.*, 33(1):10–11.

Bernal, M. E., & Padilla, A. M. (1982), Status of minority curricula and training in clinical psychology. *Amer. Psycholog.*, 37:780–787.

——— Barron, B. M., & Leary, C. (1983), Use of application materials for recruitment of ethnic minority students in psychology. *Prof. Psychol.: Res. & Pract.*, 14:817–829.

Bernard, J. L. (1975), Due process in dropping the unsuitable clinical student. *Prof. Psychol.: Res. & Pract.*, 6:275–278.

Bersoff, D. (1983), Hospital privileges and the antitrust laws. *Amer. Psycholog.*, 38:1238–1242.

Beutler, L. (1983), *Eclectic Psychotherapy: A Systematic Approach.* New York: Pergamon.

——— (1986), Systematic eclectic psychotherapy. In: *Handbook of Eclectic Psychotherapy*, ed. J. C. Norcross. New York: Brunner/Mazel.

Bigler, E. D. & Ehrfurth, J. W. (1981), The continued inappropriate singular use of the Bender visual motor gestalt test. *Prof. Psychol.: Res. & Pract.*, 12:562–569.

Blanck, G., & Blanck, R. (1974), *Ego Psychology: Theory and Practice.* New York: Columbia University Press.

Bouhoutas, J. (1983), Media psychology. *Clin. Psycholog.*, 36(2):32–34.

Brammer, L. M., & Shostrom, E. L. (1982), *Therapeutic Psychology: Fundamentals of Counseling and Psychology*, 4th ed. Englewood Cliffs, NJ: Prentice-Hall.

Brenner, C. (1973), *An Elementary Textbook of Psychoanalysis.* New York: International Universities Press.

Bromberg, W. (1975), *From Shaman to Psychotherapist: A History of the Treatment of Mental Illness.* Chicago: Henry Regnery.

Bryant, E. T., Scott, M. L., Golden, C. J. & Tori, C. D. (1984), Neuropsychological deficits, learning disability, and violent behavior. *J. Consult. Clin. Psychol.*, 52:323–324.

Budman, S. H., Demby, A., Feldstein, M., & Gold, M. (1984), The effects of time-limited group psychotherapy: A controlled study. *Internat. J. Group Psychother.*, 34:587–604.

——— Gurman, A. S. (1983), The practice of brief therapy. *Prof. Psychol.: Res. & Pract.*, 14:277–292.

Bugental, J. F. T. (1978), *Psychotherapy and Process: The Fundamentals For an Existential-Humanistic Approach.* Menlo Park, CA: Addison-Wesley.

Buller, K., Cervantes, J., & Brickhouse, B. (1977), Minority students view graduate training. *Clin. Psycholog.*, 30(3):17–22.

Buss, A. H. & Plomin, R. (1975), *A Temperament Theory of Personality Development.* New York: John Wiley.

Butcher, J. N., Braswell, L., & Raney, D. (1983), A cross-cultural comparison of American indian, black, and white inpatients on the MMPI and presenting symptoms. *J. Consult. Clin. Psychol.*, 51:587–594.

——— Kendall, P. C., & Hoffman, N. (1980). MMPI short forms: Caution. *J. Consult. Clin. Psychol.*, 48:275–278.

——— Koss, M. P. (1978), Research on brief and crisis-oriented therapies. In: *Handbook of Psychotherapy and Behavior Change: An Empirical Analysis*, 2nd ed., ed. S. L. Garfield & A. E. Bergin. New York: John Wiley.

Caddy, G. (1981), The development and current status of professional psychology. *Prof. Psychol.: Res. & Pract.*, 12:377–384.
Capsule, (1986), A newsletter from the APA Committee on accreditation and the staff of the accreditation office. Spring issue.
Carmody, T. P., & Zohn, J. (1980), APA-approved group treatment internship training opportunities: Present status and future directions. *Prof. Psychol.: Res. & Pract.*, 11:213–219.
Cattell, J. (1937), Retrospect: Psychology as a profession. *J. Consult. Psychol.*, 1:1–3.
Cattell, R. B. (1966), The meaning of clinical psychology. In: *An Introduction to Clinical Psychology*, 3rd ed., ed. I. A. Berg & L. A. Pennington. New York: Ronald Press, pp. 3–24.
——— Scheier, I. H. (1961), *The Meaning and Measurement of Neuroticism and Anxiety*. New York: Ronald Press.
Charles, D. C. (1970), Historical antecedents of life-span developmental psychology. In: *Life-Span Developmental Psychology: Research and Theory*, 3rd ed., ed. L. Goulet & P. Baltes. New York: Academic Press.
Claiborn, W. L. (1982), The problem of professional incompetence. *Prof. Psychol.: Res. & Pract.*, 13:153–158.
Cleveland, S. (1976), Reflections on the rise and fall of psychodiagnosis. *Prof. Psychol.: Res. & Practice*, 7:309–318.
Cohen, D. B. (1974), On the etiology of neurosis. *J. Abnorm. Psychol.*, 83:473–479.
Cohen, L. D., & Cooley, S. G. (1983), Psychology training programs for direct services to the aging (Status report: 1980). *Prof. Psychol.: Res. & Pract.*, 14:720–728.
——— Lubin, B., & Nathan, R. G. (1979), Graduate degree training in psychology in medical centers. *Prof. Psychol.: Res. & Pract.*, 10:110–114.
Coleman, J. C. (1956), *Abnormal Psychology and Modern Life*, 2nd ed. Chicago: Scott, Foresman.
Comrey, A. L. & Schiebel, D. (1983), Personality test correlates of psychiatric outpatient status. *J. Consult. Clin. Psychol.*, 51:757–762.
Corey, G. (1980), *Theory and Practice of Group Counseling*. Monterey, CA: Brooks/Cole.
——— (1982), *Theory and Practice of Counseling and Psychotherapy*, 2nd ed. Monterey, CA: Brooks/Cole.
Corsini, R. J., ed. (1981), *Handbook of Innovative Psychotherapies*. New York: John Wiley.
Council for the National Register of Health Service Providers in Psychology (1983), *National Register of Health Service Providers in Psychology*. Washington, DC: Author.
Crane, L. (1925–26), A plea for the training of psychologists. *J. Abnorm. Soc. Psychol.*, 20:223–228.
Cummings, N. A. (1977), Prolonged (ideal) versus short-term (realistic) psychotherapy. *Prof. Psychol.: Res. & Pract.*, 8:491–501.
——— (1984), The future of clinical psychology in the United States. *Clin. Psycholog.*, 37(1):19–20.
——— VandenBos, G. (1983), Relations with other professions. In: *The Handbook of Clinical Psychology: Theory, Research, and Practice*, Vol. 2, ed. C. E. Walker. Homewood, IL: Dow Jones-Irwin, pp. 1301–1327.
Dahlquist, L. M., & Fay, A. S. (1983), Cultural issues in psychotherapy. In:

The Handbook of Clinical Psychology: Theory, Research, and Practice, Vol. 2, ed. C. E. Walker. Homewood, IL:Dow Jones-Irwin, pp. 1219–1255.

Dahlstrom, W. G., Welsh, G. S., & Dahlstrom, L. I. (1972). *An MMPI Handbook. Volume I: Clinical Interpretation*. Minneapolis: University of Minnesota Press.

——— ——— ——— (1975). *An MMPI Handbook. Volume II: Research Applications*. Minneapolis: University of Minnesota Press.

DeLeon, P., Frohboese, R., & Meyers, J. (1984), Psychologist on Capitol Hill: A unique use of the skills of the scientist/practitioner. *Prof. Psychol.: Res. & Pract.*, 15:697–705.

——— Pallak, M. (1982), Public health and psychology: An important expanding interaction. *Amer. Psychol.*, 37:934–935.

——— VandenBos, G., & Kraut, A. (1984), Federal legislation recognizing psychology. *Amer. Psychol.*, 39:933–946.

DeMuth, N. M., & Kamis, E. (1980), Fees and therapy: Clarification of the relationship of payment source to service utilization. *J. Consult. Clin. Psychol.*, 48:793–795.

Deutsch, C. J. (1985), A survey of therapists' personal problems and treatment. *Prof. Psychol.: Res. & Pract.*, 16:305–315.

Dies, R. R., & Teleska, P. A. (1984), Negative outcome in group psychotherapy. In: *Above All Do Not Harm*, ed. D. T. Mays, & C. M. Franks. New York: Springer.

Dimond, R., Havens, R., & Rathnow, J., Colliver, J. A. (1977), Employment characteristics of subdoctroal clinical psychologists. *Prof. Psychol.: Res. & Pract.*, 8:116–121.

Doane, J. A. (1978), Family interaction and communication deviance in disturbed and normal families: A review of research. *Fam. Proc.*, 17:357–376.

Dohrenwend, B., & Dohrenwend, B. (1969), *Social Status and Psychological Disorder*. New York: John Wiley.

Dollard, J., & Miller, N. (1950), *Personality and Psychotherapy*. New York: McGraw-Hill.

Dorken, H. (1977), The practicing psychologist: A growing force in the private sector health care delivery. *Prof. Psychol.: Res. & Pract.*, 8:269–274.

——— (1979), Why the sun didn't set in the west. *Clin. Psycholog.*, 33(1):16–17.

——— (1981), Political coping strategies for psychology during a critical decade. *Clin. Psycholog.*, 34(3):35.

Draguns, J. G. (1980), Psychological disorders of clinical severity. In: *Handbook of Cross-cultural Psychology*, Vol. 6, ed. H. C. Triandis & J. G. Draguns. Boston: Allyn & Bacon.

Dryden, W. (1986), Eclectic psychotherapies: A critique of leading approaches. In: *Handbook of Eclectic Psychotherapy*, ed. J. C. Norcross. New York: Brunner/Mazel.

Dubin, S. (1972), Obsolescence or life-long education: A choice for the professional. *Amer. Psycholog.*, 27:486–498.

Dudley, G. R., & Rawlins, M. R. (1985), Psychotherapy with ethnic minorities. *Psychother.: Theory, Res., Pract., & Training*, 22:308–478.

Dunleavy, R. A. & Baade, L. E. (1980), Neuropsychological correlates of severe asthma in children 9–14 years old. *J. Consult. Clin. Psychology*, 48:214–219.

Dusay, J. M., & Dusay, K. M. (1984), Transactional analysis. In: *Current Psychotherapies*, ed. R. J. Corsini. Itasca, IL: F. E. Peacock.

Edwards, A. J. (1971), *Individual Mental Testing, Part I: History and Theories*. Scranton, PA: Intext Educational.

——— (1972), *Individual Mental Testing, Part II: Measurement*. Scranton, PA: Intext Educational.

——— (1975), *Individual Mental Testing, Part III: Research and Interpretation*. New York: Intext Educational.

——— (1954), Manual: *Edwards Personal Preference Schedule*. New York: Psychological Corporation.

——— (1964), Social desirability and performance on the MMPI. *Psychometrika*, 29:295–308.

Einstein, A. (1936), Some thoughts concerning education. Proceedings of the Seventy-Second Convocation of the University of the State of New York. *Univ. State New York Bull.*, 1100:43–47.

Ellis, A., & Grieger, R. (1977), *Handbook of Rational-emotive Therapy*. New York: Springer.

——— Whitely, J. (1979), *Theoretical and Empirical Foundations of Rational-emotive Therapy*. Monterey, CA: Brooks/Cole.

English, H. B. (1938), Organization of the American Association of Applied Psychologists. *J. Consult. Psychol.*, 2:7–16.

Erdwins, C. J., & Buffardi, L. C. (1983), Employment of recent M.A.'s in psychology: A middle rung on the career ladder. *Prof. Psychol.: Res. & Pract.*, 14:112–117.

Erikson, E. H. (1963), *Childhood and Society*, 2nd ed. New York: W. W. Norton.

Exner, J. E. (1974), *The Rorschach: A Comprehensive System*, Vol. 1. New York: John Wiley.

Eysenck, H. J. (1952), The effects of psychotherapy: An evaluation. *J. Consult. Psychol.*, 16:319–324.

——— Rachman, S. (1965), *The Causes and Cures of Neurosis*. San Diego, CA: Robert Knapp.

Fantuzzo, J. W. (1984), MASTERY: A competency-based training model for clinical psychologists. *Clin. Psycholog.*, 37(1):29–30.

Farber, B. A., & Heifetz, L. J. (1981), The satisfaction and stresses of psychotherapeutic work: A factor analytic study. *Prof. Psychol.: Res. & Pract.*, 12:621–630.

——— ——— (1982), The process and dimensions of burnout in psychotherapists. *Prof. Psychol.: Res. & Pract.*, 13:293–301.

Felipe-Russo, N. (1979), Time to focus upon women: The mental health systems act. *Clin. Psycholog.*, 33(1):18–19.

Ferber, A., & Rantz, J. (1972), How to succeed in family therapy: Set reachable goals—give workable tasks. In: *The Book of Family Therapy*, ed. A. Ferber. New York: Science House.

Fichter, M., & Wittchen, H. (1980), Clinical psychology and psychotherapy: A survey of the present status of professionalization in 23 countries. *Amer. Psychol.*, 35:16–25.

Fiedler, F. E. (1950), The concept of an ideal therapeutic relationship. *J. Consult. Psychol.*, 14:239–245.

Fisher, K. (1985), Charges catch clinicians in cycle of shame, slip-ups. *APA Monitor*, 16(5):6–7.

Flanders, P., & McNamara, J. R. (1984), Compliance issues in medicine and psychotherapy. In: *Critical Issues, Developments and Trends in Professional Psychology*, Vol. 2, ed. J. R. McNamara. New York: Praeger.

Ford, D. H., & Urban, H. B. (1963), *Systems of Psychotherapy*. New York: John Wiley.

Ford, J. D. (1977), Training in clinical psychology: a reappraisal based on recent empirical evidence. *Clin. Psycholog.*, 30(3):14–15.

——— (1979), Research on training counselors and clinicians. *Rev. Educat. Res.*, 49:87–130.

Forehand, R. (1985), Training behavioral clinicians for a non-behavioral world. *Behav. Therap.*, 8(1):5–8.

Fox, R., Barclay, A., & Rogers, D. (1982), The foundations of professional psychology. *Amer. Psycholog.*, 37:306–313.

——— Bent, R. (1984), Current status and future directions of professional psychology. In: *Critical Issues, Developments and Trends in Professional Psychology*, Vol. 2, ed. J. R. McNamara. New York: Praeger.

Foxman, P. N. (1980), Tolerance for ambiguity: Implications for mental health. In: *Encyclopedia of Clinical Assessment*, Vol. 1, ed. R. H. Woody. San Francisco, CA: Jossey-Bass.

Framo, J. L. (1979), A personal viewpoint on training in marital and family therapy. *Prof. Psychol.: Res. & Pract.*, 10:868–875.

Frank, G. (1975), *Psychiatric Diagnosis: A Review of Research*. New York: Pergamon.

——— (1984), The Boulder model: History, rationale, and critique. *Prof. Psychol.: Res. & Pract.*, 15:417–435.

Frank, J. D. (1979), The present status of outcome studies. *J. Consult. Clin. Psychol.*, 47:310–316.

Frank, L. K. (1948), *Projective Methods*. Springfield, IL: Charles C. Thomas.

Freud, S. (1911), Psycho-analytic notes upon an autobiographical account of a case of paranoia (dementia paranoides). *Collected Papers*, Vol. 3. London: Hogarth Press, 1949.

——— (1915–1917), *Introductory Lectures on Psychoanalysis*. London: Hogarth Press.

——— (1919), *Totem and Taboo*. London: Hogarth Press.

Fulcher, R., Pion, G., & Stapp, J. (1985), *Preliminary Report: 1983 New Doctorate Employment Survey*. Washington, DC: American Psychological Association.

Garfield, R. (1982), Mourning and its resolution for spouses in marital separation. In: *Therapy for Remarriage Families*, ed. J. C. Hansen. Rockville, MD: Aspen System Corporation.

Garfield, S. L. (1966), Clinical psychology and the search for identity. *Amer. Psycholog.*, 21:353–362.

——— (1978), Research on client variables in psychotherapy. In: *Handbook of Psychotherapy and Behavior Change: An Empirical Analysis*, 2nd ed., ed. S. L. Garfield & A. E. Bergin. New York: John Wiley, pp. 191–232.

——— (1981), Critical issues in the effectiveness of psychotherapy. In: *Clinical Practice of Psychology*, ed. C. E. Walker. New York: Pergamon.

——— (1982), The emergence of the scientist-practitioner model: Background and rationale. *Clin. Psycholog.*, 36(1):4–6.

——— Bergin, A. E. (1978), *Handbook of Psychotherapy and Behavior Change: An Empirical Analysis*, 2nd ed. New York: John Wiley.

——— Kurtz, R. B. (1976), Clinical psychologists in the 1970s. *Amer. Psycholog.*, 31:1–9.

Genthner, R. W. (1980), Personal responsibility. In: *Encyclopedia of Clinical Assessment*, Vol. 1, ed. R. H. Woody. San Francisco, CA: Jossey-Bass.

Gibbs, M. S. (1984), The therapist as imposter. In: *Women Therapists Working with Women*, ed. C. M. Brady. New York: Springer.

Gifford, S., & Lawlis, G. F. (1978), The professional psychology comprehensive examination: A comparison. *Amer. Psycholog.*, 33:624–626.

Gilbert, L. A. (1981), Toward mental health: The benefits of psychological androgeny. *Prof. Psycholog.: Res. & Pract.*, 12:29–38.

Gilberstadt, H., & Duker, J. (1965). *A Handbook for Clinical and Actuarial MMPI Interpretation.* Philadelphia, PA: Saunders.

Gluck, M. R., Babick, A., & Price, K. P. (1979), The use of structured situations in screening applicants to a graduate program in clinical psychology. *Clin. Psycholog.*, 33(1):7–8.

Goldberg, A. L., & McNamara, K. M. (1984), Internship training in clinical neuropsychology. *Prof. Psychol.: Res. & Pract.*, 15:509–514.

Golden, C. J., Hammeke, T. A. & Purisch, A. D. (1980), *The Luria-Nebraska Neuropsychological Battery: Manual.* Los Angeles, CA: Western Psychological Services.

——— Kuperman, S. K. (1980a), Graduate training in clinical neuropsychology. *Prof. Psychol.: Res. & Pract.*, 11:55–63.

——— ——— (1980b), Training opportunities in neuropsychology at APA-approved internship settings. *Prof. Psychol.*, 11:907–918.

——— ——— Osmon, D. (1980), Productivity ratings of psychology programs based on publications in clinical journals. *Prof. Psychol.: Res. & Pract.*, 11:797–806.

Goldenberg, H. (1983), *Contemporary Clinical Psychology*, 2nd ed. Monterey, CA: Brooks/Cole.

Goldfried, M. R. (1980), Toward the delineation of therapeutic change principles. *Amer. Psycholog.*, 35:991–999.

——— (1982), *Converging Themes in the Practice of Psychotherapy.* New York: Springer.

——— Davison, G. C. (1976), *Clinical Behavior Therapy.* New York: Holt, Rinehart & Winston.

Goldstein, A. P., Lopez, M., & Greenleaf, D. O. (1979), Introduction. In: *Maximizing Treatment Gains: Transfer Enhancement in Psychotherapy*, ed. A. P. Goldstein & F. H. Kanfer. New York: Academic Press, pp. 1–22.

Goldstein, M. J., Baker, B. L., & Jamison, K. R. (1980), *Abnormal Psychology.* Boston, MA: Little, Brown.

Goulding, R., & Goulding, M. (1979), *Changing Lives through Redecision Therapy.* New York: Brunner/Mazel.

Grace, W. C. (1985), Evaluating a prospective clinical internship: Tips for the applicant. *Prof. Psychol.: Res. & Pract.*, 16:475–480.

Graham, J. R. (1977), *The MMPI: A Practical Guide.* New York: Oxford University Press.

Graham, S. R. (1984), A national residency program in professional psychology. *Clin. Psycholog.*, 37(1):28–29.

Grebstein, L. D. (1986), Eclectic family therapy. In: *Handbook of Eclectic*

Psychotherapy, ed. J. C. Norcross. New York: Brunner/Mazel, pp. 282–319.

Green, R. G., & Kolevson, M. S. (1982), Three approaches to family therapy: A study of convergence and divergence. *J. Marit. Fam. Ther.*, 8:39–50.

Greenberg, L. S. (1983), Psychotherapy process research. In: *The Handbook of Clinical Psychology: Theory, Research, and Practice*, Vol. 1, ed. C. E. Walker. Homewood, IL: Dow Jones-Irwin.

Greenburg, S. L., Lewis, G. J., & Johnson, M. (1985), Peer consultation groups for private practitioners. *Prof. Psychol.: Res. & Pract.*, 16:437–447.

Grilliot, H. J. (1975), *Introduction to Law and the Legal System*. Boston: MA: Houghton Mifflin.

Gurman, A. S., & Kniskern, D. P. (1978), Research in marital and family therapy. In: *Handbook of Psychotherapy and Behavior Change: An Empirical Analysis*, 2nd ed., ed. S. L. Garfield & A. E. Bergin. New York: John Wiley, pp. 817–901.

——— ——— (1981), Family therapy outcome research: Knowns and unknowns. In: *Handbook of Family Therapy*, ed. A. S. Gurman & D. P. Kniskern. New York: Brunner/Mazel, pp. 742–776.

Gurucharri, C., Phelps, E., & Selman, R. (1984), Development of interpersonal understanding: A longitudinal and comparative study of normal and disturbed youths. *J. Consult. Clin. Psychol.*, 52:26–36.

Hadley, J. M. (1961), *Clinical and Counseling Psychology*. New York: Alfred A. Knopf.

Hall, C. S., & Lindzey, G. (1957), *Theories of Personality*. New York: John Wiley.

——— ——— (1978), *Theories of Personality*, 3rd ed. New York: John Wiley.

Hall, J. (1983), Respecialization, licensure and ethical conduct. *Clin. Psycholog.*, 36(3):68–70.

Halstead, W. C. (1947), *Brain and Intelligence*. Chicago: University of Chicago Press.

Hamersma, R. J. (1972), *Educational and Psychological Tests and Measures*. Dubuque, IA: Kendall/Hunt.

Hansen, J. C., & Himes, B. S. (1980), Normality. In: *Encyclopedia of Clinical Assessment*, Vol. 1, ed. R. H. Woody. San Francisco, CA: Jossey-Bass.

——— Warner, R. W., & Smith, E. J. (1980), *Group Counseling: Theory and Process*, 2nd ed. Chicago, IL: Rand McNally.

Hare-Mustin, R. T. (1983), An appraisal of the relationship between women and psychotherapy. *Amer. Psycholog.*, 38:595–601.

Hariman, J. (1984), *Does Psychotherapy Really Help People?* Springfield, IL: Charles C Thomas.

Harrison, R. (1965), Thematic apperceptive methods. In: *Handbook of Clinical Psychology*, ed. B. B. Wolman. McGraw-Hill, pp. 562–620.

Harrower, M. R. (1947), *Training in Clinical Psychology*. New York: Josiah Macey, Jr. Foundation.

Hathaway, S. R., & McKinley, J. C. (1967). *The Minnesota Multiphasic Personality Inventory Manual*. New York: Psychological Corporation.

Havens, R. A. (1979), A brief review of the current MA controversy. *Prof. Psychol.: Res. & Pract.*, 10:185–188.

——— Colliver, J. A., Dimond, R. E., & Wesley, R. M. (1982), Ph.D. and MA clinical psychologists and MSWs in public mental health settings: A nationwide comparison. *Prof. Psychol.: Res. & Pract.*, 13:654–660.

Havighurst, R. J. (1972), *Developmental Tasks and Education*, 3rd ed. New York: McKay.

Helmes, E., & McLaughlin, J. D. (1983). A comparison of three MMPI short forms: Limited clinical utility in classification. *J. Consult. Clin. Psychol.*, 52:786–787.

Helms, J. E., & Giorgis, T. W. (1982), Who trains applied psychologists for developing countries? *Prof. Psychol.: Res. & Pract.*, 13:736–743.

Henderson, N. B., Butler, B. V., and Goffeney, B. (1969), Effectiveness of the WISC and Bender-Gestalt Test in predicting arithmetic and reading achievement for white and nonwhite children. *J. Clin. Psychol.*, 25:268–271.

Henry, W. E. (1956), *The Analysis of Fantasy: The Thematic Apperception Technique in the Study of Personality*. New York: Robert E. Krieger, 1973.

Hess, A. K., & Hess, K. A. (1983), Psychotherapy supervision: A survey of internship training practices. *Prof. Psychol.: Res. & Pract.*, 14:504–513.

Hirschberg, N., & Itkin, S. (1978), Graduate student success in psychology. *Amer. Psycholog.*, 33:1083–1093.

Hobbs, N. (1964), Mental health's third revolution. *Amer. J. Orthopsychiat.*, 34:822–833.

Hogan, D. B. (1979). *The Regulation of Psychotherapists, Vol. III. A Review of Malpractice Suits in the United States*. Cambridge, MA: Ballinger.

Hosticka, C., Hibbard, M., & Sundberg, N. (1983), Improving psychologists' contribution to the policymaking process. *Prof. Psychol.: Res. & Pract.*, 14:374–385.

Houck, J. E. & Hansen, J. C. (1972), Diagnostic interviewing. In: *Clinical Assessment in Counseling and Psychotherapy*, ed. R. H. Woody & J. D. Woody. New York: Appleton-Century-Crofts, pp. 119–186.

Hutt, M. L. (1980), Adience-abience. In: *The Encyclopedia of Clinical Assessment*, Vol. 2, ed. R. H. Woody. San Francisco: Jossey-Bass, pp. 902–910.

——— Briskin, G. J. (1960), *The Clinical Use of the Revised Bender-Gestalt Test*. New York: Grune & Stratton.

Imber, S. D., Pilkonis, P. A., & Glanz, L. (1983), Outcome studies in psychotherapy. In: *The Handbook of Clinical Psychology: Theory, Research, and Practice*, Vol. 1, ed. C. E. Walker. Homewood, IL: Dow Jones-Irwin.

Inouye, D. K. (1984), VA diplomates to receive bonus. *Diplomate*, 4:2, 1.

Jacobson, G. F., Stricker, M., & Morley, W. E. (1968), Generic and individual approaches to crisis intervention. *Amer. J. Public Health*, 58:338–343.

Jahoda, M. (1958), *Current Concepts of Positive Mental Health*. New York: Basic Books.

Jensen, R. (1979), Professional development or continuing education: A choice point. *Clin. Psycholog.*, 33(1):20–21.

Johnson, J., & Culbert, D. (1984), Automated approaches to psychological assessment. In: *Critical Issues, Developments and Trends in Professional Psychology*, Vol. 2, ed. J. R. McNamara. New York: Praeger.

Jones, S. L. (1980), *Family Therapy: A Comparison of Approaches*. Bowie, MD: Robert J. Brady.

Julius, S., & Handal, P. (1980), Third-party payment and national health insurance: An update of psychology's efforts toward inclusion. *Prof. Psychol.: Res. & Pract.*, 11:955–964.

Jung, C. G. (1956), Two essays on analytical psychology. New York: Meridian Books.

Kalafat, J., & Neigher, W. (1983), Can quality survive in public mental health programs? The challenges for training. *Prof. Psychol.: Res. & Pract.*, 14:90–104.

Kalinkowitz, B. (1978), Scientist-practitioner—The widening schism. *Clin. Psycholog.*, 32(1):4–7.

Kalish, R. A., & Knudtson, F. W. (1976), Attachment versus disengagement: A life-span conceptualization. *Human Development*, 19:171–181.

Kallmann, F. J. (1953), *Heredity in Health and Mental Disorders.* New York: W. W. Norton.

Kaplan, M. S. (1980), Parenting assessment. In: *Encyclopedia of Clinical Assessment*, Vol. 1, ed. R. H. Woody. San Francisco, CA: Jossey-Bass.

Karon, B. P. (1981), The Thematic Apperception Test (TAT). In: *Assessment With Projective Techniques*, ed. A. I. Rabin. New York: Springer, pp. 85–120.

Kaslow, N. J., & Rice, D. G. (1985), Developmental stresses of psychology internship training: What training staff can do to help. *Prof. Psychol.: Res. & Pract.,* 16:253–261.

Katkin, E. (1982), On reliable knowledge and the proliferation of professional schools of psychology. *Clin. Psycholog.*, 36(1):9–11.

Kaufmann, Y. (1984), Analytical psychotherapy. In: *Current Psychotherapies*, ed. R. J. Corsini. Itasca, IL: F. E. Peacock.

Kazdin, A. E. (1980), *Behavior Modification in Applied Settings*, Rev. ed. Homewood, IL: Dorsey Press.

Kelly, E. (1961), Clinical psychology—1960 Report of survey findings. *Newsl.: Div. Clin. Psychol.*, 14:1–11.

Kempler, H., & Norman, M. (1981), Difficulties of a psychologist's participation in legislative matters. *Clin. Psycholog.*, 34(3):30–31.

Kendall, P. C., & Norton-Ford, J. D. (1982), *Clinical Psychology: Scientific and Professional Dimensions.* New York: John Wiley.

Kiesler, C. A. (1979), The status of psychology as a profession and a science. In: *Psychology and National Health Insurance*, ed. C. A. Kiesler, N. A. Cummings, & G. R. VandenBos. Washington, DC: American Psychological Association, pp. 23–39.

Kirsch, I., & Winter, C. (1983), A history of clinical psychology. In: *The Handbook of Clinical Psychology*, Vol. 1, ed. C. E. Walker. Homewood, IL: Dow Jones-Irwin.

Klein, R. H. (1985), Some principles of short-term group therapy. *Internat. J. Group Psychother.*, 35:309–330.

Kleinmuntz, B. (1982), *Personality and Psychological Assessment.* New York: St. Martin's Press.

Klesges, R. C., Sanchez, V. C., & Stanton, A. L. (1982), Obtaining employment in academia: The hiring process and characteristics of successful applicants. *Prof. Psychol.: Res. & Pract.,* 13:577–586.

Klopfer, B., & Davidson, H. H. (1962), *The Rorschach Technique: An Introductory Manual.* New York: Harcourt Brace Jovanovich.

Knapp, S. J., & VandeCreek, L. (1985), Psychotherapy and privileged communications in child custody cases. *Prof. Psychol.: Res. & Pract.,* 16:398–407.

Kogan, L. S. (1966), Research in clinical psychology. In: *An Introduction to Clinical Psychology*, 3rd ed., ed. I. A. Berg & L. A. Pennington. New York: Ronald Press, pp. 717–739.

Kolbe, K., Shemberg, K., & Leventhal, D. (1985), University training in psychodiagnostics and psychotherapy. *Clin. Psycholog.*, 38(3):59–61.

Korchin, S. (1976), *Modern Clinical Psychology*. New York: Basic Books.

——— Sands, S. H. (1983), Principles common to all psychotherapies. In: *The Handbook of Clinical Psychology*, Vol. 1, ed. C. E. Walker. Homewood, IL: Dow Jones-Irwin.

Korman, M. (1974), National conference on levels and patterns of professional training in psychology. *Amer. Psycholog.*, 29:441–449.

Kraut, A., Batchelor, W., Hefferman, J., Vyeda, M., & Greenberg, E. (1984), *1984 Legislative Wrap-up*. Washington, DC: American Psychological Association.

Kurtz, R. B., Fuchs, M., Dabek, R. F., Kurtz, S. M., & Helfrich, W. T. (1982), Characteristics of predoctoral internship in professional psychology. *Amer. Psychol.*, 37:1213–1220.

L'Abate, L., Berger, M., Wright, L., & O'Shea, M. (1979), Training family psychologists: The family studies program at Georgia State University. *Prof. Psychol.: Res. & Pract.*, 10:58–65.

——— Goodrich, M. E. (1980), Marital adjustment. In: *Encyclopedia of Clinical Assessment*, Vol. 1, ed. R. H. Woody. San Francisco, CA: Jossey-Bass.

Lachar, D. (1974). *The MMPI: Clinical Assessment and Automated Interpretation*. Los Angeles, CA: Western Psychological Services.

Lambert, M. J. (1979), *The Effects of Psychotherapy*. St. Albans, VT: Eden Press.

——— (1980), Research and the supervisory process. In: *Psychotherapy Supervision: Theory, Research, and Practice*, ed. A. K. Hess. New York: John Wiley.

——— Bergin, A. E. (1983), Therapist characteristics and their contribution to psychotherapy outcome. In: *The Handbook of Clinical Psychology: Theory, Research, and Practice*, Vol. 1, ed. C. E. Walker. Homewood, IL: Dow Jones-Irwin.

——— ——— Collins, J. L. (1977), Therapist-induced deterioration in psychotherapy. In: *Effective Psychotherapy: A Handbook of Research*, ed. A. S. Gurman & A. M. Razin. New York: Pergamon, pp. 452–481.

Landman, J. T., & Dawes, R. M. (1982), Smith and Glass' conclusions stand up under scrutiny. *Amer. Psychol.*, 37:504–516.

Lanyon, R. I. (1984), Personality assessment. *Ann. Rev. Psychol.*, 35:667–701.

LaPerriere, K. (1979), Toward the training of broad-range family therapy. *Prof. Psychol.: Res. & Pract.*, 10:880–883.

Larry v. Riles (1974), 343 F. Supp. 1306, N. D. Cal.

LaVoie, J. C. (1980), Adult development. In: *Encyclopedia of Clinical Assessment*, Vol. 1, ed. R. H. Woody. San Francisco, CA: Jossey-Bass, pp. 17–45.

Lawler, E. E., III. (1981), *Pay and Organization Development*. Reading, MA: Addison-Wesley.

Lawlor, R. J., Siskind, G., & Brooks, J. (1981), Forensic training at internships: Update and criticism of current unspecified training models. *Prof. Psychol.*, 12:400–405.

Lazarus, A. A. (1981), *The Practice of Multimodal Therapy*. New York: McGraw-Hill.

Levine, B. (1979), *Group Psychotherapy: Practice and Development*. Englewood Cliffs, NJ: Prentice-Hall.

Levinson, D. J. (1977), The mid-life transition: A period in adult psychosocial development. *Psychiatry*, 40:99–112.

Levy, C. (1981), Improving patient care. Psychologist parity with psychiatrists in hospitals. *Clin. Psycholog.*, 34(3):24–25.

Levy, L. H. (1983), Evaluation of students in clinical psychology programs: A program evaluation perspective. *Prof. Psychol.: Res. & Pract.*, 14:497–503.

——— (1984), The metamorphosis of clinical psychology: Toward a new chapter as a human services psychology. *Amer. Psychol.*, 39:486–494.

Lezak, M. D. (1983), *Neuropsychological Assessment*, 2nd ed. New York: Oxford University Press.

Lieberman, M. A. (1980), Problems in integrating traditional group therapies with new forms. In: *Psychotherapy: Current Perspectives*, ed. R. J. Cottle & P. Whitten. New York: New Viewpoints/Franklin Watts.

——— Yalom, I. D., & Miles, M. B. (1973), *Encounter Groups: First Facts*. New York: Basic Books.

Lindzey, G. (1961), *Projective Techniques and Cross-Cultural Research*. New York: Appleton-Century-Crofts.

Lippold, S., & Claiborn, J. M. (1983), Comparison of the Wechsler Adult Intelligence Scale and the Wechsler Adult Intelligence Scale—Revised. *J. Consult. Clin. Psychol.*, 51:315.

Lorion, R. P. (1974), Patient and therapist variables in the treatment of low income patients. *Psychologic. Bull.*, 81:344–354.

Louttit, C. M. (1939), The nature of clinical psychology. *Psychologic. Bull.*, 36:361–389.

Lowe, J. D., & Ritzler, B. A. (1980), Private practice practica and graduate training in clinical psychology: A survey of APA-approved programs. *Prof. Psychol.: Res. & Pract.*, 11:925–929.

Lubin, B., Larsen, R. M., & Matarazzo, J. D. (1984), Patterns of psychological test usage in the United States: 1935-1982. *Amer. Psycholog.*, 39:451–454.

Luborsky, L., Singer, B., & Luborsky, L. (1975), Comparative studies of psychotherapies: Is it true that "everyone has won and all must have prizes"? *Arch. Gen. Psychiat.*, 32:995–1008.

Luria, A. R. (1970), The functional organization of the brain. *Sci. Amer.*, 222:66–78.

Lyman, H. G. (1963), *Test Scores and What They Mean*. Englewood Cliffs, NJ: Prentice-Hall.

Machover, K. (1980), Reflections of a pioneer: A personal diary of over fifty years in clinical psychology. *Clin. Psycholog.*, 34(1):5–7.

Maddi, S. R. (1980), *Personality Theories: A Comparative Analysis*, 4th ed. Homewood, IL: Dorsey Press.

Magaro, P. A., Gripp, R. & McDowell, D. J. (1978). *The Mental Health Industry*. New York: John Wiley.

Magnussen, M. G. (1980), Child and adolescent development. In: *Encyclopedia of Clinical Assessment*, Vol. 1, ed. R. H. Woody. San Francisco, CA: Jossey-Bass.

Maloney, M. P. & Ward, M. P. (1976), *Psychological Assessment: A Conceptual Approach*. New York: Oxford University Press.

Marsella, A. J. (1979), Cross-cultural studies of mental disorders. In: *Perspectives on Cross-cultural Psychology*, eds. A. J. Marsella, R. G. Tharp, & T. J. Ciborowski. New York: Academic Press.

Martin, C. J. (1983), Public policy and the private practice of psychology. *Psychother. Priv. Pract.*, 1(1):51–54.

Martin, R. (1979), *Educating Handicapped Children: The Legal Mandate.* Champaign, IL: Research Press.

Matarazzo, J. (1980), Behavioral health and behavioral medicine. *Amer. Psycholog.*, 35:807–817.

May, R., & Yalom, I. (1984), Existential psychotherapy. In: *Current Psychotherapies*, ed. R. J. Corsini. Itasca, IL: F. E. Peacock, pp. 354–391.

McCaffrey, R. J., Malloy, P. F., & Brief, D. J. (1985), Internship opportunities in clinical neuropsychology emphasizing recent INS training guidelines. *Prof. Psychol.: Res. & Pract.,* 16:236–252.

McConnell, S. (1984), Doctor of psychology degree: From hibernation to reality. *Prof. Psychol.*, 15:362–370.

McGuire, J. M., Toal, P., & Blau, B. (1985), The adult client's conception of confidentiality in the therapeutic relationship. *Prof. Psychol.: Res. & Pract.,* 16:375–384.

Meador, B. D., & Rogers, C. R. (1984), Person centered therapy. In: *Current Psychotherapies*, ed. R. J. Corsini. Itasca, IL: F. E. Peacock.

Meehl, P. E. (1954), *Clinical Versus Statistical Prediction: A Theoretical Analysis and a Review of the Evidence.* Minneapolis, MN: University of Minneapolis Press.

——— (1956), Wanted—a good cookbook. *Amer. Psycholog.*, 11:263–272.

Meichenbaum, D. (1977), *Cognitive Behavior Modification: An Integrative Approach.* New York: Plenum.

Miller, L. S., Bergstrom, D. A., Cross, H. J. & Grube, J. W. (1981), Opinions and use of the DSM system by practicing psychologists. *Prof. Psychol.: Res. & Pract.,* 12:385–390.

Meltzoff, J. (1984), Research training for clinical psychologists. *Prof. Psychol.: Res. & Pract.,* 15:203–209.

——— Kornreich, M. (1970), *Research in Psychotherapy.* New York: Atherton.

Menninger, R. W. (1944), The history of psychiatry. *Diseases of the Nervous System*, 5:52–55.

Meyer, R. G. (1980), Legal and procedural issues in the evaluation of clinical graduate students. *Clin. Psycholog.*, 33(4):15–17.

——— Smith, S. R. (1977), A crisis in group therapy. *Amer. Psychol.*, 32:638–843.

Miale, F. R. (1977), Symbolic imagery in Rorschach material. In: *Rorschach Psychology*, ed. A. Rickers-Ovsiankina. Huntington, NY: Robert E. Krieger, pp. 421–454.

Miller, H. L., & Rickard, H. C. (1983), Procedures and students' rights in the evaluation process. *Prof. Psychol.: Res. & Pract.,* 14:830–836.

Miller, L. S., Bergstrom, D. A., Cross, H. J., & Grube, J. W. (1981), Opinions and use of the DSM system by practicing psychologists. *Prof. Psychol.: Res. & Pract.,* 12:385–390.

Millon, T. (1981), *Disorders of Personality DSM: Axis II.* New York: John Wiley.

Mindess, H. (1955), Analytical psychology and the Rorschach Test. *J. Project. Techniq.*, 19:243–252.

Miner, M. G. & Miner, J. B. (1978), *Employee Selection Within the Law.* Washington, DC: Bureau of National Affairs.

Moreland, K. L. & Dahlstrom, W. G. (1983), Professional training with and use of the MMPI. *Prof. Psychol.: Res. & Pract.*, 14:218–223.
Moreno, Z. T. (1978), Psychodrama. In: *Group Psychotherapy: Theory and Practice*, 2nd ed., ed. H. Mullan & M. Rosenbaum. New York: Free Press, pp. 352–376.
Morgan, C. D. & Murray, H. A. (1935), A method for investigating fantasies. *Arch. Neurol. Psychiat.*, 34:389–306.
Mosak, H. H. (1984), Adlerian psychotherapy. In: *Current Psychotherapies*, ed. R. J. Corsini. Itasca, IL: F. E. Peacock, pp. 56–107.
Moskowitz, S. A., & Rupert, P. A. (1983), Conflict resolution within the supervisory relationship. *Prof. Psychol.: Res. & Pract.*, 14:632–641.
Mowbray, C., Miller, B., & Schneider, L. (1983), The new federalism and state mental health agencies: Roles for psychologists. *Prof. Psychol.: Res. & Pract.*, 14:386–399.
Muehleman, T., Pickens, B. K., & Robinson, F. (1985), Informing clients about the limits of confidentiality, risks, and their rights: Is self-disclosure inhibited. *Prof. Psychol.: Res. & Pract.*, 16:385–397.
Murray, H. A. (1938), *Explorations in Personality*. New York: Oxford University Press.
——— (1943), *Manual: Thematic Apperception Test*. Cambridge, MA: Harvard University Press.
Nash, J., Norcross, J. C., & Prochaska, J. O. (1984), Satisfactions and stresses of independent practice. *Psychother. Priv. Pract.*, 2(4):39–48.
Nathan, P. E., & Harris, S. L. (1983), The diagnostic and statistical manual of mental disorders: History, comparative analysis, current status, and appraisal. In: *The Handbook of Clinical Psychology: Theory, Research, and Practice*, Vol. 1, ed. C. E. Walker. Homewood, IL: Dow Jones-Irwin, pp. 303–343.
Nichols, M. (1984), *Family Therapy: Concepts and Methods*. New York: Gardner Press.
Noonberg, G. R., & Page, H. A. (1982), Graduate neuropsychology training: A later look. *Prof. Psychol.: Res. & Pract.*, 13:252–257.
Norcross, J. C. (1986a), Eclectic psychotherapy: An introduction and overview. In: *Handbook of Eclectic Psychotherapy*, ed. J. C. Norcross. New York: Brunner/Mazel, pp. 3–24.
——— (1986b), *Casebook of Eclectic Psychotherapy*. New York: Brunner/Mazel.
——— Nash, J. M., & Prochaska, J. O. (1985), Psychologists in part-time independent practice: Description and comparison. *Prof. Psychol.: Res. & Pract.*, 16:565–575.
——— Prochaska, J. O. (1982a), A national survey of clinical psychologists: Affiliations and orientations. *Clin. Psycholog.*, 35(3):1, 4–6.
——— ——— (1982b), A national survey of clinical psychologists: Characteristics and activities. *Clin. Psycholog.*, 35(2):1, 5–8.
——— ——— (1982c), A national survey of clinical psychologists: Views on training, career choice and APA. *Clin. Psycholog.*, 35(4):1, 3–6.
——— Stevenson, J. F. (1984), How shall we judge ourselves? Training evaluations in clinical psychology. *Prof. Psycholog.: Res. & Pract.*, 15:497–508.
Nyman, L. (1973), Some odds on getting into Ph.D. programs in clinical psychology and counseling psychology. *Amer. Psycholog.*, 36:934–935.
O'Connor, W., & Lubin, B. (1984), *Ecological Approaches to Clinical and Community Psychology*. New York: John Wiley.

Offer, D. & Sabskin, M. (1974), *Normality: Theoretical and Clinical Concepts of Mental Health*. New York: Basic Books.

Ogdon, D. P. (1982), *Psychodiagnostics and Personality Assessment: A Handbook*, 2nd ed. Los Angeles: Western Psychological Services.

Olmedo, E. L., & Barron, D. L. (1981), Mental health of minority women: Some special issues. *Prof. Psychol.: Res. & Practice*, 12:103–111.

Olmsted, M. S. (1959), *The Small Group*. New York: Random House.

Palmer, J. O. (1983), *The Psychological Assessment of Children*, 2nd ed. New York: John Wiley.

Palo, N. (1984), Across the executive officer's desk. *Diplomate*, 4(2):5.

Parkinson, S. C. (1983), Family therapy. In: *The Handbook of Clinical Psychology: Theory, Research, and Practice*, Vol. 2, ed. C. E. Walker. Homewood, IL: Dow Jones-Irwin.

Parloff, M. B. (1979), Can psychotherapy research guide the policymaker? *Amer. Psycholog.*, 34:296–306.

——— (1980), Psychotherapy and research: An anaclitic depression. *Psychiat.*, 43:279–293.

Patterson, C. H. (1984), Empathy, warmth, and genuineness in psychotherapy: A review of reviews. *Psychother.: Theory, Res., Pract., & Training*, 21:431–438.

Patterson, T. (1979), The status of continuing professional development. *Clin. Psycholog.*, 33(1):22–23.

Perlman, B. (1985), A national survey of APA-affiliated master-level clinicians: Description and comparison. *Prof. Psychol.*,16:553–564.

Peterson, D. R. (1968), The doctor of psychology program at the University of Illinois. *Amer. Psychol.*, 23:511–516.

——— (1976), Is psychology a profession? *Amer. Psycholog.*, 31:572–581.

——— (1985), Twenty years of practitioner training in psychology. *Amer. Psychol.*, 40:441–451.

Petzel, T. P., & Berndt, D. J. (1980), APA internship selection criteria: Relative importance of academic and clinical preparation. *Prof. Psychol.: Res. & Pract.*, 11:792–796.

Phillips, L. & Smith, J. G. (1953), *Rorschach Interpretation: Advanced Technique*. New York: Grune & Stratton.

Pichot, P. (1984), Centenary of the birth of Hermann Rorschach. (Translated from the French by S. Rosenzweig & E. Schreiber). *J. Personal. Assess.*, 48:591–596.

Piotrowski, C., & Keller, J. W. (1984), Psychodiagnostic testing in APA-approved clinical psychology programs. *Prof. Psychol.: Res. & Pract.*, 15:450–456.

Poffenberger, A. T. (1938), The training of a clinical psychologist. *J. Consult. Psychol.*, 2:1–6.

Polster, E., & Polster, M. (1973), *Gestalt Therapy Integrated: Contours of Theory and Practice*. New York: Brunner/Mazel.

Pritchard, D., & Rosenblatt, A. (1980), Racial bias in the MMPI: A methodological review. *J. Consult. Clin. Psychol.*, 48:263–267.

Prochaska, J. O., & DiClemente, C. C. (1984), *The Transtheoretical Approach: Crossing the Traditional Boundaries of Therapy*. Homewood, IL: Dow Jones-Irvin.

——— Norcross, J. C. (1982), The future of psychotherapy: A Delphi poll. *Prof. Psychol.: Res. & Practice*, 13:620–627.

——— ——— (1983). Contemporary psychotherapists: A national survey

of characteristics, practices, orientations, and attitudes. *Psychother.: Theory, Res. & Pract.*, 20:161–173.
——— Prochaska, J. M. (1978), Twentieth century trends in marriage and marital therapy. In: *Marriage and Marital Therapy*, ed. T. J. Paolino & B. S. McCrady. New York: Brunner/Mazel, pp. 1–24.
Rabin, A. I. (1968), Projective methods: An historical introduction. In: *Projective Techniques in Personality Assessment*, ed. A. I. Rabin. New York: Springer, pp. 3–17.
Rabourn, R. E. (1983), The Wechsler Adult Intelligence Scale (WAIS) and the WAIS-R: A comparison and a caution. *Prof. Psychol.: Res. & Pract.*, 14:357–361.
Raimy, V. (1950), *Training in Clinical Psychology*. New York: Prentice-Hall.
Rapaport, D., Gill, M. M. & Schafer, R. (1968), *Diagnostic Psychological Testing*. New York: International Universities Press.
Reichalt, P. A. (1983), Location and utilization of available behavioral measurement instruments. *Prof. Psychol.: Res. & Pract.*, 14:341–356.
Reisman, J. (1976), *A History of Clinical Psychology*. New York: Irvington Publishers.
——— (1981), History and current trends in clinical psychology. In: *Clinical Practice of Psychology*, ed. C. E. Walker. New York: Pergamon Press.
Reitan, R. M. & Davison, L. A. (1974), *Clinical Neuropsychology: Current Status and Applications*. New York: Hemisphere.
Resnick, R. (1983), Medicaid: Direct provider recognition. *Prof. Psychol.: Res. & Pract.*, 14:368–373.
Rickard, H. C. & Bernaty, M. L. (1983), Delimiting subspecialty clinical training. *Clin. Psycholog.*, 36(3):75–78.
——— Clements, C. B. (1981), Administrative training for psychologists in APA-approved clinical programs. *Prof. Psychol.: Res. & Pract.*, 12:349–355.
——— Rahaim, G. L. (1982), Retrospective responses to an interview procedure by accepted and rejected clinical applicants. *Prof. Psychol.: Res. & Pract.*, 13:439–443.
Rickers-Ovsiankina, M. A. (1977), Synopsis of psychological premises underlying the Rorschach. In: *Rorschach Psychology*, ed. M. A. Rickers-Ovsiankina. Huntington, NY: Robert E. Kreiger, pp. 3–25.
Rimm, D. C., & Masters, J. (1979), *Behavior Therapy: Technique and Empirical Findings*, 2nd ed. New York: Academic Press.
Robertson, M. (1979), Some observations from an eclectic therapist. *Psychother.: Theory, Res. & Pract.*, 16:18–22.
——— (1980), Neurotic cues. In: *Encyclopedia of Clinical Assessment*, Vol. 1, ed. R. H. Woody. San Francisco, CA: Jossey-Bass, pp. 128–147.
——— (1986), Radical eclectic psychotherapy. In: *Casebook of Eclectic Psychotherapy*, ed. J. C. Norcross. New York: Brunner/Mazel, pp. 356–374.
Robyak, J., & Goodyear, R. (1984), Graduate school origins of diplomats and fellows in professional psychology. *Prof. Psychol.: Res. & Pract.*, 15:379–387.
Rogers, C. R. (1942), *Counseling and Psychotherapy*. Boston: Houghton Mifflin.
——— (1951), *Client-centered Therapy*. Boston: Houghton Mifflin.
——— (1961), *On Becoming a Person*. Boston: Houghton Mifflin.
Rose, S. D., Tolman, R., & Tallent, S. (1985), Group process in cognitive-behavioral therapy. *The Behavior Therapist*, 8(4):71–75.

Rosenhan, D. L. (1975), The contextual nature of psychiatric diagnosis. *J. Abnorm. Psychol.*, 84:462–474.

——— Seligman, M. E. P. (1984), *Abnormal Psychology*. New York: W. W. Norton.

Rosenthal, D. (1968), An historical and methodological review of genetic studies in schizophrenia. In: *Origins of Schizophrenia*, ed. J. Romano. Amsterdam: Excerpta Medica Foundation, pp. 15–26.

Rosenzweig, S. (1954), A transvaluation of psychotherapy—a reply to Hans Eysenck. *J. Abnorm. Soc. Psychol.*, 49:298–304.

Roth, D. L., Hughes, C. W., Monkowski, P. G. & Crosson, B. (1984), Investigation of validity of the WAIS-R short forms of patients suspected to have brain impairment. *J. Consult. Clin. Psychol.*, 52:722–723.

Rotter, J. B. (1971), *Clinical Psychology*, 2nd ed. Englewood Cliffs, NJ: Prentice-Hall.

Rowe, D. C. (1980), Temperament. In: *Encyclopedia of Clinical Assessment*, Vol. 1, ed. R. H. Woody. San Francisco, CA: Jossey-Bass, pp. 400–409.

Rubenstein, A. (1985), Future projections of the psychotherapy marketplace. *Psychother. Bull.*, 19(4):9.

Russo, N. F., Olmedo, E. L., Stapp, J., & Fulcher, R. (1981), Women and minorities in psychology. *Amer. Psycholog.*, 36:1315–1363.

Ryan, J. J., Larsen, J. & Prifitera, A. (1983), Validity of two- and four-subtest short forms of the WAIS-R in a psychiatric sample. *J. Consult. Clin. Psychol.*, 51:460.

Ryle, A. (1978), A common language for the psychotherapist? *Brit. J. Psychiat.*, 132:589–594.

Sank, L. I., & Prout, M. F. (1978), Critical issues for the fledgling therapist. *Prof. Psychol.: Res. & Pract.*, 9:638–645.

Saretsky, T. (1977), *Active Techniques and Group Psychotherapy*. New York: Jason Aronson.

Sattler, J. M. (1974), *Assessment of Children's Intelligence*, rev. ed. Philadelphia: W. B. Saunders.

Schacht, T. E. (1984), Toward a rational clinical training system. *Clin. Psycholog.*, 37(1):26–27.

——— Nathan, P. E. (1977), But is it good for psychologists? Appraisal and status of DSM-III. *Amer. Psycholog.*, 32:1017–1025.

Schaefer, A. B. (1981), Clinical supervision. In: *Clinical Practice of Psychology*, ed. C. E. Walker. New York: Pergamon, pp. 50–61.

Schafer, R. (1950), *The Clinical Application of Psychological Tests*. New York: International Universities Press.

Schartz, G. (1982), Testing the biopsychosocial model: The ultimate challenge facing behavioral medicine. *J. Consult. Clin. Psychol.*, 50:1040–1053.

Schauble, P. C. (1980), Facilitative conditions in communication. In: *The Encyclopedia of Clinical Assessment*, Vol. 2, ed. R. H. Woody. San Francisco, CA: Jossey-Bass, pp. 1035–1041.

Schein, E. H. (1978), *Career Dynamics: Matching Individual and Organizational Needs*. Reading, MA: Addison-Wesley.

Schmidt, J. P. (1979), Psychotherapy supervision: A cognitive-behavioral model. *Prof. Psychol.: Res. & Pract.*, 10:278–284.

Schneider, A. (1980), Psychologists in comprehensive health care settings. *Clin. Psycholog.*, 33(4):8–9.

Schneider, S. F. (1981), Where have all the students gone? Positions of psychologists trained in clinical/service programs. *Amer. Psycholog.*, 36:1427–1449.

Schofield, W. (1969), The role of psychologists in the delivery of health services. *Amer. Psycholog.*, 24:565–584.

Schwartz, F. & Lazar, Z. (1979), The scientific status of the Rorschach. *J. Personal. Assess.*, 43:3–11.

Schwartz, G. (1982), Testing the biopsychosocial model: The ultimate challenge facing behavioral medicine. *J. Consult. Clin. Psychol.*, 50:1040–1053.

Schwarz, J. C. (1979), Childhood origins of psychopathology. *Amer. Psycholog.*, 34:879–885.

Sechrest, L. B. (1985), Specialization? Who needs it? *Clin. Psycholog.*, 38: 1, 3.

Selin, J. A., & Svanum, S. (1981), Alcohol and substance abuse training: A survey of graduate programs in clinical psychology. *Prof. Psychol.*, 12:717–721.

Serafica, F. C., & Harway, N. I. (1980), The psychology department clinic: Its organization and development. *Prof. Psychol.: Res. & Pract.*, 11:741–748.

Shakow, D., Hilgard, E. R., Kelly, E. L., Luckey, B., Sanford, R. N., & Shaffer, L. F. (1947), Recommended graduate training program in clinical psychology. *Amer. Psycholog.*, 2:539–558.

Shapiro, R. J. (1979), The problematic position of family therapy in professional training. *Prof. Psychol.: Res. & Pract.*, 10:876–879.

Shectman, F. (1973), On being misinformed by misleading arguments. *Bull. Menn. Clinic*, 37:523–525.

Shemberg, K. M., & Leventhal, D. B. (1981), Attitudes of internships directors toward preinternship training and clinical training models. *Prof. Psychol.: Res. & Pract.*, 12:639–646.

Sheridan, E. P. (1981), A resident by any other name . . . is short changed: Clinical psychology training in medical schools and hospitals. *Clin. Psycholog.*, 34(2):5–6.

Shevrin, H. & Shectman, F. (1973), The diagnostic process in psychiatric evaluations. *Bull. Menn. Clinic*, 37:451–494.

Silver, L. B., & Segal, J. (1984), Psychology and mental health. *Amer. Psycholog.*, 39:804–809.

Silverstein, A. B. (1982), Two- and four-subtest short forms of the Wechsler Adult Intelligence Scale—Revised. *J. Consult. Clin. Psychol.*, 50:415–418.

Simkin, J. S., & Yontef, G. M. (1984), Gestalt therapy. In: *Current Psychotherapies*, ed. R. Corsini. Itasca, IL: F. E. Peacock, pp. 279–319.

Simon, G. (1975). Psychology and the "Treatment Rights Movement". *Prof. Psychol.*, 6(3):243–251.

Sisk, J. E., & Langenbrunner, J. C. (1985), Greater competition in health care: Likely effects on technology use. *Psychother. Priv. Pract.*, 32:2, 878–894.

Sloane, R. B., Staples, F. R., Cristol, A. H. Yorkston, N. J., & Wipple, K. (1975), *Psychotherapy versus Behavior Therapy*. Cambridge, MA: Harvard University Press.

Small, L. (1979), *The Briefer Psychotherapies*, 2nd ed. New York: Brunner/Mazel.

Smith, D. S. (1982), Trends in counseling and psychotherapy. *Amer. Psycholog.*, 37:802–809.

Smith, M. L., Glass, G. V., & Miller, T. J. (1980), *The Benefits of Psychotherapy*. Baltimore, MD: Johns Hopkins Press.

Smith, R. S. (1983), A comparison of the Wechsler Adult Intelligence Scale and the Wechsler Adult Intelligence Scale—Revised in a college population. *J. Consult. Clin. Psychol.*, 51:414–419.

Sobel, S. B. (1979), Nick Cummings reflects on psychology's future in public policy. *Clin. Psycholog.*, 33(1):13–15.

——— Russo, N. P. (1981), Sex roles, equality, and mental health: An introduction. *Prof. Psychol.: Res. & Pract.*, 12:1–5.

Spearman, C. (1904), The proof and measurement of association between two things. *Amer. J. Psychol.*, 15:72–101.

Stagner, R. (1948), *Psychology of Personality*. New York: McGraw-Hill.

Stapp, J., Fulcher, R., & Wicherski, M. (1984), The employment of 1981 and 1982 doctorate recipients in psychology. *Amer. Psycholog.*, 39:1408–1423.

——— Wicherski, M., & Pion, G. (1985), *1984–85 Faculty Salaries in Graduate Departments of Psychology*. Washington, DC: American Psychological Association.

Steinhauser, L. (1985), A new Ph.D.'s search for work: A case study. *J. Counsel. Develop.*, 63:300–303.

Sterling, M. (1982), Must psychology lose its soul? *Prof. Psychol.: Res. & Pract.*, 36:789–796.

Stern, W. (1914), *The Psychological Methods of Testing Intelligence*. Baltimore, MD: Warwick & York.

Stevens, J., Yock, T., & Perlman, B. (1979), Comparing master's clinical training with professional responsibilities in community mental health centers. *Prof. Psychol.: Res. & Pract.*, 10:20–27.

Stevenson, J. F., & Norcross, J. C. (1985), Evaluation activity in psychology training clinics: National survey findings. *Prof. Psychol.: Res. & Pract.*, 16:29–41.

Stick, R. S. (1984), Rights of handicapped children. In: *The Law and the Practice of Human Services*, ed. R. H. Woody. San Francisco, CA: Jossey-Bass, pp. 341–372.

Stigall, T. (1981), Sunset on licensure: Are professional ethics enough? *Clin. Psycholog.*, 34(3):28–29.

Stoddard, G. D. (1943), *The Meaning of Intelligence*. New York: Macmillan.

Stoup, C. M., & Benjamin, L. T. (1982), Graduate study in psychology, 1970–1979. *Amer. Psychol.*, 37:1186–1202.

Stricker, G.(1983), Respecialization in clinical psychology: The Adelphi model. *Clin. Psycholog.*, 36(3):62–63.

——— (1984), Clinical training and accountability in service delivery. *Clin. Psycholog.*, 37(1):27–28.

——— Cohen, L. (1984), APA/Campus peer review project: Implications for research and practice. *Prof. Psychol.: Res. & Pract.*, 15:96–108.

——— Hull, J. W., & Woodring, J. (1984), Respecialization in clinical psychology. *Profess. Psychol.: Res. & Pract.*, 15:210–217.

Strickland, B. R. (1983a), Responding to current concerns in clinical psychology. *Clin. Psycholog.*, 36(2):25, 27.

——— (1983b), Clinical psychology and health concerns. *Clin. Psycholog.*, 36(3):52, 54.

——— (1983c), Chance and choice. *Clin. Psycholog.*, 36(4):82, 85.

——— (1985), Over the boulders and through the vail. *Clin. Psycholog.*, 38(3):52–56.

Strider, F. D. (1980), Psychosis/Schizophrenia: Cues. In: *Encyclopedia of Clinical Assessment*, Vol. 1, ed. R. H. Woody. San Francisco, CA: Jossey-Bass.

Strole, L. (1972), Urbanization and mental health: Some reformulations. *Amer. Sci.*, 60:576–583.

Strupp, H. H. (1955), Psychotherapeutic technique, professional affiliation, and experience level. *J. Consult. Psychol.*, 19:97–102.

——— (1978), The therapist's theoretical orientation: An overrated variable. *Psychother.: Theory, Res., & Pract.*, 15:314–417.

——— (1980), Success and failure in time-limited psychotherapy: A systematic comparison of two cases (comparison 1). *Arch. Gen. Psychiat.*, 37:595–603.

——— (1982), Some observations on clinical psychology. *Clin. Psycholog.*, 36(1):6–7.

——— Binder, J. L. (1982), *Time-limited Dynamic Psychotherapy (TLDP): A Treatment Manual.* Nashville, TN: Vanderbilt University Center for Psychotherapy Research.

——— Hadley, S. W., & Gomes-Schwartz, B. (1977), *Psychotherapy for Better or Worse: An Analysis of the Problems of Negative Effects.* New York: Jason Aronson.

——— ——— (1979), Specific versus nonspecific factors in psychotherapy: A controlled study of outcome. *Arch. Gen. Psychiat.*, 36:1125–2236.

Sturgis, D. K., Verstegen, J. P., Randolph, D. L., & Garvin, R. B. (1980), Professional psychology internships. *Prof. Psychol.*, 11:567–573.

Sullivan, H. S. (1954), *The Psychiatric Interview.* New York: W. W. Norton.

Sundberg, N. D. (1977), *Assessment of Persons.* Englewood Cliffs, NJ: Prentice-Hall.

Super, D. E. (1955), Transition: From vocational guidance to counseling psychology. *J. Counsel. Psychol.*, 2:3–9.

——— (1957), *The Psychology of Careers.* New York: Harper & Row.

Swenson, C. H., & Hartsough, D. M. (1983), Crisis intervention and brief psychotherapy. In: *Handbook of Clinical Psychology*, Vol. 2, ed. C. E. Walker. Homewood, IL: Dow Jones-Irwin.

Symonds, P. M. (1946), *The Dynamics of Human Adjustment.* New York: Appleton-Century-Crofts.

Syverson, P. D. (1982), Two decades of doctorates in psychology: A comparison with national trends. *Amer. Psycholog.*, 37:1203–1212.

——— (1983), *Summary Report 1982: Doctorate Recipients from United States Universities.* Washington, DC: National Academy Press.

Telch, M. J. (1981), The present status of outcome studies: A reply to Frank. *J. Consult. Clin. Psychol.*, 49:472–478.

Teplin, L. A. (1984), Criminalizing mental disorder. *Amer. Psycholog.*, 39:794–803.

Terman, L. M., & Merrill, M. A. (1960), *Stanford-Binet Intelligence Scale: Manual for the Third Revision, Form L-M.* Boston: Houghton Mifflin.

Thomas, A., & Chess, S. (1977), *Temperament & Development.* New York: Brunner/Mazel.

Thoreson, R. W., Nathan, P. E., Skorina, J. K., & Kilburg, R. R. (1983), The alcoholic psychologist: Issues, problems, and implications for the profession. *Prof. Psychol.: Res. & Pract.*, 14:670–684.

Thorne, F. C. (1961), *Clinical Judgment: A Study of Clinical Error.* Brandon, VT: Journal of Clinical Psychology.

——— (1973), Eclectic psychotherapy. In: *Current Psychotherapies*, ed. R. J. Corsini. Itasca, IL: F. E. Peacock.

Tipton, R. M. (1983). Clinical and counseling psychology: A study of roles and functions. *Prof. Psychol.: Res. & Pract.,* 14:837–846.

Townes, B. D., Trupin, E. W., Martin, D. C., & Goldstein, D. (1980), Neuropsychological correlates of academic success among elementary school children. *J. Consult. Clin. Psychol.*, 48:675–684.

Tucker, G. H., & Annis, L. V. (1981), The ideal function of the terminal master's degree program for a Ph.D.-pursuing student. *Prof. Psychol.: Res. & Pract.,* 12:336–340.

Tuma, J. (1981), Crisis in training pediatric psychologists. *Prof. Psychol.: Res. & Pract.,* 12:516–522.

Turkat, D. (1983), Cable television and psychology: Bringing peace to the planet. *Clin. Psycholog.*, 36(2):40–43.

VandenBos, G. R., & Stapp, J. (1983), Service providers in psychology: Results of the 1982 APA human resources survey. *Amer. Psychol.*, 38:1330–1352.

Vane, J. R. (1985), School psychology: To be or not to be. *J. School Psychol.*, 23:101–112.

Vitulano, L. A., & Copeland, B. A. (1980), Trends in continuing education and competency demonstration. *Prof. Psychol.: Res. & Pract.,* 11:891–897.

Wachtel, P. L. (1977), *Psychoanalysis and Behavior Therapy: Toward an Integration*. New York: Basic Books.

Walfish, S., Polifka, J. A., & Stenmark, D. E. (1985). Career satisfaction in clinical psychology: A survey of recent graduates. *Prof. Psychol.: Res. & Pract.,* 16:576–580.

——— Sumprer, G. F. (1984), Employment opportunities for graduates of APA-approved and nonapproved training programs. *Amer. Psycholog.*, 39:1199–1200.

Walsh, K. W. (1978), *Neuropsychology: A Clinical Approach*. New York: Churchill Livingstone.

Wampler, L. D., & Strupp, H. H. (1976), Personal therapy for students in clinical psychology: A matter of faith? *Prof. Psychol.: Res. & Pract.*, 7:195–201.

Wechsler, D. (1955), *Manual: Wechsler Adult Intelligence Scale*. New York: Psychological Corporation.

——— (1967), *Manual: Wechsler Preschool and Primary Scale of Intelligence*. New York: Psychological Corporation.

——— (1974), *Manual: Wechsler Intelligence Scale for Children—Revised*. New York: Psychological Corporation.

——— (1981), *Manual: Wechsler Adult Intelligence Scale—Revised*. New York: Psychological Corporation.

Wells, R. A., & Dezen, A. E. (1978), The results of family therapy revisited: The nonbehavioral methods. *Fam. Proc. J.*, 17:251–274.

White, R. W. (1969), Adult growth and emotional maturity. In: *The Healthy Personality*, eds. H. M. Chiang & A. H. Masow. New York: Van Nostrand Reinhold.

Wiggins, J. (1984), New JCAH policy: Psychologists' victory. *Clin. Psycholog.*, 37(2):50.

Wilson, G. T., & O'Leary, K. D. (1980), *Principles of Behavior Therapy*. Englewood Cliffs, NJ: Prentice-Hall.

Wolfe, D. (1946), The reorganized APA. *Amer. Psycholog.*, 1:3–6.

Woods, P. J. (1976), *Career Opportunities for Psychologists: Expanding & Emerging Areas.* Washington, DC: American Psychological Association.

Woody, R. H. (1966), Intra-judge reliability in clinical electroencephalography. *J. Clin. Psychol.*, 22:150–154.

——— (1967), Diagnosis of behavioral problem children: Part I. Electroencephalography and mental abilities. *J. School Psychol.*, 5:116–121.

——— (1968a), Diagnosis of behavioral problem children: Part II. Mental abilities and achievement tests. *J. School Psychol.*, 6:111–116.

——— (1968b), Inter-judge reliability in clinical electroencephalography. *J. Clin. Psychol.*, 24:251–256.

——— (1969), *Behavioral Problem Children in the Schools: Recognition, Diagnosis, and Behavioral Modification.* New York: Appleton-Century-Crofts.

——— (1980a), Introduction: A conceptual framework for clinical assessment. In: *The Encyclopedia of Clinical Assessment*, Vol. 1., ed. R. H. Woody. San Francisco, CA: Jossey-Bass, pp. xxx–xli.

——— Ed. (1980b), *The Encyclopedia of Clinical Assessment*, Vol. 1. San Francisco, CA: Jossey-Bass.

——— Ed. (1980c), *The Encyclopedia of Clinical Assessment*, Vol. 2. San Francisco, CA: Jossey-Bass.

——— (1983a), Avoiding malpractice in psychotherapy. In: *Innovations in Clinical Practice: A Source Book*, Vol. 2, eds. P. A. Keller & L. G. Ritt. Sarasota, FL: Professional Resource Exchange, pp. 205–216.

——— (1983b), Techniques in handling psychologal cases. In: *Handbook of Clinical Psychology: Theory, Research, and Practice*, Vol. 2, ed. C. E. Walker. Homewood, IL: Dow Jones-Irwin, pp. 1420–1439.

——— (1984), Professional responsibilities and liabilities. In: *The Law and the Practice of Human Services*, ed. R. H. Woody. San Francisco, CA: Jossey-Bass, pp. 272–401.

——— (1985), Public policy, malpractice law, and the mental health professional: Some legal and clinical guidelines. In: *Psychology, Psychiatry, and the Law*, ed. C. P. Ewing. Sarasota, FL: Professional Resource Exchange, pp. 509–525.

——— Springer, J. R. (1985), A holistic health model for family therapy. In: *Health Promotions in Family Therapy*, eds. J. R. Springer & R. H. Woody. Rockville, MD: Aspen Systems, pp. 36–45.

Wright, L. (1983), Please don't tell my mother I'm a clinical psychologist—She still thinks I play piano in a brothel. *Clin. Psycholog.*, 36(2):49–51.

Wright, R. H. (1981a), Psychologists and professional liability (malpractice) insurance: A retrospective review. *Amer. Psycholog.*, 36:1485–1493.

——— (1981b), What to do until the malpractice lawyer comes: A survivor's manual. *Amer. Psycholog.*, 36:1535–1541.

Yalom, I. D. (1975), *The Theory and Practice of Group Psychotherapy*, 2nd ed. New York: Basic Books.

Ylvisaker, M. Ed. (1985), *Head Injury Rehabilitation: Children and Adolescents.* San Diego: College-Hill Press.

Zaro, J., Batchelor, W., Ginsberg, M., & Pallak, M. (1982), Psychology and the JCAH: Reflections on a decade of struggle. *Amer. Psycholog.*, 37:1342–1349.

——— Kilburg, R. (1982), The role of APA in the development of quality

assurance in psychological practice. *Prof. Psychol.: Res. & Pract.*, 13:112–118.
Zohn, J., & Carmody, T. (1978), Training opportunities in group treatment methods in APA-approved clinical psychology programs. *Prof. Psychol.*, 9:50–62.
Zubin, J. (1977–1978), But is it good for science? *Clin. Psychol.*, 31(2):1, 5–7.

Name Index

Subject Index